M000112645

"Jill Hunting has given us the story of a beautiful, intimate, and unforgettable journey that shows how ineffably the past is woven into the present, how our ancestors' complicated lives shape our own, and what is gained when we come face to face with our history."

—LYNN NOVICK, documentary filmmaker and collaborator, with Ken Burns, on *Hemingway, The Vietnam War, Baseball,* and *The Civil War*

"Partly a rousing adventure in pursuit of scientific discovery, partly a series of intimate ruminations on self and history, *For Want of Wings* charms the reader to explore unexpected byways of knowledge as it crisscrosses the United States through time and space."

—NANCY F. COTT, Jonathan Trumbull Research Professor of American History at Harvard University and author of *Fighting Words: The Bold American Journalists Who Brought the World Home between the Wars*

"Jill Hunting has woven together an unforgettable tapestry of family history, fossil hunting, and high adventures in the American West. This finely honed and deeply original book reminds us that the past and the present aren't as far apart as they sometimes seem to be, and the lives of Hunting's Yale-centric ancestors have surprising resonances today. A fascinating read for both dinophiles and history lovers."

—JULIA FLYNN SILER, *New York Times* best-selling author of *The White Devil's Daughter, Lost Kingdom,* and *The House of Mondavi*

"Jill Hunting's *For Want of Wings* follows a delightfully discursive and personal path across important American history, tracking the footsteps of ancestors whose adventures in scientific discovery and political change resonate to this day. I avidly followed, feeling as enriched as did Jill and her daughter, May, out on the Great Plains and the Rockies. This is a warm and touching story showing the simultaneity of past and present—just my kind of book."

—DAVID HAWARD BAIN, author of *Empire Express* and *The Old Iron Road*

"A person's life is not just a thread from birth to death, but rather a complicated tapestry interwoven with the lives of many others. In the case of *For Want of Wings*, the author's careful research has restored the fabric surrounding the life of Thomas Hubbard Russell (1851–1916), her great-grandfather. Russell was a Yale graduate who made an important, but largely forgotten, scientific discovery in 1872 while collecting fossils with O. C. Marsh in the wilds of western Kansas, and then went on to become a respected medical surgeon in his hometown of New Haven, Connecticut. His life and the background of his once-in-a-lifetime discovery of a 'bird with teeth' make for a fascinating read."

—MICHAEL J. EVERHART, author of *Oceans of Kansas: A Natural History of the Western Interior Sea* and Adjunct Curator of Paleontology, Sternberg Museum of Natural History

"Jill Hunting is a sleuth when it comes to finding details, and she has the talent to weave many threads together to create a coherent story that combines personal history, family history, national history, natural history, travel, American West, important characters, and more. She takes the reader on the search and adventure to tell the story of finding the first complete fossil of *Hesperornis regalis*. Hunting illuminates a long-buried facet of the paleontology and history of Kansas. It is a gem."

—LEO E. OLIVA, author of *Fort Wallace: Sentinel on the Smoky Hill Trail* and *Fort Larned on the Santa Fe Trail*

FOR WANT OF WINGS

For Want
of Wings

A Bird with Teeth
and a Dinosaur
in the Family

JILL HUNTING

UNIVERSITY OF OKLAHOMA PRESS : NORMAN

Library of Congress Cataloging-in-Publication Data

Names: Hunting, Jill, 1950– author.
Title: For want of wings : a bird with teeth and a dinosaur in
    the family / Jill Hunting.
Description: Norman : University of Oklahoma Press, [2022] |
    Includes bibliographical references. | Summary: "Part detective history,
    part memoir, in this book Jill Hunting tells the story of her journey
    across the United States and into the realms of prehistory, national history,
    and family history as she follows her great-grandfather's trail to the
    fossil bed where he discovered an 83-million-year-old avian
    dinosaur"—Provided by publisher.
Identifiers: LCCN 2021031932 | ISBN 978-0-8061-7661-1 (paperback) |
    ISBN 080617661X (paperback)
Subjects: LCSH: Hunting, Jill, 1950– | Marsh, Othniel Charles, 1831–1899. |
    Paleontologists—United States—Biography. | Birds, Fossil—History. |
    Fossils—Collection and preservation—Kansas.
Classification: LCC QE871 .H86 2022 | DDC 568/.23—dc23
LC record available at https://lccn.loc.gov/2021031932

The paper in this book meets the guidelines for permanence and durability of
the Committee on Production Guidelines for Book Longevity of the Council
on Library Resources, Inc. ∞

The tail [. . .] doubtless was an efficient aid in diving, perhaps
compensating in part for want of wings, which the Penguins
use with so much effect in swimming under water.
That *Hesperornis* was carnivorous is clearly proven by its
teeth; and its food was probably fishes.
—O. C. Marsh, "On the Odontornithes,
or Birds with Teeth," 1875

CONTENTS

Prologue: Caught in a Buffalo Stampede   1

Part I: ORIGINS   3

Part II: STRATA   23

Part III: THE 1872 YALE COLLEGE SCIENTIFIC EXPEDITION   61

Part IV: I GO TO KANSAS   161

Part V: DIASPORA   181

Part VI: I RETURN TO KANSAS   207

Acknowledgments   215

Notes   217

Selected Bibliography   241

PROLOGUE
Caught in a Buffalo Stampede

Professor Othniel Charles Marsh held tight and hunched low over his Indian pony, who was running at full speed. The buffalo herd had completely engulfed them. Knowing he would be trampled if his mount's strength were to fail, Marsh began edging Pawnee toward one side of the stampeding mass. The surefooted pony had been trained to hunt buffalo, but now he and his rider were racing for their lives.

After several miles Pawnee began showing obvious signs of exhaustion. Marsh drew his cavalry carbine from its saddle holster and began firing at animals near him, opening up space for the pony to work his way toward open ground. As the buffalo fell, one by one, Pawnee leaped over them.

Still racing at a terrifying speed, Marsh raised his eyes and glimpsed the edge of the vast herd. Up ahead, the valley was narrowing. But before he could think of another plan of escape, a new terror arose as droves of panicked buffalo began stumbling in the burrows of an immense prairie dog village. Pawnee, his head lowered to watch the ground, jumped over the holes and the fallen animals in his path.

Now the herd was funneling into a canyon crisscrossed by ravines. Pawnee leaped across the gullies until they grew so wide that both pony and bison were racing down one side and up the other. Through the choking dust Marsh could see the furious red eyes and flared nostrils of the great animals that surrounded him.

The ground was level again. In the distance Marsh could make out a low butte. As he drew closer to the hill, with his heels he signaled to Pawnee his intention to change course. Reaching the butte, he swung the pony into its lee side. For more than an hour they waited in the shelter of an overhang while rampaging buffalo charged past. Marsh could feel the thunder of their hoofs and the heat of their breath as the animals passed within a few feet.

At last the herd dwindled down to a few stragglers. With one shot Marsh brought down a small cow, dismounted, and quickly carved out the tongue and steaks from the hump to take back to camp. Until they heard the distant gunshot, four young graduates of Yale University, a hired scout named Edward Lane, and 2nd Lt. James Pope, based out of Fort Wallace, Kansas, had all wondered if the professor was alive or dead.

Marsh's canteen was empty. The only drink he could offer Pawnee was whisky from a flask. The pony refused. The two began walking back to camp in the direction of gunshots returned by the waiting party. After a little while Pawnee lifted his head as if to signal that his strength had returned. Marsh climbed onto his back. When at last they came into the firelight of the camp, the sky was filled with stars. The men were eager to hear what had happened and how their leader had escaped being trampled. One offered to brush down the pony. No, Marsh said, he would do it himself. Pawnee had saved his life.

The aroma of fresh meat on the fire wafted through the chill night as Marsh recounted the wild ride that had nearly killed him. The stampede had been triggered by shots from the other men, who had not realized the professor was already in pursuit of a young cow for their supper. Only a few minutes earlier, Marsh had been riding with Lieutenant Pope and talking about the day's fossil collecting. The two men had stopped on a ridgetop to look down on the vast number of bison grazing peacefully in the valley below. It was black with them. The West was changing, and soon the buffalo would be gone.

Pope used a mathematical equation he had learned at West Point to estimate the number of animals. Six to eight miles wide and a dozen miles long, the herd had numbered almost a hundred thousand.[1]

Part I
ORIGINS

– 1 –

"Do something you've always wanted to do. Something you've never done before, like jumping out of an airplane."

That was the advice my doctor, a friend, gave me as I sat in his examining room after a routine physical. He had just told me I was going to live forever, so I asked him what he would do, if he were me, to celebrate a milestone birthday.

I didn't want to parachute out of an airplane, but I did want to see Russell Springs, Kansas, where my great-grandfather Thomas H. Russell, as a member of the 1872 Yale College Scientific Expedition, discovered a nearly complete fossilized skeleton of a dinosaur that lived 83 million years ago. I thought it would be fun to take my twenty-six-year-old daughter, May, my only child, with me. I called her and asked, "How would you like to go to Kansas?" I lived in Sonoma, California, at the time and she was in San Francisco, about an hour away. The idea was a whim and yet more complicated than that. It was the kind of idea that, as soon as you think of it or say it aloud, you recognize as coming from deep within. The significance of the trip would grow on me gradually and then profoundly.

We began planning a trip for late October, two weeks shy of my birthday. We would arrive in present-day Logan County almost exactly 138 years after our ancestor unearthed his fossil there, on October 27, 1872.

That July, Thomas Hubbard Russell, whom his friends called Tom, had graduated from Yale and was about to enter medical school there. For the interim he had signed on as a member of the Yale expedition, along with two classmates and one graduate from the previous year. Leading the party was the Yale professor and eminent American paleontologist Othniel Charles Marsh. The contrast could not have been greater between the four amateur bone hunters, who had probably joined up for an adventure, and the great scientist, as serious a person in the field as there existed and soon to be one of the most famous men in America.

For four successive years beginning in 1870, Professor Marsh led groups of Yale students and graduates on fossil-collecting trips through Kansas, Nebraska, Colorado, Utah, Wyoming, and Oregon. The genesis of these westering expeditions had been Marsh's attendance, in August 1868, at the annual meeting of the American Association of the Advancement of Science, in Chicago. There the attendees were offered excursions by train to three destinations. Marsh accepted the invitation to travel to an emerging city on the Missouri River called Omaha. From there he would continue on to whatever hell-on-wheels settlement in Wyoming Territory was the terminus at that time of the Union Pacific Railroad.

It was Marsh's first visit to the American West. The broad vistas of the Great Plains reminded him of the ocean. He was in fact looking at an ancient seabed, and before long a plan of systematic exploration took hold in his imagination. At one stop he got off the train to look at a heap of fossilized remains he had heard about. As the boarding signal sounded, Marsh persuaded the station agent to save the bones that railroad workers had shoveled aside and to let him collect them on the return trip. These bony souvenirs were the beginnings of a world-famous collection for Yale.

Marsh was well aware of the discovery in 1867 of a Cretaceous vertebrate, the marine reptile *Elasmosaurus platyurus*, in Kansas. The specimen had been found by a U.S. Army surgeon at Fort Wallace, Dr. Theophilus Turner, and brought to the wider scientific community's attention in 1868 by Marsh's onetime friend and future archrival, Edward Drinker Cope of Philadelphia.

Marsh would have returned to the fossil beds of the West in 1869 had it not been for hostilities between American Indians and whites, notably Gen. Philip H. Sheridan's winter campaign against the Southern Plains tribes that year and the next.[1] He did use the time, however, to formulate an ingenious plan that would provide him with both financing and field workers for his bone collecting. His assistants would consist of Yale students and recent graduates who would shoulder a portion of the expenses for what the American naturalist George Bird Grinnell later remembered as "the hope of an adventure with wild game or wild Indians."[2]

According to Grinnell's account, several prosperous businessmen also contributed funds for the first expedition and possibly all four. He suspected that some of them were railroad men who gave Marsh free passes or discounted rates for train travel. Railroads were opening the West to white settlement, and the U.S. Army was supporting the effort. Traveling with a letter of introduction from Gen. William Tecumseh Sherman—who commended the professor's search "for the Great West" and requested "all aid to him in his interesting work"—Marsh arranged for horses, pack mules, wagons, tents, blankets, ammunition, cavalry escorts, and local guides.[3] After arriving in the West, his group would travel from fort to fort. One guide was none other than William F. "Buffalo Bill" Cody, who, though he accompanied the 1870 expedition for only a day, forged an enduring friendship with Marsh.

— 2 —

On June 30, 1870, Marsh departed by train on the first of his four expeditions. With twelve Yale men he left Union Station in New Haven, Connecticut, bound for the fossil beds of the West. Among the young adventurers were Grinnell and Eli Whitney, whose grandfather had patented the cotton gin.

Each of the Yale College Scientific Expeditions differed in its number of members, route, success in collecting specimens, and duration. Of the 1872 party, which included twenty-year-old Tom Russell and three other recent graduates, the fewest stories have survived.

The precise movements of the group in Kansas, Colorado, Wyoming, and Utah are not known. By mapping the locations of fossils they collected and matching them with dated notes they took in the field, however, and correlating these with a handful of newspaper accounts, a rough itinerary can be deduced. Despite the paucity of information, we can assume that the four young men accumulated exciting and harrowing tales equal to those of the 1870, 1871, and 1873 parties, whose exploits made their way into published articles, one private diary, a biography of Marsh, and the professor's own unfinished manuscript about his adventures.

All four expeditions also shared one important outcome: namely, the contributions they made to vertebrate paleontology. The Peabody Museum of Natural History at Yale benefited immeasurably from the many tons of bones that arrived in crates from points west. Yale was the first university in the United States to have a department of paleontology, which was established with a gift from Marsh's uncle, the international financier and philanthropist George Peabody. Marsh was the department's chairman and sole faculty member, and he had almost no teaching responsibilities.

Before they left New Haven, Marsh required the expedition members to read *The Prairie Traveler*, an illustrated guidebook published in 1859 by an army captain named Randolph Marcy. Compiled for westbound travelers, the book's twelve chapters covered such topics as clothing and footwear, sanitation and hygiene, wagon maintenance, lariat construction, and types of saddles and weapons, including breech-loading versus muzzle-loading rifles and the relative merits of the Colt army pistol and the lighter, more portable navy revolver. Captain (later Brigadier General) Marcy warned readers about stampeding animals, advised various antidotes for snakebite, described "capricious meteoric revolutions" (severe storms), and explained how to choose a campsite, ford a river (for swimmers, horseback riders, and horses), build a boat, bank a fire, and track, pursue, and attack American Indians.

Marsh and his expeditions came up against many of the hazards the book describes. Buffalo stampeded, along with the travelers' mules, which broke loose when spooked by a wolf. Lightning struck, hail and snow fell, night brought piercing winds, and summer temperatures climbed to 110 degrees in the shade. Some students couldn't swim or became separated from the group and lost their way—in one case, overnight. Parties of Sioux followed the travelers and, in one instance, set a fire on both sides of the river Marsh's men were following. The 1870 party reported seeing as many as ten rattlesnakes in a single day, and one student member took up collecting rattles to make a necklace for his sweetheart. The fact that no major accidents or life-threatening illnesses befell any of the four groups can be credited, at least in part, to the professor's careful planning.

With all the effort and hardship that accompanied their adventures, did any of the young men feel homesick, afraid, dispirited? Did anyone have a moment when he asked himself why he had signed on with the driven, unrelenting professor? After evading horse thieves and crossing especially rugged terrain one day, a member of the first expedition may have projected his own emotional state onto the landscape when he wrote, "We stood upon the brink of a vast basin so desolate, wild, and broken, so lifeless and silent, that it seemed like the ruins of a world."[4]

Marsh had instructed each member of the party to bring boxes of waterproof matches and a hat with a brim wide enough to catch rainwater. Each man was also armed with a large hunting knife, a thirty-six-caliber Smith and Wesson six-shooter, and a fifty-caliber Sharps carbine rifle. These firearms were in wide use by the U.S. Army, and ammunition for them would be supplied to the expeditions when they reached the forts in the West. Some of the men had not fired their rifles until taking target practice at the supply fort in Omaha. Some had never ridden a horse.

One man traveling with Marsh, Tom Russell, had without question left New Haven knowing how to handle a rifle. Until the age of sixteen he had attended the highly regarded Collegiate and Commercial Institute, a military-style prep school in New Haven owned and run by his father, Gen. William Huntington Russell. Tom may even have left for the West with the bullets in the waist-belt he was wearing when the group was photographed along the way.

Tom's father had been elevated to the rank of major general early in the Civil War by Connecticut governor William Buckingham. General Russell was an abolitionist, a supporter of Abraham Lincoln, and a friend of John Brown. He was an educator with no military experience in the field, and when war came Buckingham appointed him to organize the Connecticut militia. A hundred of his students, who as cadets comprised infantry and artillery companies and drilled on the New Haven Green, received commissions from the Union armies. Before the war ended, the number rose to three hundred.

Over General Russell's long life, he distinguished himself by playing an active role in civic and military affairs, including serving as his state's representative on the antislavery National Kansas Committee. He is better known today as the founder of Yale's secret society Skull and Bones. Bonesmen—who by tradition leave the room if someone outside the network mentions its name—still invoke his memory when inquiring whether someone belongs to the society, asking, "Do you know General Russell?"

− 3 −

On the second of Marsh's trips west, in 1871, he found the fossilized remains of a "gigantic swimming bird"—a remarkable find, although it was missing its skull.[5] He named the new species *Hesperornis regalis*, meaning "regal western bird." The following year Tom Russell unearthed a specimen of the same kind of Cretaceous bird, one that was better preserved and more complete. The skull resembled those of ratites, the family of birds that includes ostriches, but, unlike the ratites, its long beak contained sharp, reptile-like teeth similar to those of the monstrous aquatic lizards called mosasaurs, which shared the sea with *Hesperornis*. The head was the thing. "Russell's bird," as field notes from the expedition refer to it, is proof of the evolutionary link between meat-eating reptiles and the pretty songbirds that visit our backyards. Birds are living dinosaurs.

In his 1875 publication "On the Odontornithes, or Birds with Teeth," Marsh did not mention that the specimen he found in 1871 had no skull. He further stated that "Mr. T. H. Russell and the writer" had obtained "a nearly perfect skeleton" in 1872.[6] Marsh left the reader to suppose that his own earlier find was the groundbreaking discovery, as paleontologist Mike Everhart has pointed out in *Oceans of Kansas: A Natural History of the Western Interior Sea*. "Although this was not an outright lie," Everhart writes, "Marsh was certainly guilty of clouding the history of the discovery of *Hesperornis*."[7]

Marsh was a competitive, indefatigable, self-aggrandizing fossil hunter and a socially awkward lifelong bachelor who was most at home in the field. He devoted his adult life to collecting, cataloging bones, and publishing papers and books about his myriad discoveries. He was determined to amass not only a complete natural history collection for Yale at his own expense, but also a representative collection for the National Academy of Sciences at taxpayers' expense. His two books about toothed birds, both funded by the federal government, led U.S. congressman H. A. Herbert of Alabama to denounce Marsh's research as wasteful. "Birds with teeth" became a catchphrase in the 1890s for what we now call pork-barrel spending.

Thousands of bones collected by Marsh and his unpaid and paid helpers made their way to New Haven. The Peabody Museum received so many, in fact, that hundreds of his fossils, though carefully catalogued, still await complete study.

The importance Marsh attached to Hesperornithiforms, the order to which "Russell's bird" belongs, is evident in his monumental

1880 monograph, *On the Odontornithes, or Birds with Teeth*. The 201-page book was published as a royal quarto (10 by 12.5 inches) with forty woodcuts and thirty-four lithographic plates. Two hundred and fifty presentation copies were published, and Marsh sent one to Charles Darwin. In acknowledging the gift Darwin told him, "Your work on these old birds and on the many fossil animals of North America has afforded the best support to the theory of evolution which has appeared within the last twenty years."[8]

Today, one of the fastest-growing subdivisions of vertebrate paleontology, or the study of fossilized animals with backbones, is the origin and early evolution of birds. Despite *Hesperornis regalis*'s inestimable importance in demonstrating the link between birds and reptiles, its superficial similarity to modern waterbirds and its small size relative to better-known prehistoric creatures have limited its fame beyond the scientific community. It is not one of the giant superstars Marsh named later, including *Stegosaurus*, *Triceratops*, and *Brontosaurus*, whose names so easily roll off the tongues of five-year-olds. The children's animated television series *Dinosaur Train* introduced a character named Jess Hesperornis, yet no plush-toy version of this feathered carnivore can be found in a museum gift shop, even the Peabody Museum's. The flightless, toothy, five-foot-long prehistoric creature that lay entombed for millions of years in the gray chalk of a Kansas canyon may be the least famous of the most important finds from the Age of Dinosaurs. Even less famous is the man who found it.

– 4 –

The chances of any creature becoming a fossil are extremely rare. So little of an animal usually survives, and of that only bones and teeth, that trying to understand the living creature it once was is like solving an elaborate mystery. How did its lifeless skeleton survive? How could Russell's bird have sunk intact to the bottom of the shallow ocean that once covered a vast portion of North America? How did it escape becoming food for a scavenger? After the Western Interior Seaway receded, how did the bird's delicate skeleton evade being crushed by tons of sediment as geological forces shaped and reshaped the earth's crust? How was this small creature then lifted to the earth's surface in its tomb of chalk, to await discovery millions of years later by a novice fossil hunter from New Haven?

What led Tom Russell, who would spend his entire life in the city of his birth, to sign on for an uncertain journey into the American West? What did he think and feel when he noticed, in an outcropping the locals call Goblin Hollow, one or two protrusions in the exposure, looking less like rough sedimentary rock than smooth bone? It is hard to imagine he ever thought that a great-granddaughter would one day follow him there and, like a paleontologist arranging fossil parts, piece together fragments of his trip west in hopes of understanding what he saw and felt.

Growing up, I didn't hear much about my maternal great-grandfather. My mother's ancestors had come to North America as Pilgrims and Puritans, and her family tree included many illustrious individuals, but she wasn't curious about history. She passed on almost no facts about her family. Of the relatives she did talk about, she repeated the same few anecdotes as if the people were not flesh and blood but characters in a story. She was close to her gregarious grandmother Russell, but of her grandfather Mom said only that he was a surgeon and very reserved. She could be forgiven for feeling unattached to a man who died seven months before she was born. Even so, he was not a mystery to her. He was not even interesting.

No one in her family seemed to regard Tom Russell as a personality worthy of interest. One of my more history-minded relatives, an uncle by marriage, told me that Dr. Russell had founded the family fortune. I grew up middle class in the Midwest, far from the family seat in Connecticut, and wondered what fortune he was talking about. I asked another relative if Tom Russell or his father had kept a journal. He doubted it. "I don't think Russells have been much given to introspection," he said.

For as long as I can remember, I have been curious about the past. I have always liked old things: antiques, classic recipes, historic buildings, my elders, ancient history. I didn't know about the family connection with a prehistoric fossil, however, until a few years after college when my mother's sister sent me two clippings from the *Yale Alumni Magazine*. I had majored in American Studies at Wheaton College in Massachusetts, and she must have thought I would be interested in a bit of family history.

The first item, an interview with a geology professor, included a group photograph of the 1872 Yale College Scientific Expedition. The seven men included Professor Marsh; a local guide whom Marsh had hired to accompany the party; an army lieutenant attached to the expedition; and Marsh's four graduate assistants. One of the assistants was my great-grandfather.

The second item was a letter to the editor that appeared in a subsequent issue of the magazine. It corrected a mistake in the photo caption that had been published. The man who had been identified as the "rough-looking character" wearing a waist-belt filled with bullets, with a rifle leaning against his leg, had been presumed to be the local guide.[9] The letter-writer who submitted the correction was my mother's cousin. The man with all the bullets, she wrote, was her grandfather Dr. Thomas H. Russell, then a recent graduate of Yale and later professor of clinical surgery at the medical school.

Even dressed in western garb, the handsome fellow with the penetrating gaze was clearly a young version of the serious gentleman in a portrait I had seen in my grandparents' house.

I wonder now why my mother and her sister and brother hadn't mentioned their grandfather's time in the West or the fact that he had found a dinosaur fossil. It seems unlikely that their grandmother would not have taken them to the Peabody Museum to see her husband's remarkable find. She may have. My mother had not taken my siblings and me to see *Hesperornis regalis*, even though we spent our summers at the family farm less than a dozen miles from where the fossil is prominently displayed. My great-grandfather had seen bison when they still numbered in the millions and American Indians before they were forced onto reservations. He had found a dinosaur—something no one I have ever met has said about an ancestor. Tom Russell may have been reserved, but he was hardly uninteresting. I wanted to know more about him. Learning about his great adventure would become my own journey of discovery.

My questions would take me to the Kansas plains; to subterranean rooms in the Peabody Museum at Yale; to libraries, historical societies, a crypt, graveyards, and museums from California to Scotland. The answers I found led to revelations that many New England clergymen, including two of my ancestors, owned slaves; they led to the writings of O. C. Marsh, Charles Darwin, George Bird Grinnell, John Brown, Henry Holt, and others linked to my family history as it intersected U.S. history at pivotal moments. They opened conversations with paleontologists, historians, a biology teacher, a television producer, a herpetologist, Hollywood movie costume experts, and ten-year-old triplets.

On my odyssey, one encounter or question frequently opened onto another. These interruptions of my train of thought sent me on unexpected tangents. I decided not to avoid them but to follow them. The detours usually resulted in insights that a conventional path of research would not have led me to.

Seeking to understand the past appeals to me, while genealogy does not. So when I learned about the modern system of taxonomy known as cladistics, I was glad to know about a way to chart a family tree that does not rest on pride but on science. Among many scientists, including prominent vertebrate paleontologists, the schema of clades has replaced the classifications of kingdom, phylum, class, order, family, genus, and species that many of us studied in high school biology. A clade is a group with a common ancestor whose members share one or more particular characteristics. I came to think of Tom Russell, my daughter, and me as belonging to a clade. Our common ancestor both by blood and by the legacy he left us, namely, to live with purpose, is William Huntington Russell. The shared characteristics of curiosity and adventurousness are what took all three of us to a bleak outcropping of gray chalk in Kansas, a place as still as anywhere on earth.

When I invited my daughter to go there with me, neither of us had set foot in western Kansas. I knew from looking at Google Maps that it was flat and sparsely populated. What I didn't know was that the very earth is golden and the landscape beautiful in its starkness. Nor did I realize at the time that by inviting May there I was offering her a place to inhale deeply and look to the faraway horizon—a tonic that so many have found in the American West—at a point when she needed perspective on the life she was creating for herself. She was only a few years older than Tom Russell when he embarked on his adventure in the West.

I needed a new horizon myself. Divorced and on my own for a decade, I had just published a deeply personal book about my brother's death in Vietnam as a humanitarian aid worker. It had become my quest to learn what happened to him and to understand the effect of his loss on me. Writing the book was a departure from my work as a food and wine editor. It expanded my life and gave me a new circle of friends.

It also culminated almost ten years of starting over. They had begun with the end of my marriage to May's father after years of dreary, monotonous, and eventually acute unhappiness. We were mismatched from the start, I came to realize, and instead of finding that we were opposites that attracted, I began to feel as if I were a leach field for his emotional effluent.

In those years my work as an editor was a refuge. It kept me safely in the shadows, correcting, polishing, and sometimes rewriting the work of others so seamlessly that they seemed to think they had done it on their own. The lack of recognition was an occupational hazard, I told myself. The brilliant writers kept me going, while others occasionally drained me to the point that I wondered why I was sitting behind a desk instead of moving out into the world as a writer. Although an editor accepts and may even prefer a certain amount of invisibility, it gradually dawned on me that my work and marriage were alike in this respect. My self-regard had taken a hit. I had voluntarily allowed my own wings to be clipped.

Eventually there was a last straw, and I slipped the noose of my marriage. Like the biblical story about the apostle Peter, I followed an angel who led me past sleeping jailors and out the opened gate of a prison. Within a month, the editor in chief of the magazine where I worked asked me to begin writing feature stories with a byline.

Around this time I asked myself one day, *What do I do now?* The answer came right back to me: *Just live.*

I started again as a woman alone. May lived at home with me for two more years before she left for college. It was a time of adjustment for both of us. For sixteen years I had wanted above all to be a good mother to her and to raise a confident daughter. Now I was putting my needs if not first, then equal to hers. I was determined to be the best, most authentic me I could be. I took responsibility for being the unique person I was created to be, whoever she was becoming. My natural confidence returned. I began, in other words, to use my vestigial wings. Emily Dickinson said hope is the thing with feathers. Confidence is the thing with wings.

First-time authors are sometimes warned by literary agents that publishing a book will not change your life, but it changed mine. Life felt fuller and larger after writing the book about my brother.

But because doing that emptied me of a story I had been carrying around since I was fifteen, what felt like my big new life now also contained a large empty space. How would I fill it? Should I return to the work I had done before, editing and writing about food and wine? How did I want to spend my remaining years?

Three days in Kansas did not transform my daughter or me. The vast skies there did not magically send down answers to the life questions we had brought with us. But the trip would turn out to be, for both of us, a *reculer pour mieux sauter*—a momentary drawing back, the better to leap forward.

Our trip also set me on a course to learn more about the little-known 1872 Yale expedition, fossil hunting, U.S. history as my forebears intersected it at critical points, and the generations of my Yale-centric ancestors. I became a paleontologist of my family, looking at strata and piecing together fragments to form a more complete picture. I would discover that my clergyman forebears, who included two of Yale's ten founders, owned slaves. I uncovered the backstory of the first abolitionist in the family, whose son, the fossil hunter, became a medical man. In the present generation, my daughter is the director of 350.org, an organization working to solve the climate crisis and keep fossil fuels in the ground. My quest showed me that evolution, far from being limited to prehistoric life, also takes place in families that adapt to the necessity of their environment and their time on earth.

Along the way I came to understand history differently than what I had learned in college studying American history and literature. History is not a straight line. Only in retrospect does it seem so, when we see patterns emerging and what looks like a flow of events. History is dynamic, fluid, and alive. It is—as the Santa Fe Institute in New Mexico describes systems ranging from the economy to weather—nonlinear, complex, and adaptive.[10]

What is history if not a process that is random, accidental, and uncontrollable, a succession of chance encounters and unforeseen meetings? Interruptions. Tangents. Events in the present that circle back to an earlier time. Lost letters that reappear. Things cast off, recycled, and reused.

How did you happen to become friends with that person? Put down roots where you did? Meet the person you married? Pick up this book? Whatever the reasons, they likely involved happenstance.

If this explanation of history as random is truer than the linear definition we were taught, then history asks something of us. Lock on to this moment. Forget the expected outcome. Go somewhere on the slimmest thread of a reason. Take a whim seriously.

– 6 –

One of my earliest memories is of walking down Whitney Avenue past the Peabody Museum in New Haven, holding my mother's hand. I didn't know until much later that there in the Great Hall is the avian dinosaur her grandfather discovered.

A few years after my aunt sent me the article with the photograph of the 1872 Marsh party, another relative showed me a book with some pages about the grandfather he was named for. It said that Thomas Hubbard Russell inherited "absolutely no money, but what was far better, sound health and a good name."[11] It also said that Professor Marsh had asked Tom to stay on as his assistant and to return with him to the West. Tom declined. He wanted to commence his medical studies. He may also have sensed that working under Marsh would be difficult. In the coming years, the professor earned a reputation for holding back his assistants.[12]

The Internet had not been invented when my great-grandfather first attracted my imagination, but eventually it would lead me to his undergraduate thesis, an anatomical study of the New England lobster. Another search turned up the pine splints he used to set a patient's leg; by the time I saw them in a photograph, the auction house offering the lot had already sold it. Items like these, along with medical papers Tom presented and obituaries about him, created a silhouette if not a picture of him.

The Peabody Museum posted a list of specimens collected on the Marsh expeditions and the locations where they were found. I pored over it and examined maps to see where Tom had gone. Google Maps showed me the terrain around Russell Springs, Kansas, where the 1872 party camped and Tom found his *Hesperornis regalis*. I saw there was no shopping center, housing development, or gas station, but only the Smoky Hill River meandering across Logan County. It couldn't be much different from what my ancestor saw 140 years earlier. I promised myself I would go there. Someday.

One reason I didn't plunge into learning more about Tom Russell and the 1872 expedition sooner was that I wanted to explore something that felt more urgent: what had happened to my brother in Vietnam. It was another topic my family didn't talk about. If Tom Russell was an unknown, Pete Hunting was the elephant in the room. Newly graduated from Wesleyan University when he went to Southeast Asia in 1963 to teach English, he was the first American volunteer aid worker to die in the Vietnam War. Walter Cronkite and the Associated Press reported that he was led into an ambush by Vietnamese who posed as his friends. To ask my parents for details about his violent death and what had really happened was impossible, but the question haunted me. Years passed and life went on. I went to college and graduate school, got married, raised my daughter, and eventually found a career in food and wine.

Sometime in my twenties I asked my mother if I could read the letters Pete wrote to us from overseas. She told me they were all destroyed in a basement flood. Decades later, I found them. They were keen eyewitness observations of the escalating U.S. involvement in Vietnam, written by an altruistic young man working in rural hamlets. Writing the story that grew out of my quest to reconnect with my brother taught me that it's good to ask questions even in a family that discourages it. In 2009 my quest became a book, *Finding Pete*.

That same year, Tom Russell took up residence in my imagination after a morning I spent at the Yale Peabody Museum. My book tour in New England had begun in Boston. From there I moved on to Connecticut. I have always loved being in the state, because, although I grew up in Missouri and Oklahoma, I spent the summers of my childhood at my grandparents' home in Woodbridge, a short distance from New Haven. My grandfather, Edward, was Tom Russell's third son and youngest child. He and my grandmother lived in a house Tom bought after his eldest son contracted tuberculosis. Dr. Russell thought the fresh country air would help cure the boy, and it did.

Whenever I return to the rolling hills and lush greenery of Connecticut, my chromosomes seem to realign themselves as I think about the nine generations of my forebears who lived here. I like to pay my respects at the Grove Street Cemetery in New Haven, where many of my mother's people are buried. I walk around Wooster Square, where my great-great-grandparents lived and the Russell School faced the park's eastern side. On the New Haven Green, a few blocks away, I admire the church where my mother's ancestors worshipped for centuries. Two of them rest in tombs in the dirt-floor crypt beneath the building. Here at Center Church, my parents were married in 1940. Dad's father, a Kentucky native who attended Yale and its divinity school, served on the pastoral staff. I'm an outsider in Connecticut, but my roots are here.

My publisher had booked an interview and a talk in New Haven for me, but I had one free day that I intended to spend at the Peabody Museum. I had read up on the Yale College Scientific Expeditions and had been corresponding with a vertebrate paleontologist named Dan Brinkman. He had offered to show me the specimens my great-grandfather collected in 1872 if I ever came to New Haven.

The Peabody is one of the largest university museums of natural history in the world. It was founded in 1866 with a gift of $150,000 from the enormously generous and comparatively unrecognized George Peabody, the father of modern philanthropy. He also endowed an anthropology museum at Harvard. His sister was O. C. Marsh's mother, who died from cholera when the boy was three. Peabody financed his nephew's college education and, after Marsh graduated from Yale's Sheffield Scientific School in 1860, helped him continue his scientific studies at German universities.

The Peabody's gift shop is the place to go if you are shopping for a present for a dinosaur-loving youngster. Although it carries only a fraction of the world's thousands of dinosaur books, you can easily lose yourself for an hour browsing in the educational toys section.

The gift shop, three floors of galleries, and the Great Hall of Dinosaurs with its immense *Age of Reptiles* mural by Rudolph F. Zallinger were all I had seen there until November 9, 2009. It was the day before my birthday. I thought of the appointment I had made with Dan Brinkman as a present to myself.

We met in the lobby of the venerable Gothic structure that presides over the intersection of Whitney Avenue and Sachem Street— only a block, incidentally, from Tom and Mary Munson Russell's former home at 79 Trumbull Street. Their house was divided long ago into offices. I went there once to look around. A side door had as many locks as Jerry Seinfeld's fictional New York City apartment, but when I pushed, it opened. Although the banisters and paneling looked beat-up, I could imagine the place as a dignified residence a century earlier.

The museum was undergoing extensive renovations. Dan and I walked past construction, down stairs, and through hallways lined with shelves crammed with bones, bones, and more bones. Remains of long-ago creatures, including a tortoise shell the size of a cauldron straight out of *Harry Potter*, were crowded together like shoes in my closet back home in California. A tweedy man passed us, and Dan introduced me as the great-granddaughter of Thomas H. Russell, one of Marsh's students. The tweedy man greeted me with a friendly handshake. My own family didn't talk about Tom Russell's youthful adventure in the West, but here in these subterranean corridors I was among people who knew about the Marsh expeditions and shared my interest in them.

We entered a basement room lined with metal cabinets and floor-to-ceiling shelves. Dan is a friendly, helpful, and efficient person, and he had prepared for my visit. On a large table he had laid out every specimen my great-grandfather collected in the West. Some of them were knobby and light tan; they looked like large white truffles, a subject I had written half a dozen articles and published a newsletter about before turning my attention to the Vietnam book.

Set out with the bones were several irregular shapes of thin paper, on which a penciled hand had written these dates, names, and locations:

Sketches of Russell's bird, Oct. 27, 1 mi. W. Russell Springs.
Pelvis of Hesperornis, Sketch taken when uncovered,
Oct. 28, 1872, natural size.
Nov. 5, Russell, North Side of Smoky, 3 Miles North
of Russell Springs, portion of Bones as found.

I reached for a skull fragment. My move may have caught Dan off guard, but he didn't stop me when I picked up more bones, along with yellowed papers bearing the original field notes about the specimens. Tom Russell had found these fossils and sketched them. More than a hundred years ago, the careful hands of a future surgeon had held all these things.

My phone rang. It was my publisher asking if I could come to their offices for a call-in interview. Thus ended abruptly my visit to the Peabody Museum. I said a quick goodbye to Dan, hurried out of the building, and, feeling somewhat dreamy, went on my way. With no small effort, I brought my thoughts back to the present. Soon I would have to turn my attention to the Vietnam War and the story I was going to tell on the radio.

I had wanted to stay longer at the Peabody. I would have liked to linger, because a picture was forming in my imagination of an autumn day on the Kansas plains and a young Tom Russell noticing something imbedded in an embankment.

Tapping gingerly on the soft, gray chalk with a small hammer, he begins working. He methodically sweeps the dust from every crevice with a horsehair-bristle brush and manipulates his penknife to expose the long-entombed remains. As loose fragments are disinterred, he wraps each one in muslin. Eventually, after exposing a larger section of the fossil, he examines it carefully. Pulling a pencil from his pocket, he sharpens it with his knife. He unfolds a sheet of parchment and lays it flat on the ground. Then, his intense gaze moving from bones to paper and back to bones, Tom begins to sketch the pelvis of his regal western bird, *Hesperornis regalis*.

Part II
STRATA

– 7 –

The door of Mary and William Huntington Russell's home in New Haven closed behind John Brown as he stepped outside on March 18, 1858. It was not his first visit to the residence on Wooster Place. Nor was it the only time he would mistake his own hopes for a promise. In August of the previous year, Brown wrote to a supporter in Boston, "I was flattered with the expectation of getting one thousand dollars from Hartford City and also one thousand dollars from New Haven. [. . .] From New Haven I got twenty-five dollars."[1]

When he called on William Russell that day, Brown took with him his son John Jr., then thirty-six. The meeting occurred roughly midway between the radical abolitionist's two most infamous acts: the brutal attack on five proslavery settlers north of Pottawatomie Creek in Franklin County, Kansas, in May 1856 and the unsuccessful raid on the federal arsenal at Harper's Ferry, Virginia, in October 1859. Brown intended to seize the armory there and provide slaves in the South with both the weapons captured and a thousand deadly pikes manufactured for him in Connecticut.

Brown was secretive. Most of his supporters knew nothing of his plot to seize Harper's Ferry. Many were unaware of the murders he masterminded in Kansas. Brown never publicly admitted to having led the party that dragged five men from their beds and butchered them, one within earshot of his wife. What William Russell knew about the activities of his arch-zealot friend and how much his trust in Brown may have deteriorated over time, we can only guess, although one source states that "he had never been privy" to Brown's plans for Harper's Ferry.[2] A U.S. senate committee inquiring into the failed raid reported in 1860 that Brown's supporters did not know the actual use to which their contributions would be put.

"It does not appear," the committee concluded, "that he intrusted [sic] even his immediate followers with his plans, fully, even after they were ripe in execution."[3]

Born in Connecticut, Brown left for Kansas pious and ardent. He returned fanatical. Three years later he became the first U.S. citizen to be hanged for treason and insurrection. Abraham Lincoln would later describe the assault on Harper's Ferry as "not a slave insurrection [but] an attempt by white men to get up a revolt among slaves, in which the slaves refused to participate."[4]

William Russell's friendship with Brown and his youth in Middletown, his student days and legacy at Yale, his superintendency of a well-regarded New Haven military-style academy, his labors for the antislavery cause, and his devotion to the Union during the Civil War—these facets of a man famous in his time but now little remembered fascinated me. What was the home environment like, I wondered, in which William raised his children?

Did Tom yearn to escape a confining strictness and scrutiny, like my mother's cousin who told me that as a little boy he couldn't run to the end of the block without some Russell relative seeing him and calling his mother? Had Tom's trip to Kansas with Professor Marsh amounted to a breaking free, if only for a couple of months? I imagined that whatever his motives were in joining up, the experience must have been formative. I had a hunch that the trailhead of his western adventure was Wooster Place. Even more, I suspected that it was less a place than a person, and the person was not the leader of the expedition, O. C. Marsh, but Tom's own father.

As I read about William in books and articles I found online, I discovered that two of his ancestors, and thus mine, both clergymen, owned slaves. Knowing of his abolition work, I wondered if he was the first in his family to renounce slavery. If so, what brought this about? He was six years out of college and living in New Haven during the *Amistad* incident of 1839, when fifty-three kidnapped Africans were jailed there before John Quincy Adams persuaded the U.S. Supreme Court they should be freed.

William threw himself into the abolitionist cause. When Kansas became a focal point of the struggle, he joined like-minded citizens to help establish a colony of New Haven emigrants there. The purpose was to add antislavery settlers to the voting population so that when Kansas Territory came into the Union, it would be admitted as a free state.

As historic events of the mid-nineteenth century accelerated toward civil war, they touched the Russell household. When John Brown called there in 1858, Tom was a boy of seven. Did he shake the hand of his father's gaunt friend with the burning eyes? Did he overhear a conversation between the two men, so that a dozen years later, when he learned Professor Marsh was going to look for fossils in Kansas, the very name of the place conjured up excitement?

— 8 —

William Huntington Russell abhorred injustice. His gravestone in New Haven's Grove Street Cemetery says that he "hated all forms of oppression"—a fervency borne out by the final act of his life, at the age of seventy-six, in 1885. One Sunday morning, from his window he saw a gang of boys throwing stones at pigeons. As a school superintendent with decades of experience training up youth, he hurried to stop the boys, but they "were active and numerous, the park was large, and he was too old for such active, prolonged effort."[5] William had not been sick a single day since childhood, but he suffered a stroke and died a few days later. Of his ten children, two daughters and four sons, including Tom, survived him.

It was said of General Russell when he died that he was "a striking example of the New England life and character"; that "by his transparent integrity and native vigor of intellect he impressed himself on all his pupils and on every order of mind with which he came into contact"; and that a more distinguished ancestry than his "could hardly be named."[6] The Connecticut congressman Nehemiah Day Sperry wrote, "If there ever was a man who labored faithfully and efficiently for the cause of the antislavery party and the election of Abraham Lincoln, that man was General Russell. He put his heart and soul into the cause. Those who knew him best during the days of the antislavery excitement and the rebellion which followed will admit that he had no superior in loyalty, earnestness, and devotion to the cause. [. . .] He was one of the most courageous men I ever knew."[7]

William was a descendant in the fifth generation of another William Russell, originally from Hertfordshire, England, who came to New Haven in 1638 or 1639 during the Great Puritan Migration. His profession is given variously as ship's carpenter, joiner, and cabinetmaker from London. In 1639 he joined his fellow citizens in signing the "Fundamental Agreement" for governance of the new colony. He was said to be well educated.

This first William and his wife, Sarah Davis Russell, had a daughter and a son, Noadiah. When the children were orphaned, Noadiah was raised by a guardian, as his father's will directed, to "be devoted to God in the way of learning, being likely to prove a useful instrument in the good work of the ministry."[8] Education and piety were values held dear by many generations of Russells.

Noadiah attended Harvard and graduated in 1681, my only Russell relative to do so to this day, for at the time there was no Yale. He was "a little man in stature, pious and holy."[9] His *Cambridge Ephemeris*, in which he tracked celestial bodies for the year 1684, was considered notably "free of religious cant" and is said to be the first almanac printed in what would become the United States.[10] At the age of twenty-nine he was ordained pastor of the First Congregational Church in Middletown, Connecticut—known as Mattabeseck to the Wangunk Indians who sold portions of their land to English settlers. The church's first worshippers met under an elm tree behind what is today O'Rourke's Diner, a Wesleyan University institution. Drums summoned the faithful to "meeting." Downhill from the shady knoll where the congregants gathered, Noadiah and his wife, Mary Hamlin Russell, are buried in Riverside Cemetery.

In 1701 ten Congregational clergymen founded Yale College. Noadiah was one of them, and Yale's first diploma bears his signature.

~ 9 ~

For Connecticut's first two centuries, many leading citizens owned enslaved people. Among them were at least twenty-two ministers, including Noadiah Russell.[11] These slaves included American Indians and, increasingly, Africans brought from the West Indies or their home continent. Bringing what were called "Native" slaves into Connecticut was outlawed in 1715. The slave population reached its zenith in 1774, when a census taken for the English Board of Trade estimated the number at 6,500, some 3.4 percent of the population.[12] That same year, the importation of slaves was entirely outlawed in Connecticut.

A century later William C. Fowler observed that the prohibition on slave trading in the colony was first based on economics. Addressing the New Haven Colony Historical Society, he stated, "The people felt that every Negro imported occupied the place of a white man, and they preferred to encourage the superior race. Besides, in the language of [clergyman and historian] Dr. Belknap, 'The winter here was always unfavorable to the African constitution.'"[13] In 1784 the state passed a partial and gradual emancipation act, which provided that no child born a slave could remain enslaved after the age of twenty-five. Another sixty-four years elapsed before Connecticut freed all its remaining enslaved people.

The individuals represented by these dates and numbers were men who labored on Connecticut's stony farmlands building barns and rock walls, shoeing horses, and making barrels. Women cooked, cleaned, sewed, and milked cows.

Slavery was a reality in Puritan-era Connecticut, but its practice was different from the southern plantation institution. Here, slaves could own property and bring a lawsuit against their owners. A male slave could earn his freedom by marrying a free woman with his master's consent. Slaves attended family prayers and church services and were expected to answer questions about the Sunday sermon. One clergyman bequeathed a black maid to his daughter and asked that she or any subsequent owner "make conscience to promote her in her reading, catechism, and all Christianity, that she may profit and grow in religion and godliness and attain the end of baptism to the glory of God."[14] While the relationship between masters and slaves in Connecticut may have been different from that of their counterparts in the South, historian Michael Sletcher has pointed out that "admittedly the evidence is usually told from the master's point of view and we are left to wonder what the slave would have said if given half the chance."[15]

History is silent as to whether Noadiah and Mary Russell's eldest son, the second William Russell on this continent, owned a slave or slaves. His hometown of Middletown traded in human property. A map from the eighteenth century estimated that about a hundred families lived in the village. Twenty-two persons named their occupation as sea captain; three others were sea captains engaged in the slave trade. Three individuals were identified as slave dealers. One old-timer told of seeing a cargo of slaves jailed in town and sold at auction.[16]

This second William Russell was the first of many generations of Russells to graduate from Yale. His wife, Mary Pierpont Russell, was, like him, the child of a Yale founder.

Mary and her sister Sarah both married clergymen. Sarah's husband was another slave owner, the revivalist preacher Jonathan Edwards, whose church in Northampton, Massachusetts, was the birthplace of the Great Awakening. This movement of religious fervor swept south to Connecticut, including Middletown. There, in

1741, four thousand people attended a meeting where the visiting preacher George Whitefield (sometimes spelled Whitfield) delivered a fiery sermon.[17] Factions arose. So-called Old Lights, who stood on the side of tradition and moderation, sided against the "awakened" New Lights. Rev. William Russell, who had succeeded his father at Middletown, was sympathetic to the Old Lights, but after Whitefield spent a night at the Russell home, he said of his host, "I think him an Israelite indeed. [. . .] Oh, that all ministers were like minded."[18]

On May 14, 1730, William Russell preached a sermon before the Connecticut General Assembly that, as a seminarian, Martin Luther King Jr. would cite 220 years later as an example of clergy critiquing religious conditions of their day.[19] Russell called his message "The Decay of Love to God in Churches, Offensive and Dangerous." It was not unusual for a minister to address the legislature, as church and government were hand-in-glove locally and regionally. It has been said that the early history of the Congregational Church in Middletown, as elsewhere in New England, *was* the town's history. In fact, until the adoption of a constitution in 1818, church and state were not separate in Connecticut.

William served the Middletown church for almost fifty years. His son graduated from Yale, entered the ministry, and served a congregation in Thompson, Connecticut.

William was succeeded at the Middletown church by Rev. Enoch Huntington, who had been an eminent scholar during his student years at Yale. One of Enoch's parishioners was Matthew Talcott Russell, the grandson of his predecessor. Enoch's eldest daughter, Mary, married Matthew.

To Matthew and Mary was born William Huntington Russell. His male forebears had served the Middletown church for 148 continuous years as pastors and a deacon.

But to keep from getting ahead of our story—namely, the influence William Huntington Russell would exert on his son Tom, the avian dinosaur Tom would find, and the mother and daughter who would follow Tom to the Kansas plains—let us return to Enoch and the renunciation of slavery in the family.

— 10 —

"We have your ancestor's tricorn hat," Deborah Shapiro told me. "Would you like to see it?" Deborah was the director of the Middlesex County Historical Society at the time of my first visit, in 2015.[20] The society and its exhibit space are located in an 1810 brick building on Main Street in Middletown.

For my appointment she had set out several volumes of books and a stack of files bulging with documents about my branch of the Russell family. She warned me that a large group of third-graders was arriving in half an hour for a tour. If I wanted to look around I should begin now, she suggested, and she would join me in a few minutes.

In an adjacent room, one of John Brown's pikes was mounted on a wall. Later I would hear the pitch of children's voices rising as they imagined, I supposed, spearing a foe with the weapon's business end. Charles Blair, a blacksmith in Collinsville, Connecticut, manufactured the pikes for Brown. They had agreed on a price of one dollar per pike for a thousand pikes, paid in installments. When Brown failed to come up with the money, Blair temporarily halted production of the weapons at five hundred. On April 18, 1859, Brown visited the home of Gerrit Smith in Peterboro, New York. Another guest of the Smiths wrote after meeting him, "New Haven advises him to forfeit five hundred dollars he has paid on a certain contract, and drop it. He will not."[21]

"New Haven" we can take to mean William Huntington Russell. "He was uncompromising in his dislike for anything which was mean or which bore the semblance of trickery," one obituarist wrote of him, adding, "His independence and honesty of purpose always compelled the respect even of those who differed with him."[22] William must have been troubled by conflicting feelings of loyalty to his friend Brown and of suspicion that Brown was concealing his real plans and misusing money entrusted to him for the self-defense of Kansas settlers.

I followed Deborah up stairs and around corners. We came to a case and she unlocked it. On a box lay the stiff, brown, three-cornered hat of my great-great-great-great-grandfather Rev. Enoch Huntington. It was the kind of hat you see men wearing in paintings of the American Revolutionary War. Its turned-up brim was a little tattered. I eyed it in silence.

We walked into an alcove with framed portraits hanging in rows. Deborah shone her flashlight on a painting. "Here he is," she said of the man looking out at us. With his even features, full head of hair, and large eyes, I could see why Enoch was considered a handsome man in an era when, as one man enthusiastically claimed, Connecticut had "some of the finest-looking men at that period that ever appeared probably in our world."[23] Sheer linen preaching bands fell from his collar and lay against his black coat. One hand held a Bible opened midway.

"And here is his wife," Deborah said as she turned her light on Mary Gray Huntington. Mary had sat for her portrait wearing a high bonnet, called a mobcap, edged with a ruffle and brown satin ribbon. Her fair complexion and deep-set eyes were like mine. I texted a photo to a friend. "Whoa," she wrote back. "That is some resemblance."

Downstairs again, for hours I pored over census records and sermons of my ancestors. I examined old maps, looking for their houses. I learned that as a young man Enoch had been ardent about congregational singing, believing it to be a duty in worship, well worth learning, and "a very manly, ornamental, and useful accomplishment."[24] Visiting the Middletown church in 1771, John Adams declared the singing the finest he ever heard in his life.

You don't have to explore Middletown's cemeteries, as I have, to know that many of Connecticut's early citizens, perhaps even your own ancestors, owned slaves. Genealogy sites, newspaper articles, public records, and books are available on the Internet for those who want to find out.

The epitaph on a gravestone in the old Liberty Street Burial Ground, behind the firehouse, is now too weathered to read, but William Cooper Nell recorded the inscription in *The Colored Patriots of the American Revolution*, published in 1855:

> In memory of Jenny, the servant of the Reverend Enoch Huntington, and the wife of Mark Winthrop, who died April 28, 1784. On the day of her death, she was Mr. Huntington's property.

Angelika Krüger-Kahloula, who has written about inscriptions on historical markers, regards these sentences that define Jenny first as a servant and second as a wife as an "extraordinary piece of assertive ownership."[25] One could ask, she suggests, whether a legal matter was at issue (for example a property dispute) or whether Enoch actually meant to claim that his earthly ownership of Jenny would continue in the afterlife.

A second enslaved person, recorded only by her first name of Phillis, is listed on the rolls of the Middletown First Congregational Church as a servant of Enoch Huntington.[26]

A deed of sale in the archives of the Middlesex County Historical Society shows that Jenny was sold by a James Cornwall to Enoch Huntington in 1767. On the back of the deed is a caption written by Enoch's daughter, my great-great-great-grandmother, Mary Huntington Russell:

> The Jenny of the accompanying paper, a very respectable woman, was purchased by the Rev'd Enoch Huntington at her own earnest

request. She had a husband who was free, a blacksmith, who used to visit his wife frequently in her new home and at length took up his abode there with his two apprentices. This being found too much of a burden, he was desired to depart. Jenny was allowed to take her choice, either to stay with the family or go with her husband. She chose the latter, and lived with him till her death, the most friendly feelings always existing between her and the Huntington family. These particulars come from Mrs. Russell, eldest daughter of Mr. Huntington, now in her eighty-fourth year. [. . .] Aug. 21, 1823[27]

Did Jenny's "own earnest request" to be sold to Enoch reflect her desire to leave a harsh master for a kinder one? Can we believe that "most friendly feelings" existed between Jenny and the Huntington family? Or as an old woman was Mary still idealizing the father who had not only owned enslaved persons but actually offered Jenny the Hobson's Choice of remaining with his family or leaving the Huntingtons to stay with her husband?

From the vantage point of more than two centuries later, it is difficult to grasp how someone so "industrious, scholarly, cultivated, genial, and devout" as Enoch Huntington could reconcile owning slaves with his Christian beliefs and, particularly in the Revolutionary period, with his convictions about freedom.[28] Not all clergymen ignored the contradiction. Rev. Levi Hart of Preston, Connecticut, preached a sermon in 1774 condemning the slave trade and slaveholding. It is easy to see why Tom Paine asked, in 1775, how his fellow colonists could "complain so loudly of attempts to enslave them while [holding] so many hundred thousands in slavery."[29]

The forty-seven years of Enoch's ministry at Middletown, from 1762 to 1809, spanned a time of epochal change in U.S. history. In those years occurred the first stirrings of liberty in the American colonies; the War of Independence; the adoption of the U.S. Constitution; the Louisiana Purchase; Zebulon Pike's Southwest

Expedition; the departure and return of Lewis and Clark and the Corps of Discovery; the presidencies of Washington, Adams, and Jefferson and the election of Madison; and the passage by Congress of a law forbidding the importation of slaves after January 1, 1808.

Middletown, too, changed in this period. Once a farming village where the first white settlers and their descendants all knew each other, by the 1750s the riverfront community had begun to attract merchants and other kinds of strangers. The position of the early leading families, whose wealth lay in their landholdings, was being challenged by newcomers who dealt in commerce and questioned laws that favored the Congregational Church and gave it preferential treatment.

Enoch kept a journal, so we do not have to guess what he thought about the way Middletown was changing. In his later years he remembered his impressions of the village when he first considered living there, having heard it was respectable and peaceable. "However I soon perceived a spirit of ambition for rule and posts of honour, which could never be gratified, till it should obtain the place of the leading characters which were in its way," he wrote. "Two seasons of squirmings I have seen, in which under religious pretenses [. . .] a spirit most notoriously opposed to the whole genius and conversation of the Gospel hath been acted out which [. . .] could have nothing for its object but the gratification of mean revengeful proud passions."[30]

As abstract as Enoch sounds, he was reacting to a real challenge to the way of life of himself and people like him. The historian Peter Hall describes it as "a product of intensely personal and very concrete obstacles to [their] ability to live that way they expected to live, their inability to make meaningful or workable provision for their children's futures, the failure of the world to conform to what they expected of it."[31] The oligarchy of the town was under challenge from new arrivals with new money and new ideas. Every generation grapples with change, and Enoch and his contemporaries were no exception.

Clergymen and deacons accepted what today we see as an obvious contradiction. In his address to the New Haven Colony Historical Society in 1873, William C. Fowler explained their worldview:

They were distinguished for their Puritan piety and their high appreciation of civil and religious liberty. [. . .] They believed in the distinctions of superiors, equals, and inferiors. They spoke of these distinctions in their prayers, and acted in accordance with them, in public and private life. [. . .] As they read the New Testament they saw, distinctly, the relation of superior and inferior between God and man, in which obedience was required by the one, and yielded by the other; [and] between husband and wife [and] master and slave. While the Puritans of Connecticut thus looked into the Bible for the rules of duty and the doctrines of religion, they could not help seeing that the chosen people of God, distinguished among contemporary nations for their high civilization, held slaves under the sanctions of the great Lawgiver.[32]

At the same time, the spirit of independence was moving over the colonies. The Continental Congress set aside July 20, 1775, as a day of public humiliation, prayer, and fasting, and on that occasion Enoch—whose brother Samuel Huntington signed the Declaration of Independence and served as both a president of the Continental Congress and a governor of Connecticut—preached a sermon based on verses 8 and 9 from the Book of Nehemiah in the Hebrew Bible. The writer was, Enoch said, an excellent man raised up by God, a patriot, magistrate, and honored cupbearer to the Persian king Artaxerxes I. Pointing out that Nehemiah was born in a foreign land and loved his home country, Enoch drew an obvious comparison with his countrymen. It was a long sermon, almost eight thousand words, more than five times longer than a churchgoer of today hears on a typical Sunday.

He asserted that acts of Parliament and the speeches and schemes of English statesmen were calculated to subdue the American colonists. Had the colonists not made every reasonable attempt to point out their error, and had these attempts not been discouraged? Had not England tried to convert the colonies to "the most abject slavery"?[33] It was "now a day of peculiar trial," he continued. "We have no other new world on earth to explore, or flee to, for an asylum, from the hand of tyranny and oppression. Here we must stand or fall." The sermon was a fervent call to patriotism and courage.

— 12 —

A story circulated in colonial times about a Connecticut clergyman zealous for the cause of freedom who owned a slave named Jack. To argue for his country's liberty and yet own a slave seemed inconsistent to Jack. He said to his owner, "Master, I observe you always keep preaching about liberty and praying for liberty, and I love to hear you, sir, for liberty be a good thing. You preach well and you pray well; but one thing you remember, master. Poor Jack is not free yet." The minister is said to have been persuaded and told Jack that if he "would behave well in his service" for a year, he could have his freedom.[34]

Apart from the contradiction of the minister being persuaded and yet keeping Jack enslaved for another year is the question of his identity. There is no reason to think it was Enoch Huntington, because he owned no male slave and the story originated in a different part of the state. It is logical, however, to suppose that the story reached Enoch's ears as it coursed through Connecticut with the current of liberty.

I do not know when the hatred of slavery so evident in the life of William Huntington Russell took root. His passion may have been fueled by rejecting his mother's defense of her father and his grandfather Enoch Huntington.

I do know something about antipathy toward one's mother or her values. Although I admired many things about my mother—her cultivated manners, her easy way and ready chuckle with people she liked—we were not close. Literally. She was not a mother who hugged her children, offered a lap to climb up on, or patted a place beside her to settle in and be read to.

A cousin of my mother's told me that the Russells suffered from what he called emotional intensity. I wish I had asked that gentle man to say more and help me understand, instead of working out my healing by attempting to resolve an issue with a difficult parent, as psychologists say we do, with a spouse. My mother's intensity typically manifested in anger. One of my nieces told me she and her siblings were afraid of Mom's temper. Her doctor once advised her to get psychiatric support. She found another doctor.

I was the youngest of four children and an asthmatic, somewhat sickly little girl, inward and observant. When I reached junior high school, my mother began telling me, "Join in!" The very idea was repugnant to me. Joining in was her idea of having fun and being fun.

By the time of my senior year in high school, while I was still not a joiner, I was voted the most popular girl in my class of 960 students. I was shocked to learn I had been nominated for this actual class office, like president or treasurer. I might say that I got there my own way and not my mother's, except that I have always figured I won because the popular kids split the votes between them and I collected the rest, like a third-party candidate.

When my friends came to the house, they liked talking with Mom. She showed genuine interest in them, and they found her a good conversationalist. But behind closed doors she had a toggle switch. She could be agreeable or aloof, calm or combustible. Until I read Terry Tempest Williams's description of her own mother as "one of the deepest women I knew and one of the most shallow," I had not known that another daughter might feel as I did.[35] In my mother's defense, her rigid upbringing did not prepare her to create the easy relationship with her children that, as a young person, she told her diary she wanted someday, or to navigate her intense emotions.

When the break between us came, if it can be said there was a break without there having been real closeness, I suppose it was in my preteen years. That is when I first remember thinking I did not like her.

One summer around this time, I took tennis lessons in Woodbridge, the town near New Haven where we spent the summers with my grandmother. Her house had a tennis court across the lane in deep woods. The incentive to keep the ball in bounds was strong, as the woods were covered in poison ivy.

I made friends with a girl in my class. When I asked my mother if I could invite her over to practice, she asked her name. When I said it, she told me not to invite her. In those years, Oklahoma City was home, and all my friends were white and churchgoing. *Anti-Semitism* was not in my vocabulary, so I used the word I knew for discriminating against someone. "You're prejudiced!" I responded. We never spoke about it again.

As an early teen I was not, however, without a role model. She was my choral music teacher, a pretty Southern Baptist with flaming auburn hair. In her popular class we memorized the "Hallelujah Chorus" in SATB, heard frequent sermonettes about right and wrong, and learned never to say "cavalry" if we meant "Calvary." Margaret Haggard was righteous, and we loved her.

Backsliding was another word I heard growing up in Oklahoma. Our family did not attend church regularly, though we were members of a Congregational church, but we lived in an evangelical culture and I learned the language. A backslider was someone who strayed from the path of the religious tenets he or she had been raised with. My mother was a backslider from the social activist principles that animated her great-grandfather, who, as his epitaph states, hated all forms of oppression.

In my college years I took part in antiwar demonstrations. The distance between my mother and me widened even more. She defended the verbal attacks of Spiro T. Agnew, Richard Nixon's vice president, on opponents of their administration. She took the side of National Guard troops who fired on Kent State University students during a campus protest against the Vietnam War. In so many words, she told me that the students who were killed had it coming. I was a campus protestor.

For some long-forgotten thing I said or did, she once shouted at me, "Drop dead!" Later she apologized, but I felt that she wished my brother had lived and not me.

Did a rift exist between William Huntington Russell and his mother over the issue of slavery? She claimed that Jenny, whom her father purchased, asked him to do it and that she remained friendly with the Huntingtons. It is possible. It is also possible that William found his grandfather Enoch's ownership of another human being so indefensible and his mother's idealization of him so unacceptable that he turned to abolitionism. His gravestone states that he came to the movement early in life. He is described there as "a lover of liberty [. . .] who in youth and manhood was among the foremost opponents of slavery and in his closing years rejoiced in the triumph of freedom."

William Russell would not have been alone in opposing his parent or grandparent and taking up the cause of emancipation. The younger Jonathan Edwards published a series of papers condemning slavery, in contrast to his famous father of the same name, the theologian and president of Princeton University, who owned slaves and defended the slave trade.[36]

It is also possible that William's father, Matthew Talcott Russell, opposed slavery, but I have found nothing to suggest a position one way or the other.

Matthew was named for Col. Matthew Talcott, an uncle and the man who would finance his Yale education. Breaking with three generations of tradition, instead of entering the ministry Matthew studied law. He set up his practice in Middletown, where he served as county attorney and city treasurer but was not wealthy. When he died of a bacterial skin infection, in 1828, the care of his widow fell to their fifth son among thirteen children, nineteen-year-old William. That same year he entered Yale.

For William's mother it was not only a punishing year but a punishing decade. In 1826 her brother died after drinking away what looked like a promising career in law. As for her household, the children were numerous, and her husband Matthew's prosperity as an attorney would have depended largely on Middletown's economy, which was in decline. The city's population was not increasing like that of Hartford or New Haven, and some believed its days as a major port and major city were over. There were problems with the youth. "Young men drifted into drunkenness and gambling—and irresponsible political activity—without parental guidance," according to historian Peter Hall, and "young women fell prey to immorality as well."[37] In an effort to reverse the town's decline, public-spirited townspeople undertook several efforts at revitalization. They were determined to attract a school.

An overture was made to the future Trinity College, which went to Hartford. Middletown got instead Capt. Alden Partridge's American Literary, Scientific, and Military Academy. Partridge had his detractors, but his school was not insignificant. The education and training that young William Huntington Russell received there would so shape him that he would model his school in New Haven on it. More famously, the first buildings of Captain Partridge's academy would one day become the North and South Colleges of Wesleyan University.

— 13 —

Students of Captain Partridge were expected to obey strict rules like these:

The utmost order and regularity will be required while at meals—no unnecessary talking will be allowed at table.

Every species of low familiarity, buffoonery, and vulgarity
among the members of the institution is prohibited, under
penalty of dismission.

Every cadet addicted to habits of dissipation or profanity will,
unless he immediately reform, be dismissed.[38]

The daily routine began with morning roll call, taken fifteen minutes after the beating of reveille. Immediately afterward, cadets swept their rooms, made their beds, and stood for inspection. They attended compulsory morning prayers and Sunday church services, to which they were marched.

Every cadet was required to participate in regular parades, wearing his complete uniform and with equipment and arms in perfect order. The amount of clothing, down to the number of pocket handkerchiefs (four the first year, two thereafter), and personal items such as foolscap, quills, candles, and shoe polish was regulated. Participation in at least one long march a year was required "for the purpose of accustoming the cadets to hardship and fatigue, and also for the purpose of instructing them more perfectly in the practical duties of the soldier."[39] As if being descended from generations of devout Puritans wasn't enough, the strict personal and military-style discipline of this school would carve a deep groove in young William Russell's character.

Captain Partridge had come to Middletown from Norwich, Vermont, where he opened his first school after being discharged as head of the U.S. Military Academy. He had himself attended West Point, had stayed on as a mathematics instructor, and, before being named superintendent at the age of thirty, had risen to the rank of professor of engineering. His teaching appointment was significant because in the early 1800s a young, developing United States needed trained engineers and surveyors to build the infrastructure of canals, roads, and railroads for expanding white settlement of the country. Civil engineering was so central to the West Point curriculum that the academy was, as historian Stephen Ambrose has said, "turning out better engineers than soldiers."[40] West Point's elevation of applied science ran counter to the emphasis at other institutions of higher learning, notably Yale, Harvard, and Princeton. In 1828 the Yale faculty issued an influential report declaring that the core of the college's curriculum was and would remain classics, mathematics, and moral philosophy. In New Haven, at "the citadel of righteousness," it was not deemed the function of a college to bend to the needs of a nation.[41]

At West Point the austere and proper Partridge was never seen out of uniform, which consisted in his case of a dress hat, buttoned-up coat, sword, and sash. The cadets called him "Old Pewter." Although order, discipline, and the military drill were a holy trinity to Partridge, his demeanor toward students was fatherly. His engineering class, which he enlivened with stories of campaigns and battles, was the most popular at the academy.

He was less popular with the faculty, with whom he had frequent run-ins. He was subverted outright by an assistant quartermaster. In 1817 he was court-martialed. The court cleared him of charges related to his performance as superintendent but found him guilty of disobeying orders and mutiny following a power-grab when President Monroe appointed a successor. Partridge was treated leniently and given the choice to resign, which he accepted. The following year he stated his intention to start his own academy in his home state of Vermont. A few years after that, in 1825, his private, for-profit American Literary, Scientific, and Military Academy opened in two buildings built for him in Middletown.

William Russell attended the new academy for two years, beginning in 1826. He graduated in 1828 and entered Yale that fall. The same year, an Englishwoman visiting Captain Partridge's school described a scene of chaos. Contrary to what one would expect at a school that on paper sounded strict, she found the hallways and stairs "knee-deep in dirt; and the boys, instead of being at their studies, were romping and squealing all through the rooms, up and down stairs, nothing but loud talking and horse laughs."[42] The house was filthy, with no adult attempting to restore order. A mob of cadets chased the appalled woman to the bottom of the stairs, where she found a teacher who managed to herd the students back into their rooms. A few months later, Partridge abandoned the buildings and returned to Vermont.

- 14 -

Middletown and New Haven are twenty-six miles apart, or a long day's walk. William often traveled the distance on foot to save the stage fare and returned to Yale the next day after breakfast. He supported himself through college and may have needed to economize, but financial necessity was not the only reason he walked. He was inured to long-distance hiking from attending Captain Partridge's academy. Partridge believed that arduous exercise built character and was a vital component of education. During William's two years as his pupil, the cadets visited Washington, D.C., and upstate New York, traveling mostly on foot.

The school catalog for 1827 stated that students would visit Revolutionary War battlegrounds and the site where the British general Burgoyne surrendered to the American patriots. They would also examine navy yards, arsenals, canals, and railroads. Along the way they would experience hardship and exhaustion and cultivate self-reliance. A student account of a previous, shorter excursion to Massachusetts described how the corps, traveling entirely on foot, made twenty-eight miles some days. They marched in pouring rain and extreme heat, traversed mountainous terrain, and trudged through deep, burning sand. The archives of present-day Norwich University, which spun off from the first institution Partridge founded after he left West Point, do not contain rosters of the students who participated in the marches. We cannot be certain therefore that William took part, but, given that about half of the cadets did, there is no reason to suppose he did not and an equal chance that he did.

William's academic record before college did not signal that he would distinguish himself there. In Middletown he did not win any of the prizes for declamation, public speaking, and composition. At Yale, however, he excelled at these things. He attained the positions of class orator and first president of the Linonia literary and debate society, in addition to being secretary of Phi Beta Kappa and valedictorian of the class of 1833.

He is better known for founding the secret society Skull and Bones, which according to author David Richards, himself a member, "began with a prank, which mutated into a series of classic college bull sessions, and ended with a high educational purpose."[43] The prank, as Richards relates in *Skulls and Keys*, was William dressing up as a ghost and visiting the room of two friends, making a lasting impression if not a frightening one. Phi Beta Kappa had recently dropped the requirement of secrecy among members. William and his friends agreed that Yale needed a secret society whose benefits would supplement their education. Among these benefits would be training and practice to think on their feet and to debate and speak extemporaneously. Richards dispels some myths about the origins of Skull and Bones, including that William spent his junior year studying in Germany, where supposedly a group of Hegelian students influenced him to start a secret society at Yale; and that, as an *Esquire* magazine article put it, the society's original purpose was to convert "the idle progeny of the ruling class into morally serious leaders of the establishment."[44]

Conspiracy theories about Skull and Bones abound on the Internet, even linking it to plots of world domination. Some websites erroneously situate my great-great-grandfather in a branch of the Russell family they claim is linked to the opium trade. Much has been written about the society's rituals, dynasties, and highly networked membership roster and about the hopes of young men and, since 1991, women of being tapped in the spring of their junior year. What an

1869 graduate of Yale, Lyman Bagg, said about Skull and Bones still holds: "The mystery now attending its existence is genuine, and forms the one great enigma which college gossip never tires of discussing."[45]

If we delve no further into Skull and Bones but only glance backward to William's great-great-grandfather Noadiah Russell, the Yale cofounder; if we note that William's male ancestors were all Yale graduates since its founding; and if we consider William's achievements as a student and his role in founding the college's most famous secret society, it is clear why one historian concluded, "This remarkable record of close association with the University is perhaps without parallel in the case of any other single family."[46]

– 15 –

In 1836 William married Mary Hubbard. Her father was professor of surgery at the Yale medical college. Less than a mile from Old Campus, William opened his Family School for Boys in a building formerly occupied by the Young Ladies Institute, which Mary had attended. New Haven would be their home for the rest of their lives.

William received a medical degree from Yale in 1838, not planning to practice medicine but expecting the knowledge would help him care for students at his school. It was renamed the Collegiate and Commercial Institute (CCI) and became known informally as the Russell School. To townies, the initials CCI stood for Cabbages Contained Inside. After Gov. William Buckingham appointed William to the rank of major general, in 1862, the school became widely known as General Russell's School or General Russell's Military Academy. CCI and the adjacent Russell home were located in the then-fashionable neighborhood of Wooster Square. One newspaper called the school "one of the city jewels."[47]

William's mission was to provide his students with a general education that would prepare them for college or business. The principal emphases were "thoroughness in work; and secondly, a thorough, all-round culture, both of body and mind."[48] A military school was not his intention, but the emphasis on rigorous exercise and daily drills led to CCI's reputation as one. Its hallmark was discipline—serious discipline of the kind William internalized as a student of Captain Partridge. "The sober faces of the small cadets in surviving daguerreotypes are proof enough of the spiritual and intellectual climate," one writer noted. "The inheritance of two centuries of Calvinism lay like the snows of a New England winter upon the Collegiate and Commercial Institute."[49]

– 16 –

One of the thousands of boys who went through CCI was the future book publisher Henry Holt. In later years he recalled his secondary school days and the towering personality of the superintendent:

> Most of my fitting for college was at General Russell's in New Haven. [. . .] His ideal of education was Military Discipline. He was at heart a kindly man, but I never suspected it before a talk we had shortly before I entered college, when he came to visit me while I was ill at an aunt's in the neighborhood. At school he was little more than a soulless machine—Discipline, Discipline, Discipline. Another exception was in a Sunday evening class of the older boys [when he gave] us a good deal of friendly but sadly biased and rigidly puritanical instruction. He made me a thorough rebel against nearly everything he tried to instill. [. . .] When about half way through my eighteenth year, I entered Yale with the class of 1861. I had, of course, a colossal constitution.[50]

Holt also allowed that the best teacher he ever had taught Latin prose composition at General Russell's school.

A letter from a CCI pupil indicates the standard of conduct expected of students. Cadet A. J. McNutt wrote to General Russell on October 16, 1874: "Dear Sir: As you have asked all the boys to write a confession of their experience at Lake Saltonstall Wednesday afternoon, I will state that I rode out in cars in the company of two or three others and while on the train I smoked a cigarette. That after I got to the lake I bought a programme and watched the races part of the time. I chewed some tobacco, ate some candy and chestnuts, and smoked another cigarette. I think this all that I can think of and hoping that you will deal a little leniently with me [sic]."[51]

At the same time William was running his school and while he was impressing upon students the "stern Puritan virtues" Henry Holt was to recall, he was also raising a family. Ten children were born to William and Mary, beginning in 1837 with Lucy and followed by three more girls and six sons, including one who joined Skull and Bones. One son died in infancy. The others, like their forebears since the foundation of the college, all graduated from Yale except one who died of acute dysentery during his sophomore year.

Thomas Hubbard Russell, the third son, entered the world on December 14, 1851. That winter was one of the severest of the nineteenth century. Henry David Thoreau, in Massachusetts, noted in mid-September "a great change in the weather from sultry to cold."[52] By late November a storm was hammering the eastern United States. On Long Island Sound, which runs along the southern shore of Connecticut, "the wind blew a hurricane, the rain fell in torrents, and the sea ran high," the *New York Daily Times* reported. In New Haven the tide was the highest in ten years.[53] In low-lying parts of the city, where the Russell school and home were located, floodwaters caused extensive damage. In nearby Bristol dams gave way and inundated cellars stocked with winter fuel and provisions. By the middle of December an Arctic mass was parked over the Northeast. In New Haven the temperature fell to minus five degrees in December, and the mean temperature was only 24.9 degrees Fahrenheit. That same winter, a fire broke out in General Russell's school.

Under these trying conditions Tom Russell began life. He was probably delivered at home by his father. A winter storm will not stop an infant from coming into the world any more than inclement weather can silence a minister on a Sunday. On the day Tom was born, parishioners who braved the elements heard the pastor of the College Street Church in New Haven speak on the rousing topic "The Pulpit's Sphere and Urgencies."[54]

– 17 –

On March 28, 1857, an announcement appeared in the Hartford *Connecticut Courant*:

> Any persons in this vicinity who contemplate leaving for Kansas this spring will do well to apply to William H. Russell, Esq., of New Haven, No. 8 Wooster Place, or to H. K. W. Welch, Esq., 298 Main Street, for certificates that will enable them to obtain tickets much under the usual prices. The certificates are furnished gratis; but the applicant must either be personally known or must bring a letter of introduction from some gentleman known to Russell or Welch. A man can travel half across the continent for $31.25 by complying with these requisitions.[55]

The United States of the 1850s was proceeding toward a terrible conflict, and Kansas was central to the question of whether slavery would be dismantled or prevail. As a New York newspaper framed it in March 1856, it was "a question which affects the institutions of all States, from the Rivers to the Ends of the Earth."[56] In 1854 Congress had passed the Kansas-Nebraska Act, effectively overturning the Missouri Compromise of 1820, which prohibited slavery above a latitudinal line following Missouri's southern border. Kansas Territory was above the line, but the new law granted voters there the right to determine whether they would come into the Union as a free or a slave state. In response, a group of Easterners formed a company, the New England Emigrant Aid Society, to populate Kansas with antislavery settlers. Supporters pledged to raise money to be used in strict accordance with the law.

In 1854 the Connecticut assembly voted to change the name of the emigrant aid company to the Pioneer Association and appointed twenty-seven trustees, including William Huntington Russell, to manage the corporation. The same year, politically minded William, who had represented New Haven in the state legislature as a member of the Whig Party, joined other foes of slavery in forming a new party, the Republicans. That autumn John Brown left for Bleeding Kansas to arm four of his sons and a son-in-law against raiders crossing the border from Missouri, where slavery was legal.

In 1856 a group of slavery opponents met in Buffalo, New York. William was chosen as Connecticut's representative to this new National Kansas Committee. Abraham Lincoln was chosen as Illinois's representative but declined to serve because of other obligations. The committee raised funds and used them to outfit companies of emigrants bound for Kansas. Once they arrived, the committee sent them seeds—in 1857, a hundred tons—so they could grow crops on the land they settled.

From New Haven, eighty men volunteered to emigrate to Kansas. Charles B. Lines, who had founded the original Emigrant Aid Society, was elected president of the "colony." In a meeting at the North Church on March 22, 1856, Lines, an attorney, and Henry Ward Beecher, the famous clergyman and brother of Harriet Beecher Stowe, delivered impassioned speeches to an overflow crowd in New Haven's largest hall. Lines praised the families who had "resolved to abandon homes and their thrifty trades and sever themselves entirely from the pleasant associations of New England" to help establish Kansas as a free state.[57] Beecher appealed to the audience to arm the colonists with guns to hunt game, protect themselves from other wild animals, and defend themselves against aggressors. After he took his seat, the enthusiastic audience sang John Greenleaf Whittier's "Song of the Kansas Emigrant" to the tune of "Auld Lang Syne."

Seventy-six-year-old professor Benjamin Silliman of Yale then rose to his feet, asking to be the first to contribute twenty-five dollars for a Sharps rifle. William Russell stood second. By the close of the meeting, all four classes in Yale College had pledged rifles. Added to proceeds from the twenty-five-cent admission charge, the evening's collection for Kansas came to a thousand dollars. A correspondent for the *New York Tribune* wrote that "as cheer after cheer went up for 'freedom in Kansas' and the success of the Colony, every person present seemed to take a deeper interest in Kansas affairs."[58]

– 18 –

On March 31, 1856, the New Haven families left for the West. A waving and cheering crowd of several hundred saw their friends off on a steamboat to New York. The emigrants were described as "mostly large, athletic men, with strong hands and strong hearts, and some of them [. . .] the flower of this, the metropolis of Connecticut Yankeedom."[59] They included two former legislators, a clergyman, a physician, and a couple of theological students.

The Sharps rifles they took with them were nicknamed Beecher's Bibles because crates carrying them were labeled as Bibles to prevent their being stolen, particularly by proslavery elements in Missouri. The new settlement in Wabaunsee, Kansas, became known as Beecher's Rifle and Bible Colony. The settlers served as "conductors" and "stationmasters" on the Underground Railroad. They established a church whose numbers rose and fell over time until, in the twentieth century, parishioners reorganized to create what may have been the state's first multiracial Congregational church. The

Civil War began over Kansas and slavery, and Wabaunsee played an important if largely unrecognized role in the abolition movement.

Following the brutal attacks by John Brown's band on proslavery settlers near Pottawatomie Creek, in May 1856, Brown returned to New England to raise money. At a meeting of the National Kansas Committee in New York in early 1857, he requested money and arms for Kansas. Brown refused to be questioned about his plans. In spite of misgivings on the part of some members, Brown persuaded the committee to give him two hundred weapons and five thousand dollars. The committee deferred to its auxiliary in Massachusetts to supply the arms, explaining that the state committee controlled those. The executive committee in Chicago subsequently determined that sending seed to the settlers was more important than Brown's purpose of repelling Missouri "border ruffians." By early April, Brown stated, "I am prepared to expect nothing but bad faith from the National Kansas Committee."[60]

Later that month the Massachusetts committee authorized Brown to take possession of two hundred rifles already in Iowa. With the possibility of an accident befalling him, and perhaps some members suspecting that he was covertly planning violence, the committee took the precaution of securing from Brown a will. The document he signed on April 18, 1857, assigned the funds and property he collected for Kansas to three trustees, including William Russell:

I, John Brown, of North Elba, N.Y., intending to visit Kansas, and knowing the uncertainty of life, make my last will as follows: I give and bequeath all trust funds and personal property for the aid of the Free State cause in Kansas, now in my hands or in the hands of W. H. D. Callender, of Hartford, Conn., to George L. Stearns, of Medford, Mass., Samuel Cabot, Jr., of Boston, Mass., and William H. Russell, of New Haven, Conn., to them and the survivor or survivors and their assigns forever, in trust that they will administer said funds and other property, including all now collected or hereafter to be collected by me or in my behalf for the aid of the Free-State cause in Kansas, leaving the manner of so doing entirely at their discretion.[61]

It was a provisional will. After his arrest at Harper's Ferry on October 19, 1859, from his cell Brown penned a last will, in which he left each of his children a Bible. On the way to his execution that December, he stated, "I, John Brown, am now quite certain that the crimes of this guilty land will never be purged away but with blood."[62] Among the guards surrounding the scaffolding at Brown's hanging was an actor from Richmond, Virginia, who had recently joined Company F of his state's militia, John Wilkes Booth.

– 19 –

Every morning, about two dozen wild green parrots make their way from a roost at the South Pasadena, California, public library to various locations in Los Angeles County where they look for seeds and fruit. Around twilight they return. They fly mostly in pairs, calling what sounds to my ears like "Krr-aa-aa-aa-aak-rog! Ra-aa-aa-ak!"

These parrots comprise part of a flock—the collective noun is actually a "pandemonium"—of hundreds in the area. I have seen them perched in the trees next to a Bank of America branch, high atop my backyard neighbors' redwood, and on the branches of my next-door neighbors' tall acacia tree. Some locals consider them obnoxious. One in nearby Highland Park complained in an anonymous blog post of not being warned, when he or she bought a house, that it was located in an aviary. Me, I love the parrots' staccato screeches, the wildness they bring to city living, and the emerald-green flashes I see when I scan the skies for them.

On their way to Eagle Rock, a gentrifying neighborhood of Los Angeles, the birds set a course north and west, crossing the Arroyo Seco only blocks from my house and passing directly overhead. In this manner the wild parrots link me to my ancestors and their connections, because their flyway also crosses the place where John Brown's eldest daughter, Ruth, lived in old age. Her house, now gone, and mine are just seven-tenths of a mile apart as the parrot flies.

At the edge of the canyon, a bench marks the spot where Ruth and her husband, Henry Thompson, lived in a small cottage on what is now Arroyo Drive. They struggled to make ends meet, like Ruth's two brothers who followed them to Southern California. Jason and Owen Brown lived in the foothills overlooking Pasadena in a cabin, hermitlike and penniless.

After years of living underground, these Browns (of John Sr.'s twenty children) made California their home with the help of a nurseryman and later U.S. Indian agent named Horatio Nelson Rust. Rust was born in Amherst, Massachusetts. He accompanied his father, an abolitionist, when he went to see the Africans who had been taken captive aboard the kidnappers' ship *Amistad*. The experience horrified Horatio. He took to heart his father's dying wish that he continue the work to abolish slavery.

A few years later, in 1856, Horatio was working in a drugstore in Collinsville, Connecticut, when he met John Brown. Brown was having his thousand pikes manufactured in Collinsville. The friendship that began there lasted until Brown's execution.

Rust volunteered as a medical aide during the Civil War. He lived awhile in Chicago before settling, in 1881, in a Pasadena of five hundred residents. Here he found "good soil, pure water, a better climate . . . and a respectable community."[63] In the hospitable horticultural climate he cultivated Washington oranges, Eureka lemons, and grapes.

In 1884 Rust received a letter from John Brown Jr., then living in Put-in-Bay, Ohio, on Lake Erie. A number of John Brown's children had hidden there from notoriety and the law. John Jr. wrote that his younger brother Jason wanted to move his family to California and find a job in "fruit culture." "He is very skillful in the growing of vines and fruits," John Jr. wrote. "He is capable, industrious, and a radical temperance man."[64] The next month another letter disclosed that Jason's only living son had lost his wife to consumption. Two little grandsons might have inherited a lung weakness and would probably do better in Pasadena's climate.[65]

At the time of his execution, John Brown expressed the hope that his friends would take care of his family. Rust felt the obligation keenly.[66] Not long after his exchange of letters with John Jr., Jason and Owen Brown, along with Ruth and Henry Thompson, were living in Pasadena.

The Brown brothers were strange.

Jason Brown had sharpened swords but was not directly involved in the murders masterminded by his father in Bleeding Kansas, although he was arrested and imprisoned for a time. He was not present for the Harper's Ferry attack.

Owen Brown and Henry Thompson had taken part in the Pottawatomie Massacre. Soon afterward Henry was shot at the Battle of Black Jack. He did not participate in the Harper's Ferry raid, but two of his brothers did and lost their lives. Owen was not on the premises at Harper's Ferry during the attack but kept watch at the nearby hideout in Maryland. When he learned that the raid had failed, he made a dangerous escape. He later recounted the details to a reporter for a gripping article in the *Atlantic Monthly*.

The trauma of violence that surely stayed with them after their participation in John Brown's raids may account for why the Thompsons, Jason, and Owen only scraped by in their Pasadena years. They set out to farm. How could they not make a go of things in such an Eden, with its year-round balmy climate, where, as a physician wrote in 1883, the "soil yields fruits and vegetables every month" and there is "more of God's sunshine to the acre than in any habitable locality known"?[67] Lingering trauma may also explain the vacant expression on Owen's face in a photograph taken of him in later years. Horatio Rust did not employ the piteous survivors, but for years he tried to raise support for John Brown's widow and children. He also sought John Brown collectibles, such as letters and autographs, to sell for the family's welfare, acting as "a one-man eBay."[68]

As old men with grizzled beards, Jason and Owen came down from their cabin in the San Gabriel Mountains to support temperance activities in Pasadena. Owen did carpentry work for Ruth at her cottage, and it was here that she nursed him as he died of pneumonia in 1889. Two thousand people attended his funeral. He was buried near the cabin. The gravesite lured so many hikers that in time the headstone was removed while a committee of citizens established a more secure setting for it. Owen did not marry or have children.

Ruth and Henry Thompson lived until 1904 and 1911, respectively, and are buried in Altadena's Mountain View Cemetery. Horatio Rust's grave is not far from Ruth's. Jason left California and died in 1912 in Ohio.

What are the chances that descendants of William Huntington Russell and John Brown, old comrades from Connecticut in the struggle to end slavery, would make their home in the same city on the opposite coast? Then again, this is the nature of history: chancy, surprising, and full of unlikely intersections.

— 20 —

On January 29, 1861, Kansas was admitted to the Union as a free state. In February the Confederate States of America was formed and in March a constitution was adopted. On April 12, 1861, Confederate troops fired on Fort Sumter, South Carolina, accelerating the Civil War. When news of the attack reached West Point, northerners met in one cadet's room and loudly sang "The Star-Spangled Banner." Another student recalled the occasion as the first time he observed the southerners cowed. A few days later a visiting Union officer who had been at Fort Sumter was serenaded, as was the popular Lt. Fitzhugh Lee, nephew of Robert E. Lee, on the night he left for Virginia. The entire student body saw him off, removing their hats as he passed the barracks.[69]

In New Haven, William Russell's antislavery convictions and speeches lost him friends, backers, and southern students who withdrew from the school. He was in his fifties when the war began. With a large school, a large family, and no true soldiering experience, he declined Connecticut governor Buckingham's offer of a colonelcy. Buckingham then appointed him major general of the state militia and charged him with forwarding troops to the front. Cadets of CCI, known for their proficiency in drilling, were commonly seen in their school uniforms training companies of adult men on the New Haven Green. Others, striplings as young as twelve years old, instructed Connecticut recruits in maneuvers and the handling of arms at Camp Russell (named for William), north of New Haven near the landmark East Rock. Years later, a commendation of General Russell issued upon his death by local veterans of the Grand Army of the Republic stated, "Many of us remember that our first lessons in the school of soldiery were received from pupils of the Collegiate Commercial Institute."[70]

One hundred CCI graduates were commissioned as army officers. Before the war ended, the number grew to three hundred. While most served the Union side, more officers, Union and Confederate, came from CCI than from any institution except West Point.

Mary and William Russell's five underage sons, the eldest of whom was thirteen when war broke out, did not participate in the war. So strongly did William believe in the Union cause, however, that he hired replacements for them. Mary and other women asked for donations of yarn, socks, stockings, and woolen blankets. They collected cotton nightshirts and "drawers, made full, without waistbands, hemmed, and gathered on strong tape" along with "delicacies for the sick . . . such as jellies, farina, corn starch, cocoa, condensed milk, and nicely dried fruit."[71]

Soon after the Civil War began, a new tune began circulating in New England. A band played "John Brown's Body" at Fort Warren, Massachusetts, during a flag raising on May 12, 1861. Connecticut's Thirteenth Volunteer Infantry Regiment sang it in concert in New Orleans, and the band of the Fourteenth played it in Virginia. On November 16, 1864, from a hill above the smoldering city of Atlanta, General Sherman heard music. "Some band, by accident, struck up the anthem of 'John Brown's soul goes marching on,'" he recalled in his memoirs. "The men caught up the strain, and never before or since have I heard the chorus of 'Glory, glory, hallelujah!' done with more spirit, or in better harmony of time and place."[72]

Five months later, news of another man killed in service to his vision for the United States—this time not a fanatic but a great man—reached New Haven. Crowds poured into the streets, flags flew at half-mast, and homes and public buildings were swathed in mourning cloth as word spread that Abraham Lincoln had been assassinated. New Haven's *Daily Register* stated in an editorial on April 15, 1865, "We cannot doubt the murderer of President Lincoln will prove to be insane. It does not seem possible that a man in his right mind could be so depraved—so oblivious to the best interests of our country as to strike at the life of President Abraham Lincoln in a crisis."[73]

Some residents had seen the assassin, John Wilkes Booth, in October 1863, when he came to New Haven to play the title roles in *Richard III* and *Hamlet*.

— 21 —

How word of President Lincoln's assassination reached the Russell household we can only speculate. When the bell at Center Church on the New Haven Green pealed to alert the city to the dreadful news, did William send a runner, perhaps thirteen-year-old Tom, to learn what had happened? Did the New Haven *Palladium*, whose editor was also an antislavery man, send someone to the house on Wooster Place with the report? Did William, his family, and his students then drape the Commercial and Collegiate Institute and the Russell home in black, when only five years earlier they may have hung patriotic bunting to welcome the presidential candidate from Illinois?

Lincoln had campaigned in New Haven. Well known in the Midwest, he nonetheless needed to broaden his base of support before the 1860 nominating convention in Chicago. Two months before his party would nominate him on the third ballot, the man described by a Connecticut reporter as a "gaunt, homely figure, [with an] unpretending manner, conversational air, careless clothing and dry humor" arrived in the City of Elms on an afternoon train from Hartford.[74] The date was March 6, 1860, an occasion that my mother told me her great-aunt Martha Almira Munson, then a girl of ten, never forgot. "I want you to remember this day, Mattie," her father told her as Lincoln passed. "There goes a great man." Five years later the president would appoint Mattie's father, the New Haven attorney Lyman Ezra Munson, to the first supreme court of territorial Montana.

Congressman Lincoln spoke to a packed house at Union Hall. The *Palladium* reported: "Every seat was packed full, every aisle and every foot of standing room were crowded by the throng, and even the platform was not left, but was so covered that it seemed impossible to find room for the officers of the Club and speaker. We have never seen a more intensely excited and interested audience in New Haven."[75] The next day Lincoln made no public appearances. He may have called on Republican friends and supporters. The following evening he took a short train ride to Meriden, spoke to a packed house, and returned to New Haven. A procession and brass band led the candidate to the home of his host, the *Palladium* editor, where a thousand well-wishers gathered and sent up cheers.[76]

The death of President Lincoln leaves us to wonder about the grief and outrage of William Russell, who, as the New Haven historian

Edward Elias Atwater described him, "understood the duties of a citizen in a very profound sense, and thought of them as peculiarly sacred and binding."[77] We are left to wonder, because anything William may have written has been lost. According to his grandson and my late great-uncle Thomas H. Russell Jr., not long after William's death the family sent his collected papers, including all his letters and manuscripts, to a Yale graduate residing in a western state (otherwise unidentified), who had undertaken to write his biography. The writer sent a completed manuscript and all the source material to an eastern publisher. Supposedly it never arrived.

Even so, I allow myself to hope it will someday surface and I will meet the sympathetic character of my great-great-grandfather in his own words. I imagine a postal employee noticing a package in a cavernous warehouse or an editorial assistant at Henry Holt and Company discovering a dusty box marked *Discipline, Discipline, Discipline* and a voice on the phone telling me, "I think I have found something."

Part III
The 1872 Yale College Scientific Expedition

When he was twenty years old, Tom Russell took part in two expeditions. One was the fossil-hunting trip to the West in the fall of 1872. The other, that spring, was a dredging expedition of Long Island Sound to conduct research for his undergraduate thesis, *On the Anatomy of the American Lobster*.

Like anyone who has plunged a lobster into a pot of boiling water, he must have wondered: *Do lobsters feel pain?* According to People for the Ethical Treatment of Animals, the answer is yes. The Lobster Conservancy, based in Maine, explains on its website that while these exoskeletal creatures have stress receptors and can sense temperature changes, their receptors cannot truly be compared to ours. Lobsters are in fact distant relatives of spiders; both are members of the invertebrate phylum *Anthropoda*. Lobsters are prehistoric. Paleontologists have identified lobster-like creatures dating back 480 million years. Some were as large as humans.

Since the close of the twentieth century, the lobster population along the coast of southern New England has declined alarmingly. As our planet's rising temperatures have warmed the waters of Long Island Sound, lobsters there have been relocating to chilly coastal Maine.

Climate change isn't the only problem confronting *Homarus americanus*. In the late 1990s, an immense population of lobsters in the Sound died in a matter of days after an insecticide intended to eradicate mosquitoes, which are distantly related to lobsters, was sprayed in New York City and Long Island. One lobster distributer in New York hung a strip of tape coated with insecticide in a storage area to kill flying insects. Two days later he found dead bugs. The dozens of lobsters in his holding tanks were dead, too.

During the last vacation of his senior year, Tom Russell and his classmate Theophil Mitchell Prudden chartered a sailboat, the *Washington*, and plied the waters of coastal New England. Mitchell, as his family and friends knew him, came from an old Connecticut family, like Tom's. His father was an abolitionist and Congregational clergyman.

Their dredging expedition included others who may have been classmates or hired crewmen or both. They sailed as far as Wood's Hole and Edgartown, Massachusetts, "had a glorious adventure, and brought back much plunder."[1] One measure of their success in collecting is that Tom and Mitchell were credited with documenting previously unrecorded invertebrate habitats and being first to dredge in the waters of Wood's Hole.

Without identifying them by name the *Yale Literary Magazine*, an undergraduate publication, reported on the trip:

The Expedition to Martha's Vineyard has been very generally commented on, and perhaps nothing more can be added. It was undertaken by some Seniors for the purpose both of pleasure and science. Leaving the Wednesday after the term closed, in the Yacht *Washington*, they sailed through the Sound stopping at New London and Newport. Arriving at Edgartown, in Martha's Vineyard, on Saturday, they remained there over Sunday. While three of the party were attending a Methodist meeting in the evening, the only door in the building was mysteriously locked. [. . .] According to the general law of piety, the females present exceeded the males, their relative proportion being as thirty to three; but these three being somewhat advanced in years, it devolved upon the Seniors present to solve the problem of egress, which was accomplished in no other way than by assisting the inmates one by one out of a window. Returning to their boat, the surprise of the remainder of the party, on hearing an account of the adventure, was less than was consistent with innocence. The next day the Yacht directed its sail homeward. Dredging was pursued more or less each day with success. All reached New Haven safely, after a week's absence, well pleased with the excursion.[2]

Tom and Mitchell pulled in enough shellfish to support writing their senior theses, Tom's on lobster anatomy and Mitchell's on fiddler crabs. At graduation they shared the prize for the best collection illustrating the freshwater zoology of New Haven and its vicinity. Prudden also won a prize in botany.

They may have brought back enough lobster to share or even sell, to recoup some of their expenses. Lobster had by this time risen in status from a prison food to a delicacy. I like to picture these serious students who would rise high in the medical profession enjoying their fill of shellfish, drenching each bite in enough sweet butter to run down their chins.

– 23 –

"What to do next?" The *College Courant*, a weekly journal published in New Haven, posed this question in a headline on June 15, 1872.[3] How would the thousands of young men graduating from colleges that year put their educations and talents to use? Some might postpone their choice of a life work, the unidentified editorialist commented. Others might continue their studies or travel. The majority, however, "must take upon themselves something definite," choose a profession, and decide on a direction in life. Nearly one-third of Yale graduates in those days chose law. Theology, long a strength of Yale, was a calling to which "the preacher, of all men . . . should be sure." The third traditional vocation, medicine, demanded "such peculiar natural talents and such a turn of mind" that only a calling to the profession fitted a man to it. "If ambitious, he studies Law," the *Courant* said. "If conscientious, he studies Theology. If curious, he studies Medicine." Undecided graduates were advised to consider journalism or science.

As a freshman Tom had enrolled with his father's permission in Yale's Sheffield Scientific School. He wanted to pursue a scientific track instead of the traditional "academical" course. A young man wanting to study the sciences or engineering no longer needed to get his education at West Point.

The publisher Henry Holt, in his *Garrulities of an Octogenarian Editor*, described the Yale from which he graduated in 1862 as a place where students of the scientific school and medical school "were more or less looked upon as men of sin."[4] He recalled one wag saying that the law school was next to the jail, the divinity school was on the road to the poorhouse, and the medical school faced the graveyard. By 1872, when Tom graduated, medical studies had gained more respect. Medical students were no longer looked upon as cadaver-hunting grave robbers.

The course at "Sheff" was three years long and led to the degree of Bachelor of Philosophy, or Ph.B. Tuition was a hundred dollars a year plus another five dollars for the graduation fee. Chemistry students paid an additional seventy-five dollars for lab supplies. First-year students studied physics, chemistry, mathematics, French, German, and English. As juniors and seniors they chose one of seven majors: chemistry, civil engineering, mechanics, mining and metallurgy, agriculture, natural history and geology, or science and literature. No single major included zoology, botany, organic chemistry, and physiological chemistry, or what we now call biochemistry.

Tom and Mitchell both intended medicine as a profession. The school's governing board had approved a new curriculum for medical studies in 1868, and the faculty were thus at liberty to create a special program for Tom and Mitchell. It gave them the benefit of closer relationships with their professors than their peers had. One invited them into his herbarium at home for advanced work. They studied chemistry under another professor in his private laboratory. In the "bug lab" they worked less as students than as assistants to their zoology professors. They became familiar with Professor Marsh's rooms and the foul smell of mammals macerating in chemicals. In 1872 Tom and Mitchell finished their studies as the first premed graduates of Yale.[5]

College wasn't all work. Tom joined a reading club and the Sheff secret society Book and Snake. As a senior he sang second bass in an octet called The Crows. His pursuits were tame compared to those of others at Yale, whose activities were publicized by newspapers hundreds of miles from New Haven. In February 1872 the *Louisville Courier-Journal* ran a squib about fourteen Yale men who were engaged to the same serial heartbreaker. On March 8 the *Indianapolis News* told of a daring student who allegedly drank the alcohol preserving a toad. The *Detroit Free Press* stated, on March 27, that the average Yale student smoked five dollars' worth of cigars in a week. That year, the faculty first considered allowing students to attend a single Sunday church service instead of two.

Tom went west with Marsh in 1872, while Mitchell joined the 1873 party. Mitchell may have originally intended to join the 1872 expedition, but the death of his father that year and an offer to teach freshman chemistry for a professor traveling in Europe may have changed his mind.[6]

It seems that at first Marsh did not so much tap students for an expedition as accept them once they approached him, if the experience of George Grinnell indicates the professor's recruiting method. Three weeks after Grinnell approached Marsh to ask about the 1870 trip, he learned he was accepted as a member of the party and quickly realized he *was* the party. He then urged his own friends to apply.

For the three subsequent expeditions, Marsh may have been more selective. Some who knew him considered him good company, but he had few intimates and chose to befriend "those whom it was most desirable to know," as his contemporary Timothy Dwight put it.[7] In his mansion on Prospect Street, the first home of the forestry school at Yale, Marsh "exercised a cheerful hospitality," Henry Holt recalled, but he never married "despite a constant yearning which he confided to me for a chatelaine for his house. He wanted everything in the woman, including a fortune that would prevent her limiting his enjoyment of his own."[8]

Marsh was likewise expedient in choosing whom to take west, at least after the first expedition. According to Ernest Howe, who intended to write a biography of Marsh but did not complete it, few of his assistants became professional paleontologists—that is, competitors—and many excelled in their unrelated chosen careers.[9]

Tom Russell, the product of a deeply rooted Yale family, would have interested Marsh for his connections, for having studied the sciences, and, presumably, for his work ethic and even disposition. Tom's friend and colleague William Hawkes would praise him many years later for "his methodical thoroughness, his sober seriousness of purpose, his conspicuously quiet and sympathetic manner."[10] Tom was serious, but hopeful and cheerful, Hawkes added, with a sense of humor "which was apt to turn the point of a situation upon himself, always sparing another, unable to wound anybody's feelings." An undergraduate classmate, Charles A. Tibbals, described Tom as shy but "strong, sincere, and straightforward—a singularly pure and gentle soul." He was, Tibbals summed up, "a man to tie to."[11]

Apart from any personal qualities or credentials Marsh may have desired in his volunteers, he seems to have expected them to perform certain tasks beyond collecting fossils. In the foreword to a collection of her brother's papers, Mitchell Prudden's sister noted that his memoranda and notebooks indicate Marsh assigned him a quartermaster role, in effect, on the 1873 expedition. "Doubtless, in this way," she wrote, "he earned his expenses for this unusual experience."[12] According to Howe's notes, Marsh bore the expense for the first Yale trip. The second year, the government provided escorts and provisions, while the remaining expedition costs that season totaled some $15,000 (about $325,000 today).[13] Of his own experience on the final trip, in 1873, Henry W. Farnam, later a professor of economics at Yale, recalled that students paid not only their own personal expenses but also the expenses of the expedition, including the cost of shipping the fossils they collected back to New Haven. They also packed the fossils, despite finding it "very difficult," Farnam wrote, "to get any information from Professor Marsh on what we were doing."[14]

– 24 –

Four Yale graduates accompanied Marsh on the 1872 expedition: Tom Russell, James MacNaughton, Benjamin Hoppin, and Charles Hill.[15]

James MacNaughton had graduated the previous year and returned to his home, in Albany, New York. He began studies at Albany Medical College under his father, a dean of the school and a leading physician of the city. At the end of his senior year at Yale he had taken a prize in astronomy. Marsh may have hoped his ability to navigate by the stars and his year in medical school would prove useful.

Benjamin Hoppin was descended from an old New England family and was the son of a divinity school professor at Yale. In his second year of college he won two prizes in English composition. He was tapped for Skull and Bones. As a senior he won a third composition award, joined Phi Beta Kappa, and was chosen as a speaker for the commencement exercises, held July 8 through 12, 1872.

Later in life Hoppin would travel to the Arctic with Robert Peary (then a lieutenant, ultimately an admiral) and in 1896 publish a vivid and detailed account of that voyage. Marsh may have expected Hoppin to keep notes during the trip west, and during his interview Hoppin may have agreed or even volunteered to do it. Why he did not, or why any journal he may have kept has never come to light, and why so little is known about the 1872 expedition compared to the other three—the clue could lie in an unnerving experience Benjamin would have in Kansas when he became separated from the group and spent a night alone on the plains.

Charles Hill came from a pioneer lumbering family in New Brunswick and Maine. In the only photograph of the 1872 expedition, Hill, wearing moccasins, holds in his left hand the barrel of a rifle aimed alarmingly close to the right side of his face, foreshadowing the manner of his death.

And Tom Russell, whose abolitionist father supported New Haven emigrants when they left to settle in Kansas. The first member of his family to see the American West. A student of science instead of the traditional academic curriculum. Serious and somewhat shy, but not humorless. A man to tie to.

Benjamin, Charles, and Tom had been classmates at General Russell's School. One of them, perhaps Tom, may have persuaded the others to go west with Marsh. Their parents may have consented because they would travel in the company of known schoolmates, a distinguished professor, and, when they reached the West, armed soldiers.

– 25 –

On October 9, 1872, Tom Russell, Benjamin Hoppin, and Charles Hill left New Haven. They would travel to the Rocky Mountains by way of St. Louis, the *Hartford Daily Courant* reported.[16] There they would meet Professor Marsh and depart immediately, expecting to return that winter. For Tom to begin his postgraduate medical studies at that time would have been unusual, but he evidently had arranged to defer his admission.[17]

That same year, Yale played its first football game, against Columbia, and won 3 to 0. Henry Ward Beecher, who in 1856 had spoken stirringly in New Haven to raise money for rifles to outfit the Kansas settlers, was exposed for having an adulterous relationship with a congregant. Innovations designed for safety and convenience—the fire extinguisher, the doughnut cutter, and dried milk—were granted patents. Residents of New York City saw the opening of the Metropolitan Museum of Art and Bloomingdale's department store. Serialization of George Eliot's novel *Middlemarch*, whose first installment appeared in December the preceding year, was completed. On the political front, an 1872 report on the U.S. Census of 1870 found there was no constitutional basis for having excluded American Indians as "a constituent part of the population viewed in the light of all social, economical, and moral principles."[18] Voting and office-holding rights were restored to southern male secessionists under the General Amnesty Act, excepting Confederate military leaders. The first African American governor, Pinckney Benton Stewart Pinchback, of Louisiana, took office. In June both the Woman's Suffrage Convention and the Republican National Convention met in Philadelphia. The Equal Rights Party chose Victoria Woodhull as their presidential candidate, and Republicans nominated President Ulysses S. Grant for reelection. Grant won. Suffragist Susan B. Anthony was arrested for voting. Also in 1872, William F. "Buffalo Bill" Cody's gallantry as an army scout earned him the Congressional Medal of Honor, and he made his stage debut, in Chicago. Yellowstone became the world's first national park. A Kansas ear, nose, and throat doctor named Brewster Higley wrote a poem that achieved fame as "Home on the Range," which in 1947 was chosen as the state song of Kansas.

In New York, the three Yale graduates bound for the West became a party of four when James MacNaughton of Albany joined them. When they reached St. Louis, they met up with Marsh. Two months earlier the city had been shocked by an accident involving two flying-trapeze performers in a circus. Before five thousand spectators, Fred Lazelle was hanging by his feet from a rope and swinging toward the trapeze when the mechanism began to shake. Down went Lazelle and his fellow artist William "Billy" Millson. A third acrobat, George North, who was on the ground below, fell under their weight. Women fainted, children cried, and a crowd rushed toward the downed men. None of the three was mortally wounded, though Millson sustained serious injuries and North suffered internal bleeding.[19]

The Yale party continued on to Kansas City, Missouri. There, a sensational event had occurred less than a month earlier, on September 26, when the Kansas City Exposition was robbed. One evening at twilight the exposition association's treasurer collected the day's receipts, a sum in the low five figures. Another thousand dollars was left in the cashbox, in the care of a ticket-seller. As the crowd exited the grounds half an hour later, three masked men, including Jesse and Frank James, rode up on horseback and stole the cashbox. Three days later, an opinion piece appeared in the *Kansas City Times* expressing admiration for the bandits' frontier spirit: "Crime of which daring is simply an ingredient has not palliation on earth or forgiveness anywhere," wrote John Newman Edwards. "But a feat of stupendous nerve and fearlessness that makes one's hair rise to think of it, with a condiment of crime to season it, becomes chivalric; poetic; superb."[20] If the four young Easterners did not know the West was wild before they left home, they must have figured it out by the time they crossed the Missouri River.

The cities from which they had departed, Albany and New Haven, were tame and established by comparison. Albany, with a population just under 70,000, was the twentieth-largest city in the United States at the time of the 1870 census. New Haven ranked twenty-fifth, with a population close to 51,000. Today, neither city ranks among the top one hundred most populous U.S. cities.[21]

Located on the Hudson River and at the eastern end of the Erie Canal, Albany was a thriving commercial center, with a shipping and transportation infrastructure connecting it to New York City. Stoves, a primary export, "cooked the dinners and boiled the tea-kettles" of lumbermen in Maine, settlers in Texas, and pioneers on the frontier, a *New York Times* article stated.[22] Chartered in 1686, Albany was by 1871 the country's largest market for barley, made into malt and alchemized into beer by its breweries, and was a significant market for lumber.[23] In addition to its public schools and a law school, the city had an observatory, a two-year normal school for training teachers, and one of America's first medical schools.

The New Haven of 1872 was a 234-year-old city whose college had graduated young men for more than a century and a half. It was connected by railroad to Hartford and to New York City, where the Grand Central Depot, built by Cornelius Vanderbilt, had opened in 1871. Streetcars, originally horse-drawn, connected central New Haven to its suburban neighborhoods. An 1868 photograph shows a neat downtown with two- and three-story buildings and several church steeples. Streets were still unpaved and without electric lighting, however, and electrification of hospitals and operating rooms, public buildings, businesses, and private residences was more than a decade away.[24] Even so, the city was respected as a hub of learning and culture.

A tourist guide of the time described places and scenery that travelers crossing the continent by railroad would see. While the 1872 expedition did not follow the same route laid out in George Crofutt's guide, the advice he offered was just as apt for the journey of the four young Yale graduates: "As you are about to leave the busy hum and ceaseless bustle of the city for the broad-sweeping plains, the barren patches of desert, and the grand old mountains— for all these varied features of the earth's surface will be encountered before we reach the Pacific coast—lay aside *all* city prejudices and ways for the time [. . .] and for once be *natural* while among nature's loveliest and grandest creations. Having done this, you will be prepared to enjoy the trip—to appreciate the scenes which will rise before you."[25]

26

After some twenty-two hours, the train from Kansas City arrived in Wallace, Kansas, on October 15 around nine o'clock in the morning.[26] The journey from New Haven had taken six days. Notice of the Marsh party's imminent arrival had traveled by what American Indians called the "talking wire." On October 14 a telegram had been sent from Fort Leavenworth to Fort Wallace. The next day, orders concerning an escort for the expedition were hand-entered into the post records.[27]

Headquarters Fort Wallace Kansas

October 15, 1872

Special Orders

No. 103

I. In pursuance of telegraphic instructions dated Hdqrs. Dept. of the Missouri Oct. 14, 1872 the Commanding officer Co. "H" 3d Infantry will detail four (4) men of his Company to proceed as escort to Professor O. C. Marsh on an exploring expedition not to go beyond twenty miles from this post.

The escort will be rationed for twelve (12) days.

II. The Quartermaster's department will furnish the necessary transportation.

III. Private Herrigle Co. "D" 6th Cavalry on extra duty as teamster in the Quartermaster's department is hereby detailed to accompany the escort.

By order of Captain [Louis Thompson] Morris

Thos. S. Wallace

1st Lieut. 3d Infantry

Post Adjutant

Much as I would like to know Tom Russell's impressions when he stepped off the train at Wallace, because he did not record them it isn't possible. But by piecing together what is known about the town's history, I can picture some of what he saw.

Wallace had undergone an economic boom in 1869 with the arrival of the Kansas Pacific Railway. The population swelled to 3,600 (compared to the 2010 census figure of 57). Records of the early days of the Wallace Hotel, sometimes called the Railroad Hotel, are sketchy, but sometime before 1872 a one-story building 150 or 200 feet long by about 30 feet wide had been constructed coincident with the laying of track. A succession of proprietors ran the hotel. These included the "urbane" Henry H. Metcalf and John A. McGinty, who distinguished themselves in 1870 by serving a five-course Christmas dinner to snowbound railroad passengers.[28] Managed later by a husband and wife named Ruggles, the hotel, just steps from the rails, boasted a fountain that "[threw] its tireless, clear spray from a bronze swan's bill" and helped to create "an oasis pleasing and cheering to the tourist."[29] A few months after the Yale expedition passed through Wallace, Fred Harvey opened a dining establishment, a chain he later named Harvey Houses, in the hotel.[30]

Wallace also had a two-story telegraph office constructed of stone, a post office, and a building for the use of railroad officials and clerks. In the former stagecoach building, Thomas Madigan, an Irish immigrant who had prospected for gold in Colorado, opened a "liquor house" in 1870, believing that men needed "a place where [they] could obtain their daily supply of liquor."[31] Having learned from experience that "grub was scarcer than gold," as he put it, he expanded the tavern into a general store, foodstuffs included.

Before setting off to hunt for fossils and encamp by the Smoky Hill River, Marsh likely purchased at Madigan's such provisions as canned fruit, flour, sugar, coffee, and spirits. The previous year, the *Lawrence* (Kansas) *Daily Journal* reported that Marsh had "[laid] in well for commissary stores" at Wallace, running up a bill exceeding two hundred dollars, or more than $4,200 in today's currency.[32]

  I wondered if Charles Hill, who wore moccasins for a studio portrait of the 1872 Yale College Scientific Expedition, bought them at Madigan's.

27

Holding up the long sleeve of a man's blue shirt with piping at the cuffs, I called out to Leighton Bowers, "Was MacNaughton's shirt something like this?"

Leighton is the director of research at Western Costume Company in Los Angeles. I was following her down a long row of men's shirts in the firm's warehouse. It smelled old but clean, like a great library.

She turned around to look at the sleeve. We had just spent an hour examining the clothing worn by the seven men in the photograph of the 1872 expedition. She thought their shirts were made of a durable type of cotton, such as canvas, cotton duck, or gabardine.

"Could it have been cotton flannel, like this?" I asked.

"Not in the real West," she said. "Only in Hollywood."

Western Costume has outfitted actors for the movies for more than a hundred years. This is where costume designers can come to select clothes from more than eight miles of garment racks. Here you can see a gown worn by Vivian Leigh in *Gone with the Wind* or the ruby slippers that with a couple of clicks took Dorothy Gale home to Kansas. The warehouse seems like an archive, but it isn't. You can rent the costumes or even buy them at the company's annual spring sale. They also make costumes, from bespoke shoes to hats fashioned by milliners on the premises.

This was my second trip to Western Costume. On a previous visit I had met with Kurt Cox, a uniform specialist who in thirty years in the film business has made saddles, ridden horses in movies, and curated museum displays of military uniforms for the Autry Museum and the Ronald Reagan Presidential Library. From Kurt I learned that the accessory holding my great-grandfather's conspicuous array of bullets was not a bandolier but a prairie belt, also called a waist-belt. Tom's gusseted shirt was made from a large square of fabric, a style that permitted more freedom of movement than a tailored shirt.

Marsh was wearing a work coat, probably corduroy. Standing behind Tom Russell in the photograph, the guide Ed Lane was not carrying binoculars, as I called them, but field glasses. Precision matters in Kurt's line of work. "I try to be as accurate as I can," he told me. "Every cop and military uniform is as authentic as possible, from boot soles to handmade epaulets to helmets," he said for Western's website. "[My] goal is for you to look at a guy, and you don't know if he's in a movie or if he's real."[33]

On this visit to Western Costume, I hoped Leighton could tell me where the Yale students might have acquired their clothing. It was possible that garments like these were tailor-made back East, but how else might someone from New York or Connecticut have obtained suitable garb for the American West?

The garments were not custom-made, Leighton told me. Her assistant opened a large volume of bound *Harper's Illustrated* magazines to show me advertisements for ready-made clothing available by mail order. By 1872 there were many outfitters for western-bound travelers. The railroads distributed pamphlets to game hunters, encouraging them to get off the train at stops along the route and buy things. It was good for the local economy. Every little town had a store where merchandise was sold.

Leighton was surprised that all the men's hats were rumpled. Tom Russell and Lt. James Pope wore porkpie hats, a style named for the British culinary classic and one that Brad Pitt has been photographed wearing. I had seen an article about Pitt and Angelina Jolie's breakup, in which the writer asked at what point Jolie had realized the kind of man she was married to. As she put it, "Was it the porkpie hat?"

Professional costumers, like other kinds of professionals, often see things differently. What Kurt Cox called a work coat, Leighton Bowers called either a work coat or a hunting coat. He saw woolen shirts, she saw cotton. He saw corduroy, she saw moleskin. He saw buttons made of glass or rubber, she saw shiny, probably metal buttons.

Together we examined the neckerchiefs, lapels, ties, and tie-pins; Ed Lane's sack coat, Lieutenant Pope's frock coat, Professor Marsh's coat with many pockets; Tom Russell's high-top cavalry boots, James MacNaughton's riding boots; everyone's button-fly wool pants; Benjamin Hoppin's hat; and Charles Hill's moccasins. Leighton speculated that Hill likely purchased the moccasins from a western outfitter.

Downstairs in the warehouse we walked past dozens of porkpie hats displayed high above us. Rows of clothing were labeled, for example, "1800s–1900s Western Pants, Tan." Other trousers were grouped as assorted khaki, canvas, or black canvas. Jackets were crowded onto high racks overhead, with vests hanging still higher. To reach them, wardrobe specialists climb ladders and pull down what they need, and the company puts it on their account.

One "Western Coat" looked shredded. *The Revenant*? I thought of a story I had read just the week before about a man who was mauled by a bear in the Sierra Madre foothills in Los Angeles County. He was hiking alone when he came upon a black bear, which rose up on two legs. The man shouted and began stepping away, only to realize he was backing up to a second bear, which grabbed his wrist, knocked him down, and put its mouth on his neck. *This could be it for me*, he told himself, before thinking, *It isn't over 'til it's over*. He held perfectly still for about ten seconds. The bear let go and walked away with the first bear.

Costumes are not merely clothing. They can conjure a scene in our mind, just as the shredded coat evoked a bear attack in mine. They let loose our imagination. They help actors, and possibly even tenderfeet from the East, get into character.

28

"The great beauty of Fort Wallace is its unattractiveness, being surrounded by a desolate country, over which not a spear of grass four inches high dare show its head for fear of the wild winds."[34] So said a journalist from Missouri visiting the area in May 1870. From the local post office the four young men from Yale could have sent letters home saying they had arrived safely in Kansas. If anyone did, however, we know of no letter that has survived. We cannot say whether the first impression was of a "desolate country" or the "beautiful little village" Maj. Alfred Rochefort Calhoun described after he accompanied a railroad surveying party three years earlier.

Contrary to the image many of us have of a frontier outpost from watching westerns, Fort Wallace was not surrounded by a high, gated stockade. Instead, like other forts on the plains, the structures—including officers' quarters, barracks, laundresses' quarters, commissary storehouses, mess halls, stables, chapel, schoolhouse, hospital, and kitchen—stood in the open. To say Fort Wallace looked exposed is an understatement. Mrs. George Armstrong Custer's first sight of Fort Riley, Kansas, in 1867 gave her a similar feeling: "I supposed, of course, it would be exactly like Fortress Monroe, with stone walls, turrets for the sentinels, and a deep moat. I could scarcely believe that the buildings, a story and a half high, placed around a parade-ground, were all there was of Fort Riley."[35]

Fort Wallace was established to support what Kansas historian Leo E. Oliva has called "the Anglo-American invasion of prime buffalo country south of the Platte River and north of the Arkansas River."[36] This region of western Kansas was home to American Indian tribes whose ancestors had lived in North America for thousands of years. White settlement of these lands, supported by the U.S. Army, was tantamount to a national demand that indigenous people surrender their hunting grounds and age-old way of life. Their resistance took many forms. Telegraph wires were severed so cleverly that cuts could be discovered only by a repairman examining long stretches of line. Poles were pulled down, and wires were laid across railroad tracks to ensnare trains. Track was pulled up to disrupt the railroads' advance.

Both parties to the strife waged raids and counterraids over a vast theater from Montana to the Texas-Mexico border, and for many years. The so-called Indian Wars are often demarcated as beginning in 1864 with the Sand Creek Massacre in southeastern Colorado and ending in 1890 with the Battle of Wounded Knee in South Dakota, but conflict between American Indians and colonizing whites can be traced as far back as the arrival of European immigrants in the seventeenth century.

In the years after the Civil War, the U.S. Army supported national expansion in the West by guarding stagecoach routes, railroad construction crews, and homesteaders. The army's aim, consonant with federal policy, was to confine Native people on reservations and force them to take up farming as a way of life. An attendant aim was to bring about the extinction of the American bison. These animals were the Plains Indians' main source of food, and so much more: the bison tongue and choice meat from the hump were delicacies consumed fresh, while other cuts were dried and cured for jerky; hides were made into tipis, clothing, and parfleches; the wool served as bedding; horns were fashioned into cups, spoons, and other utensils; the bladder held water; the stomach became a cooking pot; and the sinew was used as thread for sewing as well as for bowstrings.

Reporting on his survey of the Smoky Hill Trail in 1860, Lt. Julian R. Fitch described entering buffalo country and seeing, for miles in every direction, "shaggy monsters of the prairie, grazing quietly upon the richest pasture in the world." Others with better knowledge than he, Fitch said, had estimated their number in the millions, "as being greater than all the domestic cattle in America."[37]

As the railroads brought white tourists into the West, passengers were encouraged to shoot buffalo from their coaches. The carcasses were left to rot on the plains or be consumed by wolves and other scavenging animals. The skulls were so numerous that the Western Union Company decorated their office roofs with them.

One railroad shipped more than a million pounds of bones east.[38] An old-timer from western Kansas recalled loading up a buckboard with bison and cattle bones and selling them at Dodge for a dollar a load. He was told they were used in manufacturing sugar. Years later, the man's grandson visited the Imperial Sugar Company exhibit at the Texas State Fair. A display showed the final stage of refining, called whitening. For this, the sugar was filtered through charcoal made from charred bones.[39] Another byproduct of buffalo bones was bone-meal fertilizer. Buffalo skulls were used to pave a street in Topeka.[40]

In 1871 an eastern tannery developed a method for processing bison hides on a commercial scale. For the next two years, the number of bison killed every day averaged five thousand. Buffalo hunters were paid to ship hides—a million and a quarter in 1872 and 1873 alone[41]—that were tanned for shoes or made into leather belts for machinery to power the factories of an industrializing nation. What year the immense herd of the southern plains was gone is not certain, but it was dying out as early as 1874.[42]

To tan so many hides consumed great quantities of the highly tannic bark of hemlock trees. Pennsylvania's Wilcox Tanning Company, on the eastern side of what is now the Allegheny National Forest and near a railroad, went through 63,000 tons of hemlock bark in a year and employed as many as four hundred men just to peel it.[43] The rest of the tree, which was considered unsuitable as a building material, was left to rot. Forcing American Indians onto reservations, slaughtering bison, and destroying hemlock forests was a knot of subjugation, despoilment, and loss. There were many such knots in the history of the West.

We know what the United States gained by developing the interior of the country. But when the great herds of buffalo disappeared, the Plains Indians' traditional way of life was subverted, and what seemed like inexhaustible natural resources were converted into commodities, what did we lose?

29

Fort Wallace was one of several Kansas forts established in the 1860s to protect commerce and white travelers on the Smoky Hill Trail, which followed the Smoky Hill River through much of Kansas. Gold seekers joining the 1859 rush to mining camps in Colorado could cross the central plains sooner by following the Smoky Hill Trail, which was shorter by a hundred miles and several days than the Santa Fe Trail to the south and the Oregon-California route to the north. The available water was less alkaline, and buffalo grass was plentiful for grazing animals in both summer and winter.[44] The trail was also situated within a vast sweep of land where nomadic Indians had long hunted buffalo and made camp. The choice campground and burial site Big Cottonwood Grove, or Big Timbers, near the present-day border of Colorado and Kansas, was only twentysome miles west of Fort Wallace. It was this grove, a prominent landmark resembling a cloud of smoke, that George Bird Grinnell said accounted for the name given by American Indians to the region, Smoky Hill.[45]

From Fort Wallace, comparatively small garrisons patrolled a larger territory, aided more scouting and escorting parties, and engaged in more violent confrontations with Plains Indians than troops at any other post in Kansas. The post acquired the infelicitous name "the fightin'est fort in the West."

In the years 1865 to 1869, raids in Kansas were particularly violent. The Indians were defending lands they considered theirs. The terror reached a crescendo in 1867 following Gen. Winfield Scott Hancock's capture and destruction of a Cheyenne and Oglala Lakota village west of Fort Larned. In retaliation, whites were scalped and brutally attacked, their corpses sometimes identifiable only by their teeth, or, in one case, by the neckband of a shirt made by the wearer's mother. Workers quarrying and hauling stone to construct buildings at Fort Wallace were killed. Tents and wagons were set afire. Horses, mules, and livestock were stolen or run off.

That year, General Hancock reported that armed and active Indian warriors between the Platte and Arkansas Rivers, an area encompassing parts of both Kansas and Nebraska, numbered between fifteen hundred and two thousand.

Lt.. Col. George Armstrong Custer responded in force. After mounting a campaign against Cheyennes in 1868–69, he reported on May 31, 1870, that a scouting party had found evidence of a large group on the Republican River in northern Kansas. He advised alerting troops patrolling the Republican, Solomon, and Saline Rivers in Kansas and Nebraska. A large detachment of cavalry and infantry would, he said, scout the country between Fort Wallace and the Platte River, in Nebraska, which could drive the Cheyennes toward white settlements. "Don't let our people be caught napping," he urged.[46]

A month later, on June 30, 1870, the first Yale College Scientific Expedition left New Haven. From Fort McPherson, in west-central Nebraska, they set out with six well-stocked army wagons, guides to scout the country a mile ahead (including, for one day, Buffalo Bill), and a guard of soldiers to bring up the rear. Charles Betts, a member of the party whose account was published in *Harper's New Monthly* magazine, described "a country infested by hostile Indians."[47] The soldiers acted as both guards for the expedition and, as it progressed, collectors. The Pawnee guides were initially reluctant to handle bones, supposing some were human remains and therefore untouchable, but eventually they too entered into collecting fossils. Betts wrote about night fires set increasingly close to their encampments by Sioux, followed by day marches over scorched prairie. Grasshoppers, cactus, and grass—which the soldiers had counted on as feed for the stock—all were charred.

A report of the Secretary of War for 1870–71 included a recommendation by Gen. John Pope that Fort Wallace, along with two other forts, be closed. The buildings were in disrepair, and American Indians were living, in the main, on reservations in Indian Territory (present-day Oklahoma). He proposed that only a small contingent of soldiers remain. In the same report Pope attributed Indian raids on railroad workers to the latter's defenselessness, carelessness, and lack of common sense. Their condition was, he claimed, "an irresistible temptation to the Indians."[48]

In 1871 the departments of the Platte and the Missouri were merged, and General Pope was given command of the district. Between late February and mid-May that year, settlers expressed alarm that a large band of Cheyennes had received permission from the Indian Bureau to hunt off their reservation. General Pope warned forts in the vicinity to be prepared in case of attack. Several killings by American Indians were reported that year; none were in Nebraska but Kansas saw three or four.

– 30 –

On July 2, 1871, Professor Marsh and ten others, including a returning member of the 1870 party, traveled directly to Fort Wallace. The previous fall Marsh had been intrigued by finding two knucklebones of a giant flying reptile in the region. With five army wagons and an escort, this second Yale expedition began with further exploration of the Smoky Hill River environs, looking for more of the giant flying reptiles. To call it a river was something of an exaggeration, according to a member of the party whose account appeared in the *College Courant* the following February. "The whole country was," he said, "almost entirely destitute of water." By mule- or horseback, the unidentified writer continued, the fossil hunters examined the yellow and blue-gray Cretaceous ground amid labyrinthine and disorienting canyons:

> With scientific instinct sharpened by curiosity [. . .] and by ambition to discover something new, [one] would occasionally perceive upon a shelf of rock a skeleton fully exposed to view. To

dismount, examine, and secure the prize was the work of but a short time. But not always did these objects of search so readily reveal themselves. Sometimes it was only a projecting vertebra or rib, or bone of the foot or tail, that revealed the presence of the fossil within; and more often a piece of bone had become detached and having rolled a few feet down the cañon, was discovered quietly lying where the storms and gravitation had left it. When such a piece was found, the work of trailing began. The discoverer crept on hands and knees up the slopes, minutely scanning every inch of the rock.[49]

The 1871 party journeyed on to Denver, then to the Green River Basin in Wyoming, Salt Lake City, and, in Oregon, the John Day Basin and Portland. There the group split up. Those who did not start back home by rail accompanied Marsh to San Francisco, where they spent two weeks sightseeing. This contingent sailed home by way of Panama, crossing the isthmus and giving Marsh the chance to acquire the ancient Chiriquí pottery collection of a French consul. Marsh subsequently collected the valuable antiquities in quantity.[50]

In January 1872, when graduation from Yale's Sheffield Scientific School was within sight for Tom Russell and Mitchell Prudden, Fort Wallace was center stage for a famous buffalo hunt. The honored guest was His Imperial Highness Grand Duke Alexis Alexandrovich Romanov, the twenty-two-year-old son of Tsar Alexander II of Russia. Seventy-five cavalry horses, six mule teams, and four ambulances were provided for the grand duke's party. A large herd of buffalo was located in eastern Colorado about sixty miles west of Fort Wallace. Estimates of the number of animals taken ranged from about forty to two hundred.[51] A journalist imbedded with the imperial party observed that, unlike the sluggish bison of Nebraska, the Colorado prey "were disposed to make a desperate effort for escape" and fled at a speed "worthy of an express locomotive."[52]

On March 13, 1872, the hospital at Fort Wallace caught fire. Strong winds quickened the blaze, and the building was nearly destroyed.

The resultant rude conditions gave the sick no privacy or quiet, and the make-do setup included neither a bath nor a sink and no laundry facility.

That same spring a young woman named Mary Jordan told her mother she was going to join her husband on one of his buffalo hunts. She had lost a baby and thought it would be good for her to accompany him. Her mother tried unsuccessfully to dissuade her. The Jordans left their home, about a hundred miles east of Wallace, Kansas, with two other hunters. They headed to the Smoky Hill River and followed the watercourse upstream. After they failed to return as planned, a scouting party found three male bodies and Mary's bonnet. Taken captive by a band of Cheyennes, she tore off bits of her skirt and dropped them along the way as clues to her whereabouts, but she was never found.[53]

– 31 –

Of all the stories of terror visited upon whites passing through Kansas, none is more harrowing than the fate of a family named German, in 1874. This family of nine, originally from Georgia, was bound for Colorado. As they crossed Kansas they were told that Fort Wallace was but a day's journey and that the best route was to follow the old stagecoach tracks on the Smoky Hill Trail. Just west of present-day Russell Springs they stopped for the night and camped on a plateau above fingers of canyons. Just two years earlier, Marsh and his assistants had examined these canyons on their hands and knees. The campsite chosen by the Germans is within hailing distance of the fossil bed where Tom Russell unearthed his *Hesperornis regalis*.

As morning broke on September 11, a party of Cheyennes rose up from a canyon to attack. The leaders were Medicine Water and his wife, Buffalo Calf Woman. His first wife and her first husband had been killed in 1864 by Colorado militia in the massacre at Sand

Creek. After that, Medicine Water, Buffalo Calf Woman, and their family declared war on whites. They fought on the plains until they were captured and sent to prison in Florida for their crimes against the Germans.[54]

John German, his pregnant wife, Lydia, and their only son were killed immediately. One daughter was burned alive, along with the family's wagon and some of its contents. The other five daughters were carried away on horseback. The captors had not gone far when they stopped to kill another daughter. Of the four remaining girls, two ended up with one band. Their two little sisters were taken by another and eventually abandoned on the prairie. All four were abused and tortured. All four miraculously survived and were rescued by soldiers. They were reunited six months later, on March 2, 1875.

The sisters chose to remain in Kansas instead of returning to their grandparents in Georgia. All four married and lived long lives. Catherine German, the eldest, was once asked by her great-niece if she hated Indians. No, she replied, because she had seen how they went hungry, suffered, and died of exposure. "Besides," she said, "I am a Christian and cannot live with hate."[55]

In 1990 more than a hundred descendants of the four German sisters and about a dozen Cheyennes gathered in Russell Springs for a peace ceremony. The late John Sipes Jr., then a researcher for the Oklahoma Historical Society, was one of the organizers. Sipes was the great-great-grandson of Medicine Water and Buffalo Calf Woman. The other organizer was Arlene Jaucken, the great-granddaughter of Sophia German, the second-eldest daughter.

The ceremony began with a Cheyenne blessing of the dead. Observers watched from a respectful distance as smoke from a ceremonial pipe sent prayers to heaven.

"Today I would like to say Peace to the Cheyenne people and to five generations of the German family," Arlene Jaucken said.[56] Her great-grandmother had kept a single memento of her months in captivity, the moccasin she was wearing when soldiers found her. Jaucken gave Sipes a framed picture of the moccasin.

"It's high time we all came together and forgot the past, although we can hardly do that because it is part of our lives, our history, our culture," Sipes said, as if to acknowledge the tension between wishing the sins of the past could be forgotten and realistically accepting their influence. "I hope we all leave here with a better understanding of the Cheyenne ways," he said, "and the non-Indian ways."[57]

Linda Denning, who covered the ceremony for the *Salina Journal*, told me that of all the events she reported on for that newspaper, this was in the top tier. "I remember it as very emotional," she said. "In a dignified way."[58]

Bob Hopper, another German descendant, described the peace ceremony's atmosphere as free of bitterness. Someone had brought along the German family Bible. A soldier with the detachment that buried the first four victims had pulled it from the ashes gone cold. Finding nine names inscribed within its pages, the soldiers realized that five persons must have been taken by the Cheyennes. The search for the girls began. Thus did the family Bible save four lives, Hopper said, and from that the entire family had learned the greatest lesson, forgiveness.[59]

John Sipes noted that Medicine Water's job as the leader of his warrior society was to stop intruders who entered the Cheyenne homelands. In another place and time, Sipes acknowledged in an interview the anger he felt he would always carry for the wanton killing of his ancestors at Sand Creek. "That's why I have to utilize the sweat [lodge], because I think about it and I think it's only part of anyone that would have lost people at Sand Creek. You still are going to carry a bit of anger with you. [. . .] If America wants to preserve her culture, her history, like they say they do, they need to know both sides of Sand Creek," he said. "They need to know the feelings. There's two different types of feelings here. The Cheyennes who lost people there, they're not going to forget. And we're going to mourn and mourn."[60]

The German family ordeal thus has a postscript but not a resolution. For the German descendants, forgiveness has been the path to peace. For John Sipes, remembering his people and their history was what counted. A peace ceremony can be a meaningful gesture. But whether it is possible to go beyond a single ceremony and to hold forgiveness and remembering in tension, to ask forgiveness as well as offer it, and to consider what a vision of peace might look like to Cheyennes and other American Indians is as complex as any issue facing our country.

– 32 –

The dangers to white travelers in the West were well known to Americans living far from Kansas. Newspapers in Connecticut and New York kept New Haven's citizens abreast of national events. *Harper's Weekly* magazine, which reported on the progress of railroad construction and clashes between the army and American Indians, had in the nineteenth century a hundred thousand subscribers and half a million readers.[61] The editorial cartoons of Thomas Nast were a popular feature. Widely distributed in the East, *Harper's* was a source of current events, opinion, illustrations, and poetry—something like a cross between *Time* and the *New Yorker*.

Even though the army reported no engagements with Indians in Kansas in 1872, a climate of uncertainty existed and would not subside until 1878. That year, the last skirmishes between federal troops and Indians occurred after Northern Cheyennes escaped from the reservation in Indian Territory and fled north to their ancestral homelands in present-day northern Wyoming and southern Montana. Tom Russell's parents would have been aware of the risks in letting their son travel to a place far from home—unstable, dangerous, and remote in case of emergency. A letter mailed from Fort Wallace in 1870 reached departmental headquarters in St. Louis thirty hours later; even with communications improving, to send a letter to New Haven or receive one could have taken several days.[62] A telegram would have arrived sooner. In any case, when William and Mary Russell saw Tom off, it might have crossed their minds that they would not see him again.

How could they have let him go? As soon as the question occurred to me, the answer came back to me. *The same way your parents let Pete go.*

Like Tom Russell, my brother Pete Hunting had just graduated from college when he left for his great adventure, as he called it, in Vietnam. The United States had not yet committed combat troops to Southeast Asia, only military advisors. When troops were sent, not only GIs but any American, even a noncombatant like my brother, could be a target—or as a North Vietnamese veteran who fought the Americans said to me, circling his eye with an index finger, "Round eyes. All same."

Certain areas of the West were more dangerous for whites than others. By 1872 most Cheyennes and Arapahos were living on a reservation in Indian Territory. An authority on the history of Kansas in this period, Leo Oliva, told me, "There were a few Indians out, mostly from the north coming down into Smoky Hill country to hunt bison. The fear of Indians was often greater than the actual danger, but if you were in the wrong spot at the wrong time (like the German family), it was deadly. So the Indian threat was not serious in 1872, but military escorts were still provided for Marsh and others."[63]

My brother wrote from Vietnam, on February 10, 1965, just before U.S. ground forces landed on China Beach: "Pleiku is a very bad area, where Phan Rang is not." Pleiku is about 240 miles from the city where Pete lived at the time, Phan Rang, and approximately the distance from Santa Barbara, California, to the Mexican border town of Tijuana. At that distance, Pete felt safe from the worst violence, or so his letters home claimed. "Physical danger was a constant fact of life for us," a former American provincial representative working for the Agency for International Development (USAID) has written of that period in Vietnam. "At first, I was very concerned about the danger, but after a short while, and especially because we were extremely busy, I put it to the back of my mind."[64]

The USAID magazine *Front Lines* attempted to assuage the jitters of its readers. "Working in areas where danger can and does break out unexpectedly, and where the problems are enormous, the American advisers must learn a new way of life, eat unaccustomed foods, speak strange languages, make friends at all levels and regard Vietnamese problems as their own. They are usually men like [Pete] Hunting who can temper vigor with reason, gravity with humor, and initiative with self-restraint. They have proved fearless, dedicated, and dynamic."[65]

You didn't want to be in the wrong place at the wrong time. It was dangerous, but you got used to it.

How could they have let their son go somewhere so dangerous?

In Kansas, Tom Russell would find an avian dinosaur whose wings, over millions of years of evolution, had atrophied. It was an excellent swimmer and diver, but *Hesperornis regalis* could probably propel itself on land only by scooting on its belly or walking awkwardly, because its wings were vestigial and virtually useless.

What of our sons' and daughters' wings? If we hold our children back, hoping to shield them from every risk and danger, how will they ever learn to fly?

William and Mary Russell did not keep Tom from leaving the nest, and my parents did not stop Pete. I ask myself: Is this in my DNA, too? Is this a healthy parental instinct, or a biological imperative, or both of these? For want of wings—which our sons and daughters are born with but may never use if we are afraid—they may live the secure life we wish for them, but not a full life of their own.

A detachment from Fort Wallace may have brought a wagon or mounts to meet the 1872 Yale expedition's train in Wallace and take them directly to the post. Or Professor Marsh and his four young assistants may have opted for a restaurant meal and comfortable bed at the Wallace Hotel before going to the fort, knowing they would be roughing it for most of the next two months.

The soldiers who greeted Marsh's party would have been dressed in surplus garments left over from the Civil War. The uniform worn in Kansas was light blue trousers and a dark blue shirt with sky-blue piping. The fabric was not of highest quality. A single uniform worn against the extremes of heat and cold typical of Kansas offered limited protection from the elements.[66]

The young men's first sight of Fort Wallace would have been buildings of local, chiefly yellow limestone or wood-frame con-struction. In 1867, in the rush to complete the first of the barracks before winter set in, ventilation, light, and space were not given due consideration, according to the post surgeon.[67] Additional bar-racks built later, officers' quarters, the post chapel, and other build-ings were constructed of wood brought from distant locations. The newer barracks had crude bathrooms, but some troops preferred living in wood-frame, semipermanent tents.

Soldiers at the frontier posts usually slept two to a bed, head to toe. This was one way of keeping warm when army-issue blankets were either scarce or scarcely enough, provided you could sleep at all with your bunkmate's feet near your face and the smell of hay from the stables stuffed into your makeshift mattress.[68]

Sanitation was ever an issue, even though surgeons at Fort Wal-lace considered the climate healthful and the dry air a boon to heal-ing. Regularly inspecting the soldiers' food and keeping records about the state of the barracks, kitchens, latrines, and water drawn from the Smoky Hill fell to the post surgeon.[69] In summertime the men took baths in the river, about a half mile south of the post. The

1870 Yale party, while in Nebraska, reported seeing rattlesnakes slither over their clothes on a riverbank while they bathed. Kansas also had its share of rattlers.

By order of Fort Wallace's commanding officer in 1868, troops were required to wash and, in dry weather, to air out their clothing and bedding at least once a week. Mattress bags were to be laundered and filled with fresh straw or hay once a month. Blankets were to receive a good shaking every day in the out of doors. In his memoir of serving on the frontier, Corporal Emil A. Bode recounted carrying his blankets out to the parade ground and discovering a nest of snakes in the folds. He supposed they had shared the blankets with him for four or five days.[70]

Disease and low morale were constant adversaries of soldiers in the West. In his book *Fort Wallace: Sentinel on the Smoky Hill Trail*, Leo Oliva lists fevers, colds, bronchitis, toothache, pneumonia, scurvy, constipation, diarrhea, dysentery, and venereal diseases as frequent ailments, to say nothing of sunstroke, frostbite, broken bones, cuts, and gunshot wounds.[71] Antibiotics had not yet been developed to treat these and other medical conditions. A monument in the Fort Wallace cemetery testifies to the many lives claimed by cholera.

In joints located beyond the fort's boundaries, getting drunk, gambling, and visiting prostitutes broke the monotony for soldiers at Fort Wallace, as at other frontier posts. As many as a quarter of the officers and enlisted men on the frontier were alcoholics.[72] The desertion rate was high.

Not surprisingly, soldiers complained about the food. To say menu choices were limited evokes too little empathy for the men. A store at the fort sold canned goods, and even at high prices soldiers bought them to supplement their miserable diet. Foods shipped from distant sources could spoil or, once in storage, attract vermin. Forts were instructed to plant a vegetable garden. By 1870 the effort at Fort Wallace had failed three years in a row. Attempts were made to irrigate. The onions looked promising until June brought a plague of grasshoppers. This was not a one-off; three years earlier a lieutenant writing from Fort Wallace said that in some places the grasshoppers were an inch deep.[73] In 1871, however, the garden was successful enough for the fort to share some of its produce with the Wallace Hotel.

It doesn't take much imagination to guess what kind of impression Fort Wallace made on Tom Russell and his three companions from back east. Sheer pluck may have outweighed the shock, but Marsh was wise to have required them to read Randolph Marcy's *The Prairie Traveler* in advance. Instead of discouraging Marsh's protégés, Marcy's comprehensive, can-do guidebook may have emboldened them. Their preparation may also have included reading published accounts of the 1870 and 1871 Yale expeditions. Moreover, word-of-mouth tales about the earlier trips were likely circulating in New Haven, possibly growing more colorful with each retelling by a former expedition member or by Marsh himself, who was something of a raconteur. If the men of the 1872 Yale College Scientific Expedition did not greet the realities of frontier life with a cheer, at least they had been forewarned. Still, it is one thing to have information and another to have firsthand knowledge.

– 34 –

On October 15 or 16 the expedition left Fort Wallace with enough rations for twelve days. Their military escort was led by James Worden Pope, a Kentucky native and 1868 graduate of West Point. His class rank was thirty-nine out of fifty-four.[74]

Upon graduation, Pope was commissioned second lieutenant, 5th U.S. Infantry, and assigned to a company at Fort Lyon, Colorado. He spent his first years as a soldier defending workers on the Kansas Pacific Railway, who were under attack from American Indians whose lands they were entering. In the months before accompanying the 1872 Yale party, he served on a military expedition to the Cucharas River in Colorado when hostilities arose between Ute Indians and Cuchareños, the Spanish settlers in the area.

Pope was twenty-six years old and fifteen years younger than Marsh at the time of the 1872 expedition. His military record does not indicate how he came to be assigned to the Yale party. It is possible that his second cousin once removed, Gen. John Pope, who was at the time the commander at Fort Leavenworth, may have been responsible for assigning James to the scouting duty with Marsh's party.

A journal James Pope kept during his first winter on the plains makes it clear why Marsh might have appreciated the company of this young officer. In frank and not unfeeling language, Pope recorded the hardships of soldiering on the plains.

On November 30, 1868, he slept in the open for the first time. That same night, a soldier who was swearing was "finally tied up until he declared he was freezing and stopped his noise."[75]

A week later, sleet turned to snowfall so heavy that the accumulation covered the company's trail, forcing the men to stop and make camp with "the wind blowing fearfully. At night the mules made a terrible noise from the cold," he continued. "One died."

On December 18, Pope reported following a canyon for several miles before riding up onto a plateau, where he killed two buffalo.

The first New Year's Eve of Pope's long military career found him both down-to-earth and philosophical:

Weather misty and hail still covering ground. [Animals] dying rapidly for want of grazing. Remained up to see the old year out. Gloomy and solemnly, without a murmur amidst a soft dreary drizzling, he gave up the ghost, burying with him many pleasant associations and hopes and fears. How little did I expect at this time last year to be out in this desolate region with only a tent for a shelter against wintry weather and a soldier's arms to lie upon. Many, how many goes an episode in the life of a soldier. Still, bright hope adorns the horizon.

What qualifications might be desirable in an army officer assigned to protect a Yale professor and four novices from back east? He would know the necessity of finding wood, water, game, and a good campsite. He would understand what direction he is traveling at all times and how to measure distance and read tracks. He would be a good hunter. He should bear severe cold and other hardships without complaint. He must be a good observer.

The escort for Marsh's party in Kansas also included eight more soldiers and a guide named Edward S. Lane, a sombrero-, spurs-, and buckskin-wearing twenty-six-year-old originally from Pennsylvania.[76] Fort Wallace furnished eight wagons and riding mules. Marsh rode the same pony, Pawnee, he had ridden on his two previous expeditions.[77] From Fort Wallace they proceeded downstream along the South Fork of the Smoky Hill River.

Nearest to the fossil deposits Marsh wanted to work was what he later described as "a dismal water-hole, nothing more nor less than a large buffalo wallow."[78] He subsequently learned that an old bull had become trapped in the mire and died. The water was green and slimy, but being the only water available, it was used for brewing coffee. The group were "contented if not happy."[79]

They made camp near the river in Sibley tents. These had been used during the Civil War but were phased out because they were costly, cumbersome, and inefficient to transport. The air inside was "of the vilest sort," in the words of one man who breathed it and was surprised "to see how men endured it as they did."[80] The conical tents had the smallest of flaps. Even if they were left open, ventilation was poor.

At the top of the tent was a hole to let in air in hot weather or to accommodate a stovepipe in cold weather. "It was not an unusual sight in the service," according to one veteran, "to see the top of one of these tents in a blaze caused by someone having drawn the cap too near an over-heated stove-pipe."[81] From the supporting tripod a chain could be suspended to hang a kettle.

The tent was heated by an accessory Sibley stove, an appliance made of iron. Its pipe was government-issued and too short to reach the opening above. If the pipe was not lengthened "after market" by a clever soldier, the tent's ceiling was soon a sooty mess. The stove was impractical for cooking. It shot sparks, and if water was not at the ready to extinguish a blaze, tent-mates used their hands. The Sibley stove received "more petting and was fed more wood than any of the large boilers heating thousands of people," one soldier complained. "Some very rare remarks were hurled at that stove when it became balky and petting failed."[82]

Inside, the atmosphere was noxious. One man wrote, "In cold or rainy weather, when every opening is closed, they are most unwholesome tenements, and to enter one of them of a rainy morning from the outer air, and encounter the night's accumulation of nauseating exhalations from the bodies of twelve men (differing widely in their habits of personal cleanliness) was an experience which no old soldier has ever been known to recall with any great enthusiasm."[83] Was it the Sibley tent itself, the polluted air inside, the fetid odor upon awakening, a generalized morning grumpiness, or no provocation at all that caused the guide Ed Lane to scramble out of his tent in the morning and curse? "He was very apt to begin the day with a long volley of profanity," recalled Henry Farnam of the 1873 expedition, "doubtless to put his mind in tune for the work before him."[84]

Campers slept with their feet facing the center of the tent. The man with first dibs positioned himself opposite the door and out of the way of traffic, but he unavoidably inconvenienced others when he went out or came in. No one could sit up straight or stand except in the center of the tent.

Although less is known about the 1872 expedition than the preceding two and the fourth that followed, the *Hartford Daily Courant* published an account of it when the party returned to New Haven in December.[85] From this article, along with Schuchert and LeVene's definitive biography of Marsh; some newspaper notices of the expedition as it progressed along its route; a list of topics and a handful of stories Marsh intended to include in a book; and lists of specimens collected and later catalogued at the Peabody Museum, there is enough written down to create an outline of the expedition. Some of what happened we must infer.

The daily routine was to rise around daybreak. The men looked after their mules and breakfasted on buffalo meat, deer meat, or grouse. The government provided coffee, tea, and flour, so their meal may also have included biscuits or hardtack. Then they set out for the Smoky Hill canyons and spent the day searching for fossils.

No mention of evening menus was made in any account of the expedition, apart from Marsh saying that after surviving the buffalo stampede, he cut out the tongue and hump steaks from an animal for the party's supper that night. It might be hard to imagine five Yale graduates and their professor singing college songs around the campfire, but that is what the twelve members of the 1870 expedition did when they celebrated Thanksgiving on the plains. Perhaps it was the wine of Kentucky—that is, the whiskey—talking.

Each fossil hunter was armed with a rifle, handgun, knife, waistbelt, and ammunition. Marsh, who grew up on a farm, was a good shot.[86] Their army protectors, however, were not necessarily good marksmen. Because of a shortage of ammunition, soldiers in the West did not typically have the benefit of firearms training. Only in 1874 did the War Department authorize twenty rounds per man per month for regular target practice.[87]

Professor Marsh's directions for collecting vertebrate fossils are not as extensive as those of a modern-day paleontologist, but they represent more than just a list. They reveal a scientist who was emphatic, particular, and less concerned about shipping costs than the contents of a shipment. Judging from the fact that Marsh later offered Tom inducements to become his assistant and urged him to take up paleontology as his lifework, my great-grandfather must have followed instructions.

In these directions, set out in 1875 for hired collectors after he was no longer taking students on expeditions, we can hear Marsh's voice and picture the work in the field:

1. On leaving camp to collect, always take proper tools, and also sacks, paper cotton and twine, so as to pack specimens where found. Otherwise they may be badly injured in getting them to camp.

2. The best way to find fossils is to go over all the ground on foot, slowly and carefully. Haste makes waste in collecting, as the best specimens may easily be overlooked.

3. It is of the greatest importance to keep the bones of each animal by themselves, separate from all the others, and to save all the pieces, however small or weathered.

4. Collect carefully all the loose bones and fragments, on the surface or covered with earth, before beginning to dig out the rest of the skeleton. Otherwise valuable pieces are sure to be lost.

5. Never remove all the rock from a skull, foot, or other delicate specimen. The more valuable the fossil, the more rock should be left to protect it. Better send 100 pounds of rock than leave a tool mark on a good specimen.

6. When an entire foot is found, keep the bones of each toe together, and separate from the rest; then the foot can be put together again with certainty. A complete foot is often more valuable than a skull.

7. Get all the bones of every good specimen, if it takes a week to dig them out. The absence of a single tooth or toe bone may greatly lessen the value of a specimen.

8. When a rare bone cannot be got out of the rock entire, it is important to measure its exact length on a piece of thick paper, and pack this, properly marked, with the pieces saved. A drawing of such a bone, however rude, may prove of value.

9. Small specimens are often more valuable than large ones, and should always be carefully sought for, when a good locality is found. Bird bones, which are usually small, and very hollow, are among the rarest of fossils, and should be preserved with great care.

10. Single bones, if one end is perfect, are worth saving. If freshly broken, look carefully for all the pieces. When two or three bones are found together, they should always be kept together.

11. In packing, a skull should be rolled up in cotton, and then in one or more sacks, closely tied or sewed up. Teeth and other delicate specimens should be put in cotton, and if very fragile also in cigar boxes, or in tin cans. Every bone should be wrapped separately in paper. If broken, the ends should never be together when packed.

12. Each skeleton, or part of a skeleton should be put in one sack, with a label inside, and a tag outside, giving locality, formation, collector, and date. If one sack is not large enough, use two or more, properly marked, and tied together when packed in the box.

13. Pack fossils in boxes of moderate size, and made of inch boards. Plenty of hay or straw should be put in the bottom, and closely around the sacks of fossils, so that they cannot move when the box is turned over. Always put a large label inside, just under the cover, stating the number of the box, contents, locality and collector. Hoop all boxes at both ends, with iron, wood, rawhide, or leather.

14. All boxes should be numbered, and plainly directed, not on a card, but with *marking ink* on the cover as follows:

    Yale College Museum
    With Care
    New Haven, Conn.

15. Send boxes as freight. Small boxes with very valuable contents should be sent by express. Keep [a] full list of boxes

sent, but always send the R.R. receipts direct by mail to Prof. O. C. Marsh, Yale College, New Haven, Conn.[88]

~ 35 ~

In the Smoky Hill country Marsh and his party saw bison by the thousands as well as deer and antelope in great numbers. During their twenty-five days in the region, they shot fifty bison. Some of the meat may have been taken back to Fort Wallace by Private Herrigle, a teamster detailed from the quartermaster's department. Midway through the expedition, Herrigle evidently returned to the post to restock a wagon with rations and supplies for twelve more days. With the wagon restocked, he left the fort again around Monday, October 28. The supplies he brought back to camp carried the party through to November 8 or 9, when they returned to Fort Wallace.[89]

According to descriptions entered into ledgers after the boxes reached the Peabody Museum, twenty-six specimens were discovered on the first day in the field. Five were credited to Marsh, one to Marsh and Ed Lane, one to Marsh and Lt. James Pope, sixteen to the Yale party as a whole, and two to Tom Russell, the only student credited with finding fossils on day one.[90] Five of these finds were remains of an aquatic lizard. Three were the flying reptiles *Pteranodon*, which Marsh called "dragons" in notes for the book he intended to publish about his Kansas adventures.[91] One was a fish. Many more fish skeletons were found in this long-ago ocean bed, but they were not deemed valuable enough to collect. Field notes from that first day described all the fossils as Cretaceous or Late Cretaceous specimens from the Niobrara Formation, a vast geologic feature that has since been identified as holding major oil and gas deposits.

Marsh's luck held for the next three days. On October 19, 20, and 21 he collected fossils of five different vertebrates in the Niobrara Chalk and at Butte Creek. He may have worked by himself. He may have worked near or with others in the party but put his own name to what he found. Lieutenant Pope collected remains of an aquatic lizard on October 21.

A four-day gap from October 22 to 25 is unaccounted for. Collecting resumed on October 26.

The next day, October 27, Tom Russell found his nearly complete skeleton of a large bird. In July of the previous year, Marsh had discovered a headless individual of the same species—the holotype, or specimen upon which the description of a new species is based—and named it *Hesperornis regalis*. Whether the individual Tom discovered was male or female cannot be determined, but it had both a skull and teeth. It was a stunning find that would bring Marsh worldwide fame.[92]

– 36 –

Down the street from my house in Pasadena, California, lives a family with three young girls, the Jones triplets. On hot days they often set up a card table on the corner and sell lemonade. When I see them, I always buy a cupful. Stopping at a lemonade stand is like a religion with me.

One day not long ago, I invited the three sisters and their mother over to talk about dinosaurs. It had been many years since I served lemonade and cookies to young girls. Back then, it was my daughter and her friends. Listening to their lively conversation and watching whatever they were up to, from doing cartwheels to dropping water balloons off the roof for a science project, amused and delighted me.

On this day Lily, Mia, and Everest Jones were at my house to talk about the television show *Dinosaur Train*. I have heard it said that little boys love dinosaurs. As a child, I myself loved dinosaurs, and so did other women I have talked to. To counter the gender stereotype, I wanted to hear what some girls had to say about them.

I thought of the triplets down the street. I introduced myself to their mother and asked if her daughters ever watched the PBS animated series *Dinosaur Train*. They did, and we set a date for the girls to tell me about it. I knew that the show has a character named Jess Hesperornis. I watched a few episodes to prepare for our interview.

Dinosaur Train is the brainchild of animator Craig Bartlett, who got the idea after watching his preschooler play with a dinosaur and a train at the same time. Why not create a show that has both?

A TV producer named Sue Bea Montgomery entered the picture and pitched the show to the Jim Henson Company. PBS Kids picked it up. I learned she was from Tulsa, and on the slender thread of having lived in Oklahoma myself I invited her to my house to talk about our mutual interest in *Hesperornis*.

Where did the idea for Jess Hesperornis come from, I asked. Sue Bea's team had brought a paleontologist, Dr. Scott Sampson, in on the project. *Hesperornis* was one name on a list of dinosaurs he submitted. Sue Bea was intrigued by the suggestion of a bird that couldn't fly. She recalled thinking it was goofy in an appealing way. Jess was introduced in the show's third season.

Dinosaur Train centers on a family of five *Pteranodons*, including a mother, father, and three children. They adopt Buddy, a *T-rex* who comes to live with them. They take train rides, time-travel through the Mesozoic era, and meet other kinds of dinosaurs at the Cretaceous picnic grounds. One of the show's themes is tolerance. Buddy and his adoptive family learn there are all kinds of dinosaurs.

The *Pteranodon* daughter, Shiny, has pronounced long eyelashes like her mother's. Jess Hesperornis is purple and has a long neck, wings, small feet, and a gold beak. He has a surfer accent. Introducing himself, he says, "I'm a dinosaur *and* a bird."

I located the actor who voices Jess and asked him about the character's gender. He checked both the character breakdown he'd been given and the audition reel he submitted. Jess had been categorized as male. The actor gave him a young-sounding, higher-pitched voice than his own.

Since the name Jess could arguably be a boy's or a girl's, I asked Sue Bea why she had envisioned the character as male. The question seemed to surprise her.

The Jones sisters, on the other hand, were certain that Jess was female.

"How do you know?" I asked.

(Sister 1) "She had a girlfriend."

(Sister 2) "My brain tells me."

I asked them to describe the show. They talked fast and sometimes all at once.

"The main character is a *T-rex* in a family of flying dinosaurs. They are green, blue, and orange. It was a show for when we were younger."

I asked what the *T-rex* was like.

"The *T-rex* didn't eat the others because they raised him and he wanted to fit in. It was a typical story with kids and two adults. They went somewhere on a train. It used to be my favorite show. I used to watch it every day."

"Why are the dinosaurs cartoons?" I asked. "Why didn't they use real dinosaurs?"

"If they used a real *T-rex* it would eat them to pieces. They have gone extinct. The meteor struck earth, and they died due to starvation. There was dust everywhere. The plants died, then the plant-eating dinosaurs didn't have anything to eat, then the meat-eating predators didn't have anything to eat. Some knew a volcano was going to erupt. They felt the shaking and tried to run away."

"How long ago did dinosaurs live?"

(One sister) A billion years ago. (Another sister) Human history hasn't been around that long. Two million years ago. The world existed, but humans didn't until cavemen came along.

One of the girls introduced the topic of centaurs. A discussion among them followed as to what part of a centaur is human and what part is "a horse butt."

"Centaurs are real. I have a feeling a horse can breed with a human."

At this point their mother, Carol, interjected that they were getting off the topic of dinosaurs.

I asked, "Did dinosaurs ever live around here?"

They all agreed yes. "They lived everywhere, all across the globe. Some were more adapted to the environment. Some adapted to the heat, like succulents do."

"Do you think there will ever be dinosaurs on earth again?"

"Yes. Chickens are dinosaurs, and sharks and some lizards and sea turtles. Living dinosaurs will keep evolving. They keep breeding."

I asked where they had learned all this.

"At school. A kid in our class, Jackson, comes in one day and starts screaming, 'Hey! Chickens are dinosaurs, people!' One time we overheard a conversation other children were having about dinosaurs."

After the girls left, I thought about how dinosaurs and centaurs had intersected in their minds. Centaurs, mermaids, unicorns, dinosaurs—these are creatures no one has ever seen in the flesh. We have seen dinosaur fossils and mounted skeletons in museums, but, bones aside, what we have seen of dinosaurs are scientists' best attempts at reconstruction, and artists' conceptions. It wasn't so far-fetched for three bright girls to make the connections they did. I know because my brain tells me.

– 37 –

One of the best stories to come out of the 1872 expedition—or any of Marsh's four in the West—was his account of being caught up in a buffalo stampede and saved by his fleet-footed pony. Marsh did not forget his debt. When Pawnee died the next year after a rattlesnake struck his nose as he grazed, "he was buried with full military honors," Marsh wrote, "and a double salute fired over his remains."[93]

Marsh included another tale, "Lost on the Plains," on a list of Kansas stories he intended to tell.[94] Only years later, in 1931, was the tale set down and published, when the Yale economics professor and 1873 expedition member Henry Farnam recounted it for Marsh's biographers.[95] By that time none of the 1872 expedition members— O. C. Marsh, Tom Russell, Charles Hill, James MacNaughton, or Benjamin Hoppin, whom the tale concerns—was still alive.

The incident may have occurred during an unexplained hiatus in collecting, from October 22 to 25. The hiatus did not fall on the Sabbath or over a weekend, which might justify the break, but spanned a Monday through Thursday. Bad weather could account for the incomplete record. The gap could also be explained by Marsh and the students failing to log their discoveries on these days or spending them searching without success for new fossils, even though there was no shortage of specimens to be found or fossil prospecting to do in Kansas. It could be attributed to errors made half a continent away in New Haven, either when the specimens were first accessioned or decades later, when information was added to the Peabody Museum's records and, later, its computerized database.

One can only speculate why work stopped for four days and when what happened to Benjamin Hoppin happened. There is no doubt, however, that the hiatus fell during a dark spell in the lunar cycle, when the moon shrinks from a waning gibbous phase into the last quarter. The night sky over Kansas was dark, and by late October the cold had set in.

As the hunt for fossils was proceeding one day, Benjamin saw an animal, possibly an antelope, and took off in pursuit. He may have been the individual whose gunshot triggered the buffalo stampede that nearly cost Marsh his life. He may have wanted to prove himself as a hunter, especially if the incident happened prior to October 26, when he had yet to discover a fossil.

He followed the animal, armed with his rifle and only one bullet. He was wearing no coat and carrying no matches. He may have fired his one round before heading back in what he thought was the correct direction to rejoin the outfit. At some point he realized he was lost. He began walking in a southerly direction, knowing he would eventually intersect the Kansas Pacific Railway. From there he could follow the tracks to a station. As night fell he had not found the railroad tracks.

The hide from a buffalo's carcass would shelter him until morning. "He shook the bones out of the skin and crawled in to spend the night," Farnam wrote. "The next day he reached the track and started to walk along the rails. Professor Marsh had, of course, sent word all through the state that one of his men was lost, and offered fifty dollars' reward for anyone who would find him."[96]

At length a telegraph operator saw someone walking along the tracks, carrying a rifle and wearing no coat. Without waiting to confirm who it was, he sent a message to Marsh: "Your man is found. Send on the fifty dollars." In today's money, it was more than a thousand dollars.

How Benjamin experienced this incident we have no way of knowing, because he left no written account of it. No doubt he spent an uneasy night. There was plenty to dread: an attack by Cheyennes or Sioux; rattlesnakes and wolves; the shame he would feel when he rejoined the others in the party, were he to survive.

According to Farnam, Benjamin suffered a complete mental breakdown a few years later.[97] Though he was brilliant, Farnam said, his mind was "unhinged." He entered law school at Yale in 1873 and dropped out the same year. He drifted around Europe. He returned to New Haven and took a job as a tutor at the college but gave up the position for health reasons. Although in later years he continued to pursue his interests in genealogy, languages, history, and Arctic exploration, he retired permanently in 1880 at the age of twenty-nine.

– 38 –

Because Marsh never married and spent so much time in the company of men, some have suggested that his sexual preference was for males. But according to Richard Conniff, in *House of Lost*

Worlds: Dinosaurs, Dynasties, and the Story of Life on Earth, it is more likely that Marsh was solitary, perhaps even autistic, and less interested in intimacy than in "the tantalizing discipline of work."[98] The Yale president Timothy Dwight described him in *Memories of Yale Life and Men* as "a man quite by himself."[99] He was peculiar and somewhat selfish, George Bird Grinnell once said of him, but "where his own interests were not involved, he was most kindhearted, and was often ready to take great trouble to be helpful to others."[100] If Benjamin Hoppin did suffer a nervous episode, a stress overload, even a panic attack from his night alone on the plains, did Marsh, with a sympathy not widely credited to him, call off collecting fossils for four days, placing the young man's welfare above the all-important scientific mission?

When work resumed did Marsh, ordinarily a man quite by himself, and Tom Russell, a man to tie to, try to help Benjamin by keeping him close by as they worked, even helping him find specimens to which he could put his name? On October 26, possibly with someone's kind assistance, Hoppin discovered his first fossil, a specimen of the marine lizard *Platecarpus*. On October 30 he and Marsh, working the same fossil bed, found remains of one or more additional *Platecarpus*. On November 5, working in proximity, he and Tom found remains of mosasaur-type reptiles, smaller versions of the monstrous creature that in the film *Jurassic World* leaps out of the water to snatch a shark.

What if Benjamin did keep a journal while on the expedition, but his companions knew it could not be published without exposing its writer as unhinged, to use Henry Farnam's word? Could it be that Marsh treated him as his protégé in the literal sense of someone protected and that he had to surrender any hope of the 1872 expedition being chronicled?

Benjamin Hoppin's story brings to mind another, earlier explorer of the West, Meriwether Lewis. One of America's great expedition journalists, Lewis was a protégé of Thomas Jefferson, who invited him to live in the White House as his personal secretary. In choosing him to lead the Corps of Discovery, along with William Clark, the president was aware of Lewis's inclination to depression and too much drink. In 1809, three years after he returned from the expedition and without writing a final report, he took his own life. "I fear the weight of his mind has overcome him," Clark told his brother upon learning of his friend's death.[101]

The man to read Meriwether Lewis's report most closely would have been his mentor, the brilliant former president. As monumental a figure as Jefferson was, even more monumental was Lewis's subject: namely, the many experiences he and Clark underwent and the vast wilderness itself.

Considering what happened to Lewis raises a question the late environmental writer Barry Lopez posed: How far can you venture out and still successfully come back? He concluded that Lewis went too far. He had trouble reentering the world and a life that once had been familiar to him. "It was Lewis," the historian and first-person Thomas Jefferson interpreter Clay Jenkinson has said, "who really let the American West percolate into his innermost soul."[102]

Was it like this for Benjamin Hoppin? For a person who only a few years later would suffer a complete breakdown, perhaps the expedition was a venture too far. The strangeness, the uncertainty, and the wildness of the West may have been too much to come back from successfully.

When Hoppin got home and settled again in New Haven, he may have intended to write a book about the expedition from a journal he kept, if indeed he kept one. It may have been daunting to measure up to his father, a professor and writer on theological topics. Trying to meet Professor Marsh's expectations and prove himself a competent fossil hunter, a good shot, and a chronicler of the expedition may have been too much for him. He may have hoped that he would find afterward, in his European travels, the wherewithal to set down the story, but the energy and inspiration evaded him.

Written in longhand on a yellowed sheet of parchment paper are the words "Sketches of Russell's Bird" in Tom's handwriting. Someone else, possibly Marsh, has written, "1 M W [mile west of] Russell Springs, Oct. 27."

These locality notes about the site where *Hesperornis regalis* was found are sketchy compared to the precise coordinates available today by GPS or even in light of Marsh's instructions about properly recording data in the field. But the information Marsh himself recorded about where he found a specimen was sometimes imprecise. The contextual information about a fossil was generally considered less important than the specimen itself.[103] As his biographers Schuchert and LeVene explain, "Professor Marsh, from the beginning of his field work, was careful to note the general superposition of the strata from which he was collecting vertebrate fossils; but, curiously, in none of his publications do we find that he ever actually measured or described in detail a stratigraphic sequence. He was satisfied with noting that his fossils came from the lower, the middle, or the upper part of a formation or even a series of beds."[104]

Tom Russell left no account of his reaction to finding a fossil that day. One can guess how excited he might have felt, however, by reading the account George F. Sternberg, of the Kansas fossil-collecting family, wrote about his discovery of a duck-billed dinosaur at the age of twenty-four.[105]

In the summer of 1908, Charles H. Sternberg took his sons, George, Charlie, and Levi, with him to look for dinosaur remains in Converse County, Wyoming. Finding fossils there was more difficult and was taking longer than he expected. Charles decided he must return to the nearest town for supplies, taking Charlie with him. Meanwhile, he left George and his little brother Levi in camp.

One evening George happened to see some large bones protruding from a ledge. To expose the fossil looked difficult to the brothers, but they went to work, removing a little bit of rock at a time. What if they couldn't find the skull, they wondered. "For it so often happens," George wrote many years later, "that after finding an articulated skeleton one finds the head has been severed from the body before burial and is nowhere to be found. This practically destroys the skeleton for museum purposes."[106]

George and Levi were down to the last of their food, a bag of potatoes. They had no salt. It could be several days before their father and brother returned. They kept working. By the third evening, George had exposed a large portion of the skeleton. He removed a piece of sandstone and, to his surprise, saw in the rock the perfect impression of skin. "Imagine the feeling that crept over me," he later recalled, "when I realized that here for the first time a skeleton of a dinosaur had been discovered wrapped to its skin. That was a sleepless night for me."[107]

Two days later, around dusk, Charles and Charlie returned. George excitedly told his father about the bones and head they had found and the superbly preserved impression of the dinosaur's skin. Away the two of them went:

Darkness was nearly upon us when we reached the quarry and there laid out before us was the specimen. One glance was enough for my father to realize what I had found and what it meant to science. Will I ever forget his first remark as we stood there in the fast approaching twilight? It thrills me now as I repeat it. "George, this is a finer fossil than I have ever found. And the only thing which would have given me greater pleasure would have been to have discovered it myself."

I do not remember what we had for supper that night. I do not remember what news was brought from home and loved ones. I do remember, however, that it was another restless night for not only myself but for my father as well. I could hear him roll in his bed and cough or make some noise which told me he too was spending a sleepless night. [. . .]

It was not until 1911 that I again had the privilege of seeing my prize specimen. There it lay in that great institution [the American Museum of Natural History] just as it was when I found it resting on its back with the head bent down under its body and its fore limbs stretched out on either side. [. . .] Could there be a greater thrill in the life of a man than to know he has been able to discover one of these buried treasures of bygone days and to have it placed before the world as an everlasting memorial?[108]

George Sternberg's *Anatosaurus* specimen was placed before the world by Professor Henry Fairfield Osborn, then president of the great institution in New York City.

Parallels between the discoveries of *Anatosaurus* and *Hesperornis regalis* help us imagine what it was like for Tom Russell and not Marsh to make the discovery: The young man realizing his great luck in finding an exceedingly well-preserved, important fossil. The older man recognizing that this specimen is superior to anything he has discovered, and wishing he had found it himself.

From the camp on the Smoky Hill River, Tom Russell packed the specimen into two boxes, probably with Marsh supervising, for the wagon ride back to Fort Wallace. They were labeled as boxes two and three of six and readied for the long journey to New Haven. The unusual cortège then traveled east by rail. The fossils arrived at the Peabody Museum on November 29, while the 1872 expedition was still in the West.

Parts of "Russell's bird" would be placed before the world by Marsh in 1881 in the form of plaster-cast reproductions sent to selected museums and universities for study. From 1914 to 1915, more than a decade after Marsh's death, the fossil was mounted for exhibition at the Yale Peabody Museum by the famous dinosaur collector Barnum Brown and his technicians at the American Museum of Natural History, under the direction of Yale curator and professor Richard S. Lull. Tom Russell was still alive, with an active surgical practice.

The discovery of *Hesperornis regalis* in its sepulcher of chalk in a Kansas fossil bed was cause for two thrills in the life of twenty-year-old Tom: finding a nearly complete fossil and finding this particular fossil, which double-underscored that birds evolved from reptiles. Charles Kingsley, a nineteenth-century naturalist, warned that a discovery so important carries a danger. "The pleasure of finding new species is too great," he wrote in *Glaucus: Or the Wonders of the Shore*. "It is morally dangerous; [. . .] as if all the angels in heaven had not been admiring it, long before you were born or thought of."[109]

– 40 –

Hesperornis was not the first bird with teeth to be discovered in Kansas. That distinction went to *Ichthyornis*, a small flier whose remains were collected in the Smoky Hill Chalk in 1872 by Benjamin F. Mudge. An 1840 graduate of Wesleyan University, Mudge passed the bar and served two terms as a mayor in Massachusetts before moving to the abolitionist settlement of Quindaro, Kansas.

Mudge was not a university-educated scientist, like Marsh, but he was a professor at the Kansas State Agricultural College and the first person to systematically collect fossils on lands that once had formed the floor of the Western Interior Sea.[110] He sent many of his first specimens to Edward Drinker Cope, Marsh's archrival in Philadelphia.

In 1870 he was collecting fossils from the area around Fort Wallace. He forwarded them to Cope for study. The following year, Cope traveled to Manhattan, Kansas, to view Mudge's collection.

In September 1872 Marsh wrote to Mudge expressing interest in what he had collected that summer. Instead of sending a box to Cope with the fossilized bird bones that he had found, Mudge changed the label and sent the box to Marsh. Rivalries between paleontologists, notably Cope, Marsh, and Joseph M. Leidy, an anatomist from Philadelphia, were so intense in this period that they became infamous as the Bone Wars.

When Marsh received the delicate bones of the yet-unnamed fossil bird, he realized it was markedly different from the headless *Hesperornis* he had discovered on the 1871 expedition, and not just because it was smaller. At first he thought the jaw belonged to a different animal, a reptile. His description in the *American Journal of Science* stated that this aquatic "fish bird," which he named *Ichthyornis dispar*, differed "widely from all known birds."[111] In another publication the following year, the previous description was clarified: it "differ[ed] from all known birds in having *teeth* and *biconcave vertebrae*" (Marsh's emphasis). The vertebrae were more primitive in shape than those of modern birds and signaled one step in the evolutionary transition from reptiles to modern birds.[112]

It has been suggested that Marsh did not intend to return to the west in 1872.[113] Seeing Mudge's little bird may have changed his mind. In any case, his reports on toothed birds in western North America did not dazzle the scientific community until Tom Russell's *Hesperornis regalis* led him to establish a new subclass and order of toothed birds. Marsh would go on to discover and describe the much more famous *Brontosaurus*, *Stegosaurus*, and *Triceratops*. It was, however, the Odontornithes, or birds with teeth, that first brought him worldwide renown for demonstrating their place in the evolution of reptiles into birds.

To think that *Deinonychus*, the "grabber" dinosaur on which Michael Crichton and Steven Spielberg loosely based their *Velociraptors* in *Jurassic Park*, is related to robins and hummingbirds requires a leap of the imagination. Unless, that is, you are a paleontologist. "Not all dinosaurs went extinct," Dan Brinkman told me. "We call them 'birds' today."[114] Paleontologists now believe that some small meat-eating dinosaurs with grabbing "hands," a group called maniraptorans, survived. Because of a mutation to their feathers—which developed asymmetrical leading and trailing edges capable of generating lift—the predatory motion of some of these dinosaurs' feathery, grabbing forelimbs evolved over time to enable flight.

Hesperornis regalis, whose name compared to other dinosaurs' has been called "particularly felicitous," held Marsh's attention for years.[115] This "most interesting bird [. . .] yet discovered," as he called it, had the unique, saddle-shape vertebrae of a modern bird and the teeth of a reptile.[116] Much larger than *Ichthyornis* but smaller than most of the marine reptiles with which it shared the waters, *Hesperornis regalis* has been called "the only marine dinosaur" and "the only feathered dinosaur for which we have a fossil record in the Western Interior Sea."[117] Because of its inability to fly and its presumed wobbliness on land, it has been compared to a penguin. Loons and grebes are also considered somewhat similar in their ability to propel themselves under water using their hindlimbs and feet.

Its time spent on land was limited to breeding, nesting, laying eggs, incubating, and raising its young. In the water it dived for fish, the lower limbs providing maneuverability but hardly a defense against sea monsters such as mosasaurs and plesiosaurs. In a specimen from present-day South Dakota, scientists found a *Hesperornis* individual that narrowly escaped becoming a meal. Evidently the predator opened its jaws to get a better purchase on the juvenile diver's leg. Bite marks on its left tibiotarsus matched up with the teeth of a plesiosaur, according to a study published in the journal *Cretaceous Research*. Although the intrepid bird escaped, its leg did not completely heal and later developed osteoarthritis. "Fossils are not static bits of information, but actually tell you about the behavior of the animal," said Bruce Rothschild, a coauthor of the study. "It shows the resilience of the bird to survive the injury."[118] Other *Hesperornises* were not so lucky. Fossils of some have been found in the stomachs of mosasaurs.[119]

The odds against Tom Russell's *Hesperornis* surviving tens of millions of years under any circumstances—then to be unearthed by a twenty-year-old amateur fossil hunter visiting a prehistoric boneyard for a couple of weeks in 1872—are incalculable. How did little Hesper, as I have come to think of her, escape becoming the prey of a shark or a larger marine reptile, let alone become a fossil?[120]

The lack of skeletal evidence of trauma or predation indicates that she died of natural causes. She did not drift ashore to be devoured there by scavengers. "Floating on the surface would have been an invitation to sharks," Mike Everhart told me. "The fact that it was found nearly intact supports the idea of it sinking to the bottom quickly."[121]

Although it is impossible to know how Hesper died, the "bloat and float" hypothesis explains how her body could remain intact after death. As it decomposed and gases formed, *Hesperornis* must have floated awhile on the water's surface, but once the gases escaped and her lungs deflated, she sank fairly rapidly. Unlike the lightweight bones of a flying bird like *Ichthyornis*, which would tend to remain for a time on the surface, Hesper's bones were heavier, and she sank undisturbed to the seabed.

– 41 –

O. C. Marsh was personally acquainted with Charles Darwin and once visited him at his home in Kent, England. He became "an out-and-out evolutionist," according to his biographer Charles Schuchert, and stated in an address of 1877 that "to doubt evolution is to doubt science, and science is only another name for truth."[122] Marsh's discoveries in the West elevated the theory of evolution from a hypothesis to what Schuchert, himself a paleontologist, called "a living truth."[123] His study, lectures, and published writings about birds with reptilian characters, notably solid bones and teeth set in jaws, provided additional evidence of the relationship between these vertebrate groups and brought about a sea change in the understanding of evolution.

Marsh's collection of fossil horses from the Rocky Mountain region underpinned his view of their evolution as well, which advanced the doctrine of evolution by natural selection. The fossil evidence also led him to conclude that the American continent was the true home of equine mammals. His claim that horses predated Spanish explorers by millions of years found him a friend in Brigham Young, because it supported the Book of Mormon assertion that horses were known in the Americas before the Christian era. When Marsh's student assistants visited Salt Lake City, they reaped the reward of this connection in hospitality.

But we are getting ahead of our story. Let us return to the 1872 expedition as it wrapped up its explorations in Kansas.

– 42 –

There were many more finds in Smoky Hill country. Marsh found the most specimens. On October 27, the same day "Russell's bird" was discovered, he found three *Pteranodon*, or flying dragon, fossils.[124] Two days later he found another *Hesperornis regalis* and on October 30 more *Pteranodons*. Also on the 30th, working in proximity, Marsh and Hoppin found mosasaurian *Platecarpus* specimens. As for the other two student assistants, Charles Hill discovered fossils on October 31 and November 1, 3, 6, and 7, while James MacNaughton turned in lackluster results, finding only one fossilized marine lizard in Kansas.[125]

The party returned to Fort Wallace, where they packed their specimens and shipped them by rail to New Haven. They then left for Denver around November 10 on the Kansas Pacific Railway. On November 14 the newspaper *Out West* reported that "the Yale Scientific Party," accompanied by Lieutenant Pope and Ed Lane, was in Colorado.[126]

They may have just missed an unusual incident reported by the *Denver Daily Times* on November 13. Between ten and eleven o'clock at night, somewhere west of Wallace, the train was passing through a severe storm when a man on board was awakened by "a loud report, even above the howling of the storm." When day broke, he found oysters scattered all about the car, "several packages having been bursted open and thrown around promiscuously."[127] Something had passed through several inches of hard wood and torn a large hole near the floor, though no projectile could be found to explain the cause of the damage. As surprising as a quantity of oysters in a landlocked region in 1872 may seem, bivalves were not uncommon on menus of the day. In 1873 the Christmas dinner menu of the Tefft House Restaurant in Topeka offered seven varieties of oysters.[128]

The Denver newspaper also reasoned that "buffalo down the railroad are now so much in the habit of being shot at that they don't appear to mind at all."[129] In the same issue, a few residents at Cheyenne Wells, just west of the present-day border between Colorado and Kansas, reported they had killed four bison the previous morning.

The Yale party spent three days in Denver. The weather was "very cold," the local paper reported, with "snow on the plains as well as on the mountains."[130] Fifteen inches of snow blanketed the city.

When the transcontinental railroad was completed in 1869, it had bypassed Denver. Between 1860 and 1870, the city's population had grown by only ten persons, but in 1870 its prospects improved with the linking of the Kansas Pacific and Denver Pacific railroads.[131] The year 1872 saw a boom in the city's growth, with 237 brick and 447 frame buildings erected. That same year the city added a line of "horsecars," horse-drawn trolleys that traveled a two-mile route downtown. The number of schools and students in Denver and Colorado Territory was growing. The Denver Board of Trade was already extolling the city's merits as a winter resort. In November, the first of the cold winter months, the temperature was half a degree above freezing day and night, the association stated, while eastern cities of the same latitude were "almost buried in snow and frozen up."[132]

We do not know where in Denver Marsh and his party lodged and waited out the snowstorm before beginning the next leg of their journey, but a new hotel claimed that year to be the first in the city to offer a lock on every one of its rooms. "Guests may lie down to peaceful slumbers," a newspaper said of the amenity, "undisturbed by the apprehensions of getting their heads blown off."[133]

– 43 –

One riddle about this least-documented of the four Yale expeditions has been the identity of the person who photographed the men, and where.

Mike Everhart, who included the photograph in his book *Oceans of Kansas*, suggested to me that it might have been taken in New Haven. Because my impression of my sober-minded great-grandfather did not square with him dressing up in western clothing in his home city, I was doubtful. It seemed even less likely that Lieutenant Pope and the guide Ed Lane, who first joined Marsh's party in Kansas, had ever come to New Haven.

Since I was ruling out Connecticut, could the photograph have been taken in Wallace, Kansas? The town had a photography studio, someone told me, but this trail led nowhere. Traveling photographers visited western forts. Could it have been taken at Fort Wallace?

Many itinerant photographers worked in the American West in the nineteenth century, documenting the work of geological surveys and recording important occasions such as treaty signings. They captured images of the famous and the not famous, of railroads under construction, and of nascent cities. The website Langdonroad

.com lists 186 photographers working in Colorado alone in the nineteenth and early twentieth centuries.[134] My correspondence with museums, universities, newspapers, and history archives turned up nothing, however, to narrow the search.

Barbara Narendra, the longtime archivist of the Yale Peabody Museum, had little information about the print that O. C. Marsh donated to the collections. It is one of only two known extant prints. Marsh did not provide the photographer's name.

My first clue to his or her identity came in two sentences in *Out West* magazine. "The 'Yale College Scientific Party' have arrived in Colorado," the publication reported on November 14, 1872.[135] Both Lieutenant Pope and Ed Lane were named as members of the party. Since they were still with the group after Kansas, the photograph could have been taken in Denver or somewhere else farther along the way.

Itinerant photographers traveled with props, such as clothing, backdrops, and rugs. The rug in this photo had an ornate geometric pattern. Thinking that was a lead, I turned to Jenny Watts, the photography curator at the Huntington Library in San Marino, California. With one look, she determined that the photograph was taken in a studio and not a makeshift setting. She showed me the direction from which sunlight entered the room. Electric lighting was years away, so photography studios were situated on the top floor of buildings to admit the maximum natural light. Illumination came from skylights and large windows. Natural light was also used in the process of making prints. Solar cameras were used to enlarge photos.

Jenny mentioned someone on her staff who with some digging might be able to turn up the photographer's name. Did I have any other information I could send her?

I did. The second extant print is one I had seen on the website of Cowan's, an auction house. It was the same photograph as the Marsh copy, except that someone had written the subjects' names at the bottom. The Cowan's page showed the "price realized including buyer's premium" of the albumin print as $3,408.[136] No photographer was named in the description of Lot 445, but there was plenty more information. Tom Russell was correctly identified, for example, as the individual holding a Model 1867 Sharps carbine, wearing a cartridge belt, and armed with a holstered handgun. "Interestingly," the description stated, "the students are heavily armed, all with handguns and three with visible long guns. [. . .] It was a dangerous time in the West."[137] The provenance was given as "Archive of Brigadier General James W. Pope."

Next I reached out to Katie Horstman, the director for American history at Cowan's.[138] Jenny Watts had told me that auction houses sometimes will help fill in parts of a research puzzle. When I explained to Katie that I was trying to determine who took the photograph and that I was a descendant of the man identified as Russell, she agreed to contact the consignor.

A couple of days later, Mark Greaves contacted me. He had bought the photograph at an estate sale. He keeps thorough records about every sale he goes to, including the date and time, and he itemizes everything he purchases. At four o'clock on November 12, 2009, twenty-nine people were already in line when he arrived at what was called the Pope Estate sale, in Denver. Had he known what a good sale it would be, he said, he would have arrived much earlier.

Mark remembered that the friend he went with, who was ahead of him in line, bought some diaries that Pope had kept in the late 1860s. "The diaries, the photo, and a lot of other photos and papers were on a big table pretty close to the front door as you went in the house," he said. "I originally bought the photo because I thought it was a neat photo of guys holding their guns. Later, I showed it to a friend who noticed the rock hammer and saw the name Marsh. He said, 'That's O. C. Marsh. That could be valuable.'"

When Mark got home, he found the same image on the Internet. It was the Marsh copy on the Yale Peabody Museum's website. He learned it had been taken in 1872. His print was identical except that, in addition to having names, it had age spots.

The total cost for the items he purchased that day came to $189.60. They included a collection of Pope's military papers dated 1911; five watch fobs; scenic photographs of Colorado; maps; photo albums; photo postcards; one stuffed duck; and the photograph of "seven men with guns." Mark kept some items, sold some, and consigned some, including the 1872 expedition photo, for which he had paid $2.00. He consigned it to Cowan's.[139]

One question remained: who was the photographer? The riddle was solved one day when I heard from Anita Weaver at the Huntington Library. She thought she had found something.

She had come across photos taken at Fort Wallace, proving that studio photographers were working there, but she had found something more interesting. From past research she remembered noticing considerable variation in carpet patterns in nineteenth-century photography studios. The carpet in the Denver studio of W. G. Chamberlain looked like the carpet in the Yale expedition photo.

It was in fact the identical carpet. Chamberlain (sometimes spelled Chamberlin) photographed a number of Ute Indians, including their chief, Ouray, standing or seated on chairs on the same carpet. One of the backdrops in a photograph of Utes was the very backdrop behind the Marsh party.

William Gunnison Chamberlain was born and raised in Massachusetts. At the age of twenty-four he left for South America. At that time, the government of Peru was moving to establish a silk industry. Chamberlain accepted the challenge and imported mulberry trees from the United States, silkworms from France, and a spinning machine from his father. Although the enterprise failed, Chamberlain met his wife, the daughter of English residents of Lima, there. He also chanced to meet two Americans traveling in Peru who were selling their daguerreotype camera equipment. He purchased the equipment and mastered the process, although photography was not yet his profession.

After several moves, from the United States to Peru and back with his wife and children, Chamberlain set up shop in Chicago as a daguerreotype artist. The toxic chemicals used in the process forced him to give up the business for a time. The family settled in Denver in the 1860s, and Chamberlain began taking annual trips to the Rockies to photograph mountain scenes.

In 1862 he moved his studio to the 1400 block of Larimer Street in Denver. The *Denver Weekly Commonwealth and Republican* reported that Chamberlain had "an elegant room for taking pictures, a side room which is fitted up as a laboratory, a neat little parlor as retiring room, and a petite lady's sanctum. The suite of rooms is tastefully fitted up, and in every way qualified for the business for which it is devoted. From the window is a beautiful view of the mountains and the western part of the town."[140]

By the time the 1872 Yale expedition stopped in Denver, Chamberlain had earned a reputation as a top photographer in the city. That June he had expanded his studio. It was equipped with a glass room, changeable backdrops on casters, movable curtains, and seven cameras.

Only two prints of the photograph Chamberlain took of the fossil hunters and their escorts are known to exist. And the negative? Sadly, Chamberlain's collection, which had passed to another Denver photographer, was destroyed in a fire on October 31, 1883, after a lamp exploded and ignited flammable chemicals.[141]

– 44 –

"He has a lovely face, doesn't he," Dawn Bowery said. "He looks very comfortable, very relaxed. Calm. Or determined."

Dawn and I were sitting in the warm sunshine of a February morning in Los Angeles. She is a British photographer who now lives here. We were studying Tom Russell in the photograph of the 1872 Yale expedition.

I had found Dawn by Googling "best portrait photographer in LA," an honor that voters in the 2018 LA Hot List contest accorded her. I wanted to show the photograph to a professional who works behind the camera and could tell me what she saw in the seven subjects' faces. I thought a portrait photographer might offer an insightful perspective on the men.

The four students in the photograph have been misidentified in at least one magazine article and three books, and on a website. The photo caption in a 1975 *Yale Alumni Magazine* says Tom is a local guide. In Alan Feduccia's *Riddle of the Feathered Dragons: Hidden Birds of China*, he is identified as Benjamin Hoppin. All four students are named incorrectly on a Brooklyn College web page devoted to O. C. Marsh. In the definitive biography of Marsh by Charles Schuchert and Clara LeVene, the students' names are listed in reverse order. In *The Scientific Contributions of Othniel Charles Marsh*, Mark J. McCarren names only one student in the group, T. H. Russell, but mistakes him for Charles Hill.

Just as Tom Russell has been misidentified, he is enigmatic insofar as he is not known to have left any personal papers, a journal, or correspondence. I found his medical school thesis on *talipes equinus*, or club foot, and transcripts of some talks he gave at medical meetings. I have turned up newspaper articles that mention his surgical cases and patients he attended. The minutes of the New Haven Hospital board on April 9, 1903, recorded that a physician absented himself without permission from an operation Dr. Russell was performing. Afterward, Tom informed the hospital board and the delinquent doctor was fired. Tom Russell's personal voice, however, has passed out of existence. I hoped his face might reveal something to Dawn Bowery.

When I asked if she would take a look at the photograph, she suggested we meet for coffee at the Canyon Country Store in Laurel Canyon. This neighborhood in the Hollywood Hills is famous for the musicians who lived here in the 1960s and '70s.

The composition of the photograph was good, Dawn said as she studied the image. It was very natural. Marsh, standing in the middle, was clearly the leader. When a group or a family is photographed, she said, you usually see how they are connected. Here, the only persons connected physically were Benjamin Hoppin and Charles Hill. Hill's hand is resting on Hoppin's shoulder.

Wondering if that were a sympathetic gesture, I asked if Hoppin looked like he had recently undergone a traumatic experience. I told Dawn about the night he had spent under a buffalo hide, lost on the Kansas plains. She didn't read anything in his facial expression.

Pointing to James MacNaughton, she said, "This one looks like a handful." In Kansas he had collected only one fossil, a specimen of a marine lizard. He also found a rodent fossil, but not until the party reached Colorado.

The photograph would not have been an instantaneous exposure, she continued. At this time a photograph couldn't be "fluid." "You couldn't catch a moment," she said.

Facial expressions in nineteenth-century photographs were typically serious. Open smiles—made possible by faster shutter speeds and, thanks to improved dental care, better-looking teeth—were not seen in portraiture until the twentieth century. In early photographs, moreover, a grin was "characteristic of peasants, drunkards, children, and halfwits," writes Christina Kotchemidova, an expert in media analysis and symbolic interpretation. A big smile suggested "low class or some other deficiency."[142] In the 1860s blank facial expressions and vacant stares grew less common as the exposure time needed to make a negative became shorter. Photographs became more casual. In 1867 a gallery in Denver advertised "Good pictures taken of children in one or two seconds—adults in four to six seconds."[143]

Dawn pointed out that the other students were leaning back but Tom was leaning forward. "Tom is ready. He is prepared." I thought about the obituary his colleague Dr. William Hawkes wrote. He described Tom as so prepared for his work that he routinely carried with him an "armamentarium" of surgical instruments.[144]

"He's confident. He's self-assured." Dawn placed an index finger on Tom. "If I'm going on an expedition, he's the one person I'm going with. He's smart, he's ahead of his time. He's adventurous and trailblazing. But it was all internal. He was not shouting and bragging about."

Looking up from the notes I was taking, I noticed a man sitting at a nearby table. On the bench beside him a big dog sitting stock-still on all fours was observing me with intense interest. The animal's forelegs stretched straight ahead, like the Sphinx's, in my direction.

"Are you looking at me?" I asked the dog. Its tail wagged heavily from side to side. I love dogs, but this was a pit bull, a breed I am a little afraid of.

"You *are* looking at me, aren't you," I said. With its entire body now wiggling, the Sphinx pushed its paws closer to me. The owner held the leash. I asked the dog's name.

"Mama," the owner said. He had rescued her at five months.

"Does she know you saved her life?" I asked.

Yes, he was sure she did. Her coat was shiny and the same color as the Weimaraner's who lives across the street from me. Mama was a loved dog.

She was named for Mama Cass of the Mamas & the Papas, who had once lived in the basement of the store where Dawn and I, the dog and her owner, and several more regulars were all enjoying the warm winter day. Laurel Canyon was the home of Joni Mitchell's ladies who wore gypsy shawls, baked brownies, and sat surrounded by cats and babies. When Joni came to Los Angeles in 1968, a friend told her about a book he'd found in a flea market. It said the craziest people in America lived in California. The craziest people in California lived in Los Angeles. The craziest people in Los Angeles lived in Hollywood. The craziest people in Hollywood lived in Laurel Canyon. The craziest people in Laurel Canyon lived on Lookout Mountain. So she bought a house there.[145] Lookout Mountain Avenue intersects Laurel Canyon Boulevard, where Dawn and I sat drinking coffee and Mama flirted with me.

In the course of learning about Tom Russell and the 1872 Yale expedition, I had come to understand the importance of chance meetings and unexpected intersections. They often shape history, and I was alert to them. Here I sat on a sunshiny day at the literal intersection where some of the most influential musicians of the late 1960s and early '70s met. It was also the intersection, figuratively, of a music mecca, a friendly dog, a nineteenth-century photograph, a portrait photographer, and, well, me.

Jim Morrison, the lead singer of the Doors, lived in a house behind the store and supposedly wrote "Love Street" there.

Glenn Frey, of the Eagles, said in a *Vanity Fair* interview that on his first day in Southern California he drove to Laurel Canyon. The first person he saw, standing on the porch of the Canyon Country Store, was David Crosby of Crosby, Stills, and Nash. Jennifer Aniston worked the cash register and made sandwiches here. Canyon residents, visitors, and more celebrities than one can count hang out here for the artist vibe and the espressos that Lilly Falakshahi serves at her cart on the patio.

It was all internal. As I drove home in the slow-moving traffic of a Los Angeles afternoon, I thought about Dawn's words as she studied Tom Russell's face.

What is a man like who is internal? He keeps things to himself. He may be uncommunicative. Instead of bubbling over with excitement about the possibility of going west with Professor Marsh, Tom may have thought it over long before he told his parents. Did he announce one day that he was joining up? Were there family conversations about the danger, the expense, the gear and advance reading that Marsh required, the postponing of medical school until after the expedition returned in December?

My mother said that her grandfather was very reserved. Could Tom have been so inward that as a mature man even his wife and friends had to guess what he was thinking and what he wanted out of life? Did he ever tell his children that, as George Sternberg wrote, discovering a prized fossil had been the thrill of his life? What did he expect of his three sons and two daughters, and was their relationship intimate?

If a father is internal, his children may be eager to please him without knowing how to do it. Henry Holt said that until he was ill and William Huntington Russell, Tom's father, visited him in his sickbed, he had been unaware that the man had a kindly side. Was Tom like that?

These are questions without answers, or answers that can be known. As Joni Mitchell suggested in her elegiac "Sweet Bird," we cannot recapture the past or even fully know it.[146] As she put it, our thoughts about time and change are but guesses.

Of Tom's three sons, one followed in his footsteps, one was disappointed with his vocation, and another was himself something of a disappointment. Tom selected their professions, according to a custom of the day. The eldest son, Thomas H. Russell Jr., became a physician and surgeon, like his father. My mother told me that although her uncle Hunt, the second son, became a lawyer, he had really wanted to be a teacher. Her father, Edward, was supposed to enter the ministry but instead became an entrepreneurial businessman. Instead of marrying the right girl, he eloped with my grandmother, who was not even from Connecticut.

Neither of Tom's two daughters was permitted to attend college. One married and had children. The other fell in love with a man beneath her station and never married.

Internal. I was grateful for Dawn's word. Who knows if by studying Tom's face she had sized him up accurately, but in any case she had enabled me to let him down from a pedestal. I would always admire him, but now I could also ask questions about him that I hadn't considered. I once heard Gloria Steinem say that the problem with being put on a pedestal is that the only place you can go is down. It is easy to idealize someone we know little about. Sometimes we prefer that to truly knowing the complex, flawed, fascinating person. It was fair to consider Tom's possible shortcomings, because to understand who he really was—that's what I was after.

For the photograph taken in William Chamberlain's studio in Denver, Charles Hill wore moccasins. On my visit to Western Costume, Leighton Bowers had said that Hill likely purchased them from a western outfitter.

He might have bought them at Madigan's when he stepped off the train in Wallace, Kansas, or purchased them from a catalog. Could they have been genuine and made by Indians? I found a map of the United States showing thirty-seven varieties of moccasins made by American Indians. The styles range from Plains Indians' soft-soled, two-piece footwear to eastern tribes' moccasins with a center seam, some with a hard sole and some with a pucker-toe design, or puckered stitching. I studied the map looking for moccasins like Charles Hill's.

As I explored my ancestors' history in this country, time and again I realized how little I knew about the Natives whose lives they intersected and whose lands they inhabited. In childhood I lived near the prehistoric mounded dwellings and burial sites of indigenous people in Missouri, never knowing about them, let alone visiting them. In junior high school, when I lived in Oklahoma City, the teacher in Oklahoma history class required us to learn the names of the state's governors but not the thirty-nine tribes and nations living there during and before those governors' terms. Narragansett, Quinnipiac, Seneca, Mohawk—these were names children like me learned from Disney movies, television programs, and books. In Connecticut, where my family stayed with my grandmother in the summers of my childhood, I cannot recall previous Indian inhabitants being mentioned at all. Missouri, Oklahoma, and Connecticut are all Indian names. How limited was my knowledge of this country's history. How meager and bland was my education.

The pattern on the upper of Charles Hill's moccasins was not geometric, like designs I had seen in fifteen summers of visiting Santa Fe, New Mexico, as an adult. The pattern had curved lines. The map of moccasins had not shown a design like this.

Now that I knew the expedition photograph was taken in Denver, I turned to the Denver Art Museum, whose collections include moccasins representing several tribal groups. My email reached a curator named John Lukavic, who wrote his doctoral dissertation on Cheyenne moccasins and moccasin makers. I sent him my notes:

> Charles Hill's moccasins do not appear to have a separate hard sole sewn onto a soft sole of animal skin or hide. The pattern on the moccasin upper is not geometric but has curlicues. It looks as if a separate beaded or otherwise decorated strip forms a cuff. Hill may be wearing his own light-colored, woolen, calf-high socks for warmth; it was cold in Colorado by mid-November when they arrived there. If not woolen socks, could they be Cree deerskin leggings, which were attached to their footwear? Hill's right foot seems to show, in lieu of a cuff, a leather thong encircling the foot around the instep. The moccasins do not look like warm moccasins. The uppers look, possibly, painted.

At first, John thought the moccasins were what Ojibwe people call "chimookomanag makizin," or "whiteman moccasins," which he said were made by non-Natives in the Northeast or somewhere around the Great Lakes. "He must have picked them up somewhere or brought them with him from back east," he speculated. "They are styled after Ojibwe moccasins, but not Native. I hope this helps."

Later the same day, John ventured that they might be Micmac pucker-toe moccasins, especially since the Micmacs' homeland was in the Northeast, "not too far off from Yale. If the image of the moccasin designs were clearer, it would be easier to make a solid attribution." He attached a photograph of intricately detailed moccasins with the same design of curved lines on the upper.[147]

The Micmacs are a First Nations people whose homelands are in eastern Canada and Maine. They are also sometimes called Mick Mack, but the name and spelling preferred by their governing body, the Grand Council, is Mi'kmaq (pronounced meeg maw).[148]

The early Mi'kmaq were a migratory people who often traveled to present-day Maine. From the time of first contact with Europeans, they regularly traded or sold items they made. These handcrafted items often had distinctive designs, including the double-curve motif seen on Charles Hill's moccasins. Charles came from a family in the lumber business in Maine, which points to the likelihood that he acquired genuine Mi'kmaq moccasins there.

The double-curve motif was not strictly ornamental. Vera Longtoe Sheehan, an artist and expert in traditional clothing, has explained that this motif is meant to protect the wearer. Often a mirror image of two curving lines, the design may depict plants with healing or protective properties, sometimes shown opening in springtime.[149]

Why Charles Hill brought these moccasins from the Northeast along on a fossil-hunting expedition in the West one can only guess. The explanation may be as simple as a young man having an idea of a costume, or moccasins like these having proven warm enough for cold, snowy Maine and therefore up to the task as autumn turned to winter in the Rockies.

– 46 –

The expedition continued on to Cheyenne, in the far-southeastern corner of Wyoming Territory. It had been nicknamed "The Magic City of the Plains" after springing up seemingly overnight when the Union Pacific Railroad came through. The temperature was minus 15 degrees Fahrenheit. "Very naturally, they did not care to do much outdoor work in such an atmosphere," the *Hartford Daily Courant* reported. "Water was all frozen up, and the most bitter winter weather was experienced."[150]

They stayed either in town or at Fort D. A. Russell, three miles west on Crow Creek. The officers and women of the fort held a hop in the eastern men's honor, with "some thirty ladies" in attendance.[151]

Boredom was a fact of life on military posts, and visitors and home-spun entertainment provided a diversion. In her account of family life on the frontier, *Glittering Misery: Dependents of the Indian Fighting Army*, Patricia Stallard states that in the early 1870s men and women at Fort Russell produced plays, such as *Lend Me Five Shillings* and *Faint Heart Never Won Fair Lady*.[152] Males outnumbered females and sometimes took their roles. On the dance floor men sometimes wore a kerchief to signify they were standing in for women.

Despite the frigid temperatures that greeted the fossil hunters, for troops at Fort Russell winter could be an enjoyable season. American Indians were not on the move, the soldiers were not on scouting duty, and there were more social activities in town and on the post.[153] Relations between the post and town were, after a fashion, bilateral. During a blizzard in 1872, coal from the fort was shared with Cheyenne. Certain elements in town offered soldiers various forms of dissipation, including what one journalist referred to as "a house of loose architecture."[154] The year 1872 also brought Cheyenne a public library, the first in Laramie County.

At Fort Russell a large freight depot had been established in December 1867, just after the Union Pacific reached Cheyenne. Supplies from the sixteen warehouses were distributed from this depot to twelve army posts and government agencies. A hundred wagons were based there, and a thousand mules.[155]

On November 14, Special Order No. 190—written in a cursive hand so beautiful as to be worthy of a document of state—provided for a detachment led by 1st Lt. Jesse M. Lee to escort "Professor Marsh in his Geological Expedition."[156] "The Post Quartermaster will furnish Lieut. Lee a horse with equipments and such other facilities as may be necessary," it continued. "The Post Commissary will sell to Professor Marsh such Commissary Stores as he may desire adding to the articles purchased the Cost of their transportation." The escort would be armed and equipped with forty rounds of ammunition per man and ten days' rations. The *Hartford Daily Courant* reported that the detail also included a dozen soldiers, twenty horses and mules, and two six-mule wagons, presumably strong enough to carry heavy loads.[157] The immense weight of the collected fossils was due primarily to the fact that the bones had been petrified, and many specimens, including Hesper, were left in blocks of rock.

Marsh made a note to himself in 1870, preparing for his first expedition with students: "Jackson Abney Cheyenne Knows loc[ation] & will collect."[158] Abney was a leading stockman in the area. By 1871 Cheyenne counted sixty to eighty thousand cattle within a hundred-mile radius.[159] Sheep ranching was also a major industry.

Traveling southeastward out of Cheyenne, they camped for a week in Colorado Territory and explored the country around Crow Creek on the eastern side of the Rockies. Their explorations took them within distant sight of a place sacred to the Ute, called Tava, or Sun Mountain, before it was renamed Pikes Peak.[160]

On this second leg of the expedition, instead of collecting fossils from Cretaceous-aged marine deposits, Marsh and his party spent a week exploring geologically younger, terrestrial deposits. Their explorations yielded upward of 250 specimens, including a legless, snakelike lizard, rhinoceros teeth, rodent bones, and turtle parts so ubiquitous that they were left uncollected.[161] The temperature dropped to zero. Presumably none too soon for the students, they returned to Fort Russell in late November and parted with their army escort.

– 47 –

An article in the *Deseret Evening News* dated November 27, 1872, stated that Marsh's students were in Salt Lake City from Wednesday through Friday, November 27–29, and had called on the newspaper at its offices there.[162] "They were handsomely entertained by the Mormons, were introduced to Brigham Young and shown the temple and other sights," the *Hartford Daily Courant* reported.[163] On the first of the Yale expeditions, in 1870, the "boys," as Marsh's biographers called them, had "flirted with twenty-two daughters of Brigham Young in a box at the theatre, and overcome by the effort, immediately crossed the Sierra Nevada to San Francisco."[164]

In 1871 the *New York Herald* reported that telegrams from Salt Lake City brought word of Brigham Young's arrest. Young expressed a willingness to appear in court to answer the charges against him, "the most conspicuous of which at the present moment, is 'for lewd and lascivious cohabitation with sixteen different women, under the statutes of Utah providing against offences against morality and decency.'"[165] More dispatches followed, one stating that Young was ill and unable to appear in court. On January 2, 1872, he was arrested on a murder charge and sent to prison to await trial. On April 25, by a decision of the U.S. Supreme Court, he was released.[166] He was thus a free man when the 1872 Yale party came through.

Thanksgiving Day fell on the second day of the group's stay in Salt Lake City. Like looking for a star in the night sky and seeing it indirectly by focusing on another star, we know from an account written the same year how fine a holiday feast was possible. Elizabeth Kane and her husband, Thomas, had traveled to Utah from their home in Pennsylvania. They accepted an invitation to Thanksgiving dinner at the home of Utah's territorial librarian, William C. Staines. Brigham Young and one of his wives, Amelia, were also invited.

Mrs. Kane, a Presbyterian, described the occasion in a letter to her daughter. She was confused at first, because she had remembered seeing the host's home near the train station. Why, then, did the carriage driver turn east, in the wrong direction, instead of west? She held her tongue long enough to realize that Mr. Staines had more than one household. If these domestic arrangements did not favorably impress Elizabeth Kane, the Thanksgiving meal did. After a starter of soup came an elaborate second course of roast beef and roast turkey with sides of stewed tomatoes, peas, corn, horseradish, and potatoes. Mr. Staines's two wives had put up the vegetables from their own gardens. Dessert consisted of mince pies, plum pudding, fruit cakes, and raspberry tarts.[167]

Russell, MacNaughton, Hoppin, and Hill backtracked to Fort Bridger, where they had left Professor Marsh to work while they visited Salt Lake City. When they returned to Wyoming, one final adventure in the West awaited them. Their one day in Green River country, where they went to search for fossilized fish and insects, coincided with the exposure of what the *San Francisco Chronicle* called "the most gigantic and barefaced swindle of the age," the Great Diamond Hoax of 1872.[168] Marsh played a part in the unmasking of the hoax. His friend Clarence King, the Yale-Sheffield–educated geologist, led the effort, a feat that would affirm the importance of science in a country emerging as a world power.

The deception was the idea of two Kentucky cousins, Philip Arnold and John Slack. Arnold had sought his fortune in California as a forty-niner. By 1870 he had landed in the accounting department of the Diamond Drill Company in San Francisco. The industrial-grade diamonds used in the drills gave Arnold an idea. By November of that year he had amassed a quantity of diamonds, likely ill gotten, along with rubies and other precious stones. Some of the colored gemstones were evidently purchased in Arizona from American Indians.

Arnold and Slack targeted a San Francisco businessman named George Roberts. They cagily divulged to him that a leather bag they carried with them contained uncut diamonds from a deposit they had found. When they urged secrecy upon him, they had him. "Roberts was very much elated by our discovery," Arnold admitted to the *Louisville Courier-Journal* after the fraudulent scheme was exposed, and "promised Slack and myself to keep it a profound secret until we could explore the country further and ascertain more fully the extent of our discoveries."[169]

Roberts invited investors to get in on the "opportunity." The thieves received an initial sum, from which they spent $20,000 to purchase uncut gemstones in London under an assumed name.

Pretending they had found more gemstones at their secret location, they showed some of them to the investors, who in turn asked the founder of Tiffany & Company to appraise them. Two days later Charles Lewis Tiffany placed their worth at $150,000, more than $3 million today. Arnold and Slack used more stones to salt a remote location in northwestern Colorado in the Green River region.

The miscreants were counting on their victims' unfamiliarity with the geography. They undoubtedly did not know that their "diamond field" lay in an area where one of the great western survey parties had just completed extensive fieldwork. They certainly could not have anticipated that a member of this very survey party would be on the same train as a mining engineer whom the investors had sent to examine the diamond field.

While Marsh was exploring the American West for fossils, Clarence King was exploring stratigraphy and mineral resources along the fortieth parallel. King, an eminent geologist, had proposed the survey, which the Army Corps of Engineers sponsored and for which Congress appropriated funding. The field of study encompassed an area from the eastern border of California to eastern Wyoming along a wide swath of the transcontinental railroad route. Beginning in 1867, King and his hand-picked team worked their way eastward, creating topographic maps as they progressed.[170]

King knew from previous experience in the West that "metal deposits occurred in parallel, longitudinal zones that followed the same patterns as the western mountain ranges" and that they "occurred in the same geological layers."[171] The survey identified and mapped the mineral deposits in great detail, along with their location and geologic history.

The survey's fieldwork was almost completed when one of King's men, a geologist named Samuel F. Emmons, was seated aboard a train bound for Oakland and happened to encounter some men talking about diamonds and showing samples of them. Rumors of diamond fields in Arizona and New Mexico had been circulating, but that area was not within the bounds of the survey headed up by King. From the remarks Emmons heard, however, he deduced that the field was in northwestern Colorado close to the Wyoming border, near where he had been working. If it were true, four years of scientific work would be cast into doubt.

Emmons, King, and their topographer A. D. Wilson met at Fort Bridger, Wyoming, and in the November chill set off on a 150-mile trip. In the area where they thought the stones had been found, they made camp and went to work. Following posted claim notices as clues, they came to an expanse of sandstone and began examining it. In no time Emmons found a ruby. King collected forty-three rubies with one scoop of a sieve.[172] Emmons noted in his diary that he and his companions went to bed that night imagining the wealth soon to be theirs.

The next day's work led to a different conclusion. King observed that wherever a diamond was discovered there were a dozen rubies, and that the same ratio occurred everywhere a diamond was found. Worse, the stones were found only in anthills that looked as if they had been poked with a stick, and only where footprints appeared nearby. Where there were anthills with no footprints, or no anthills at all, there were no gemstones.

King and his topographer hurried back to San Francisco and arrived on November 10, 1872. King spent most of that night explaining to a mining engineer what they had found. They were just in time to prevent a planned stock offering of ten million dollars, but not too soon for one of the duped investors to suggest that it could profit King to wait a few days before making his findings public.[173] The *San Francisco Chronicle* mocked the investors and acknowledged King for having prevented "a great financial calamity."[174] In Johnson County, Kansas, the *Olathe Mirror* published a one-sentence jeer: "For being fool enough to believe in the diamond fields of Arizona, a San Francisco man loses to the amount of $160,000."[175]

There in Green River country the Yale party found itself in the midst of the excitement and saw some of the rubies that had been collected. Professor Marsh examined the stones. On November 28,

1872, the *Wyandotte Herald*, in Kansas City, Kansas, reported, "The Professor pronounces the stones genuine diamonds but is convinced that they have been 'salted' by capitalists. His advice is not to be 'gulled' by the reports."[176]

King's exposure of the diamond swindle underscored the importance of his survey and made him a celebrity scientist. "Let it not be said that geological surveys are useless," the editor of *Colorado Mining Review* wrote in the December 1872 issue. "This one act has certainly paid for the survey of the 40th Parallel and has brought deserved credit to Mr. King and his assistants."[177]

The duty of a newspaper to report on science was taken up by the *New York Tribune* in an editorial the following year. It acknowledged that education had undergone a transformation: science and the classics were now ranked equally in importance. "Without neglecting in the slightest degree its principal function as a purveyor of news, *The Tribune* has succeeded in adding a department of theoretical and practical science far in advance of the most ambitious attempts of any other daily publication," the paper stated. Coverage of "Prof. Marsh's remarkable discoveries in the Rocky Mountains" and other scientific topics, moreover, had "not only met the wants of strictly scientific readers, but [had] created a deep interest in scientific subjects among the miscellaneous public."[178] With advances in scientific understanding coming quickly, a great newspaper was bound and even proud to lead the way in reporting on them. Science was now accessible. There was no refuge in ignorance.

With the serial publication of King's multivolume *Report of the Geological Exploration of the Fortieth Parallel*, the hoax-buster became a bestselling author. The seventh and final volume in the series was Marsh's groundbreaking monograph, *Odontornithes: On the Extinct Toothed Birds of North America*.

The Great Diamond Hoax of 1872 is a story of schemers gulling investors and counting on their greed and ignorance. It is a story of a remarkable coincidental meeting on a train that allowed scientists to prove the necessity and urgency of their work.

Ironically, about fifteen years after Clarence King exposed the diamond fraud, he embarked on an elaborate personal deception of his own. Only in 1901, when he was dying, did he reveal his true identity to Ada Copeland Todd, who had been his wife by common law for thirteen years and was the mother of his five children. From a letter he wrote to her, she learned that her blond, blue-eyed husband was not, like her, African American. His name was not James Todd. He was not a Pullman porter whose job on the railroad accounted for his long absences from their home in Brooklyn.[179]

In his other life, King moved in elite circles as a bachelor, celebrated explorer, author, and scientist and the first director of the U.S. Geological Survey. He had managed for years to gull his own family, as well as friends and colleagues.

− 49 −

The 1872 expedition broke up in Ogden, Utah. James MacNaughton and Benjamin Hoppin took the train to San Francisco. Although details of their return are not known, if they followed the route Clarence King took five years earlier, they would have boarded a steamer in San Francisco, crossed the Isthmus of Panama by rail, and reached New York after an eleven days' sail.

Professor Marsh, Tom Russell, and Charles Hill returned by the overland route. They spent one day in Omaha and another in Chicago. The *Chicago Tribune* reported that Marsh—so, too, presumably Tom and Charles—stayed at Sherman House, a luxury hotel by any standard, but especially compared to tent life.[180] They returned to New Haven on December 7.[181] A week later, on December 14, Tom turned twenty-one.

The expedition's scientific success was widely reported. In Pennsylvania the *Reading Times* told its readers, "A remarkable discovery has been made by Prof. O. C. Marsh in the upper cretaceous shale [*sic*] of

Kansas. It is no less than the link between the bird and the reptile, in the shape of a skeleton of an animal bearing the peculiar marks of both orders. In this discovery the Darwinians have a very valuable proof of their theory."[182]

In Washington, D.C., the *Evening Star* reported that the party had found more than two hundred previously unknown, extinct vertebrates. A vast region previously regarded as a desert, and an uninteresting one at that, the newspaper said, could now be understood as "a historic ground once peopled with the most grotesque and diverse forms of animal life, a Wonderland of dragons and monsters."[183] Further, the discoveries of the 1872 expedition had narrowed gaps in the understanding of comparative anatomy and were superior in number and variety to anything Europe could offer to explain the evolution of life on earth.

Appleton's Journal reported on the "treasures secured" by the expedition, including *Hesperornis regalis*. Another accomplishment, and not the least important, the magazine said, was "to put to a severe test the nerves and energies of a class of young men who are not always credited with the physical powers they really possess." Their safe return was evidence that colleges were not developing students' minds at the expense of their physical stamina. "Wanting in neither zeal nor pluck," the *Journal* concluded, "their success is worthy of national congratulation."[184]

The 1872 Yale College Scientific Expedition with the local scout and the army officer who accompanied them in Kansas and Colorado. Seated, left to right, are the author's great-grandfather Thomas H. Russell, James MacNaughton, Benjamin Hoppin, and Charles Hill. Standing, left to right, are scout Edward Lane, Professor O. C. Marsh, and 2nd Lt. James W. Pope. Photographed by William Gunnison Chamberlain in Denver, Colorado Territory, in November 1872. Courtesy Peabody Museum of Natural History, Yale University.

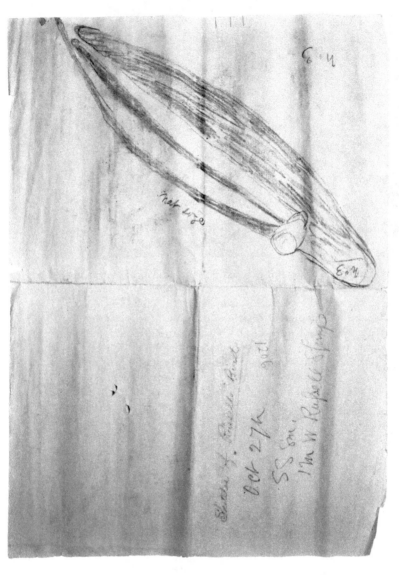

The field sketch made in western Kansas on October 27, 1872, of the pelvis of "Russell's bird," *Hesperornis regalis*, YPM VP.001206. Courtesy Peabody Museum of Natural History, Yale University.

Cadets and cannons on the parade grounds of General Russell's Collegiate and Commercial Institute, facing Wooster Square in New Haven, circa 1862. Thomas H. Russell attended his father's military-style school. Collection of the author.

Gen. William Huntington Russell, father of Thomas H. Russell.
Collection of the author.

Thomas H. Russell with his mother, Mary Elizabeth Hubbard Russell,
in 1856 or 1857. Collection of the author.

Thomas H. Russell in 1872, the year he found his *Hesperornis regalis* fossil.
Collection of the author.

The Seventh Cavalry on parade at Fort Wallace, Kansas,
from *Harper's Weekly Magazine*, July 27, 1867.

May Boeve, left, with her mother, the author, in the Goblin Hollow fossil bed near Russell Springs, Kansas. Photograph by Michael J. Everhart. Collection of the author.

May Boeve on an outcropping in Logan County, Kansas.
Photograph by the author.

Leighton Bowers, director of research at Western Costume Company in North Hollywood, California, among miles of racks of garments. Photograph by Amber Morris. Courtesy of Western Costume Company.

The Jones triplets of Pasadena, California, know their dinosaurs.
Photograph by the author.

John Brown's sons Owen and Jason Brown on muleback outside
their cabin in the San Gabriel Foothills. Courtesy Pasadena
Public Library, Pasadena, California.

Thomas H. Russell, MD, circa 1901, early in his tenure as professor of clinical surgery at Yale Medical School. Collection of the author.

O. C. Marsh and Oglala Lakota Chief Red Cloud (Maȟpíya Lúta) in New Haven, Connecticut, in 1883. Courtesy Peabody Museum of Natural History, Yale University.

Benjamin Hoppin with a trophy polar bear on board the *S. S. Hope* during Robert Peary's 1896 Arctic voyage. Courtesy Beaton Institute, Cape Breton University, 94-939-25454.

Brig. Gen. James W. Pope. Photograph by Theodore M. Brown. Courtesy
Special Collections, United States Military Academy Library.

Hesperornis regalis Marsh.
Zahntragender Vogel aus der Kreide-Zeit (nach Hutchinson und Smit).

A trading card from Series 1, *Tiere der Urvelt* (Creatures of the Primitive World), circa 1902, depicted two *Hesperornis regalises*. The cards were distributed by the Theodore Reichardt Company of Hamburg, Germany, with its product, chocolate. Collection of the author.

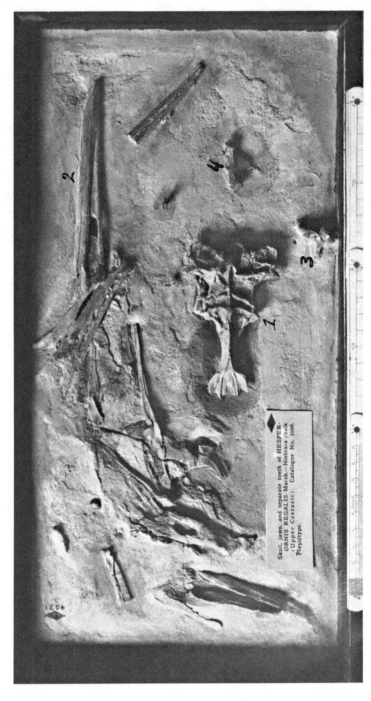

Skull, jaws, and separate teeth of HESPER-
ORNIS REGALIS Marsh.—Niobrara chalk
(Upper Cretacic). Catalogue No. 1206.
Plesiotype.

The skull, jaws, and teeth of Thomas H. Russell's *Hesperornis regalis* specimen in its original chalk matrix — literally, its mother rock — from western Kansas. Courtesy Peabody Museum of Natural History, Yale University.

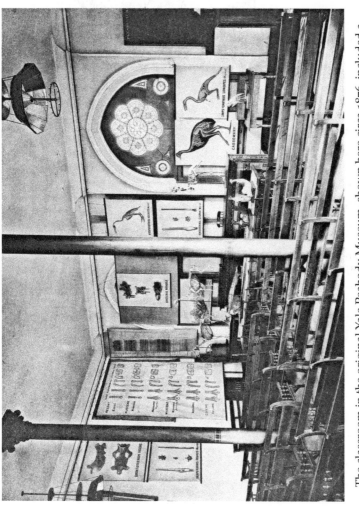

The classroom in the original Yale Peabody Museum, shown here circa 1876, included a drawing of *Hesperornis regalis* in a standing position (immediately right of the center pole). Illustrations of a cassowary and *Compsognathus*, the smallest known dinosaur at the time, indicated the animals' similarities. Courtesy Peabody Museum of Natural History, Yale University.

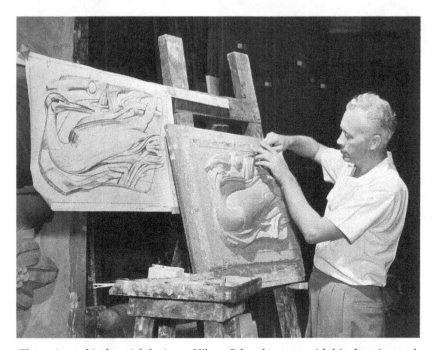

The artist and industrial designer Viktor Schreckengost with his drawing and presentation model of *Hesperornis regalis*. The Cleveland Metroparks Zoo commissioned Schreckengost to create tiles depicting avian history for a Birds of the World tower on its bird building, which opened in 1950. Photograph courtesy Heritage Auctions.

Helen Umbehr, one of the Wabaunsee County (Kansas) Historical Society "quilting ladies," and the author. The quilters have met twice a week for twenty years and have created hundreds of quilts. Photograph by Bob Aicher.

Part IV
I Go to Kansas

— 50 —

Early on the morning of October 29, May and I pulled away from our hotel in Denver listening to the theme from *How the West Was Won*. I had made a mixtape of Western music for our three-hour drive to Sharon Springs, Kansas.

Both of us lived then in the San Francisco Bay Area, May in the city's Mission District and I an hour north, within walking distance of the plaza in downtown Sonoma. California is of course geographically western, but for the true feeling of the West and particularly its open spaces, my adoptive state has nothing on Colorado. Once you leave metropolitan Denver traveling southeast, place names evoke the history and people who preceded you here: Arapahoe County, the town of Kit Carson, Cheyenne County.

Extending in every direction were flatlands, their tawny expanse interrupted only by an occasional pond or windmill. No jets or contrails streaked the sky. We saw no fields planted in rows, no herds or even lone animals. Close on our right, a freight train paralleled the road without gaining on us. We entered Lincoln County at Limon.

"Look at that," May said as we drove through the next town, Hugo. I made a U-turn so she could take a photo of the sign she had spotted: "33 Years of Cold Beers." I slowed to a crawl and she lowered her window to get the shot. A bowlegged man was walking on the sidewalk, carrying a mug of coffee, presumably. As we passed, he called out to no one we could see, "Two good-lookin' women just turned around to take my picture!"

Our plan was to meet up with a paleontologist named Mike Everhart when we reached Sharon Springs, population 763. Dan Brinkman, the vertebrate paleontologist from the Peabody Museum, had introduced me to Mike by email after I inquired whether any universities were actively hunting fossils in western Kansas. None that he knew of, Dan said, but Mike knew the area well and had written a book about it.

Mike is an adjunct paleontology curator at the Sternberg Museum in Hays, Kansas, and an expert on the Late Cretaceous. As the author of *Oceans of Kansas*, a natural history of this region and the prehistoric life that dwelled in the Western Interior Sea, he has thoroughly explored western Kansas for fossils. He is well acquainted with the work of O. C. Marsh, the collections of the Yale Peabody Museum, and Marsh's rivalry with Edward Drinker Cope.

I had sent him a list of locations where Tom Russell collected his *Hesperornis regalis* and other specimens in the Smoky Hill country. Mike thought we could get permission to walk on the property where the famous bird with teeth had been found. He knew some people in the area and said he would look into it.

He had told me I could not pay him for his time as our guide, so I was planning to buy his lunch when we met him in Sharon Springs. I was thinking about this lopsided deal, Mike's fossil-hunting expertise in exchange for a sandwich, as May and I pulled up to the Kit Carson Trading Post and Restaurant, some forty miles west of the Colorado-Kansas border.

A sign out front said "6OOO Pies." Given the small size of the town, this quantity amazed me. May pointed out that it actually said "GOOD Pies." A much larger sign over the building proclaimed, "Somehow, nothing satisfies like BEEF!"

May wanted to stop eating meat when she was in preschool. I thought it was a phase she would outgrow, but her teacher encouraged me to keep an open mind because children begin their moral development at an early age. In first grade, May asked me to help her send a letter to President George H. W. Bush asking him to make cruelty to animals, including bugs, illegal. When she was still in primary school, she sold lemonade on a street corner and sent the proceeds to PETA. Later she would say that selling lemonade had given her something more valuable than the twelve dollars she earned. She told an interviewer, "What I got was [. . .] the sense that with a little group of friends, some signs, and an afternoon, I could contribute to something."[1]

— 51 —

Inside the trading post the homey aroma of fresh-baked pie filled the room. As a food editor I had learned a lot from culinary professionals I worked with, and over the years I had turned out a fair number of pies, but in no way had I mastered the skill of pie making. I greatly admire a baker who can turn out a golden, flaky crust—someone who can gauge the right proportions of flour, shortening, and water by sight and touch, without relying on a scale or measuring cups and spoons, and who can roll out the pastry with a soda bottle if no rolling pin is available. Here in the Kit Carson Trading Post and Restaurant was such a cook, and her name was Norma.

I was excited to be starting a road trip with my daughter and to have found a first-rate piemaker in a whistle-stop on the plains. As I chatted with our waitress about the variety of pies on the menu and which ones had just come out of the oven, May looked on without speaking. She seemed tense.

She may have been wondering what kind of town and restaurant would name themselves for Kit Carson, a frontiersman as complex as he is famous. He twice married American Indian women, one Arapaho and one Cheyenne. He was responsible for relocating thousands of Navajos, two hundred of whom died on a "Long Walk" across New Mexico. In 2014, after a presentation by American Indians to the city council of Taos, the Kit Carson Park there was re-named Red Willow. "We have got to change the wreckage of the past," one council member said, "and Kit Carson is part of that."[2]

The past that May and I had come to explore did not involve personal strife. It was our familial past. But this place is political. Conflict is as much a part of western history as fossil hunting.

We had stopped in a town named for a fighter in the so-called Indian Wars, and what's more we were deep in cattle-ranching country. This restaurant with good pies prominently advertised its membership in the Colorado Beef Board. Soon we would cross into Kansas, whose bovine population is more than double that of humans. Its number of "commercial cattle processed" ranks second in the nation.[3]

If like May you are a climate activist, you know Kansas to be a battleground for renewable energy versus Big Oil. A state law passed in 2009 required utilities to generate, by 2016, at least 15 percent of their power using wind and solar, increasing to 20 percent by 2020. Opponents of the legislation fought to repeal renewable portfolio standards, such as a tax credit for wind production. In 2015 the Kansas legislature approved a bill making the 20 percent standard voluntary.[4]

Although fossil fuels—crude oil, natural gas, and coal—are a significant driver of the state's economy, Kansas ranks second only to Oklahoma and is tied with Montana for wind capacity.[5] In 2014 rural Kansans farming wind received more than $13 million a year in royalties.[6] Proponents of this technology cite the nearly four thousand manufacturing jobs that only nineteen wind farms created in the state.[7] Before May and I would conclude our time in Kansas, we would imagine what it would be like to buy acreage in Logan County and start a wind farm.

— 52 —

May is the executive director and a cofounder of a climate advocacy group called 350.org. The organization's genesis was a friendship among six students at Middlebury College, in Vermont.

From her first semester at Middlebury, May found values like her own in the friends she made. They were progressive, they took each other's ideas seriously, and they loved the outdoors. Her first year, she went snow camping for the first time and learned to ski and snowshoe, even if snowy winters were new to her. One day while we were talking on the phone, she looked out the window and said, "It's really coming down hard." Her roommate, from Maine, said something in the background. "Oh." May said. "I guess not."

When the Second Gulf War broke out, in 2003, she was disappointed not to find more opposition to it on campus. During my college years in New England, I had protested the Vietnam War, felt the sting of tear gas in my eyes, met three of the Chicago Seven defendants, attended a rally at Yale in support of Angela Davis, and marched with Gloria Steinem in support of equal pay and equal rights for women. May's expectations of college life were doubtless colored by her knowledge of my experience.

As a class project some of her friends invited the several environmental groups on campus to join forces. Calling themselves Sunday Night Group, they began devising strategies for concrete steps they could take right away to address campus environmental issues. They arranged with the dining services director to grow vegetables for the campus dining rooms. Joining the effort, May ordered composting worms and worm castings (an organic fertilizer, also called vermicompost) for the school's greenhouse from friends of mine in Sonoma who owned a worm farm. As activism on campus began to grow, May found her community and her political stride.

In 2004 Middlebury inaugurated a new president, Ronald Liebowitz. Early in his tenure Sunday Night Group urged him to make Middlebury the leader among green campuses nationwide. President Liebowitz accepted the challenge and convinced the trustees that going green was an essential course correction for the more than two-hundred-year-old institution. Middlebury became the first school of its size to go carbon-neutral. In 2009 *Time* magazine named Liebowitz one of the ten best college presidents in the nation.[8]

When Montreal hosted the United Nations Climate Conference, in 2005, the college supported Sunday Night Group by helping send three buses of students to the climate talks 130 miles away. The group also protested the burning of tires in a nearby paper mill and created sculptures out of recovered paper waste from the mill. One classmate, after attending his first Sunday Night Group meeting, wrote in the campus newspaper, "These guys walk the walk more than they talk the talk."[9]

During a three-month cross-country tour in a school bus converted to run on used vegetable oil—Project BioBus—May and her friends spoke to students at sixty-five high schools, local officials in twenty cities, and countless radio listeners about alternatives to the fossil-fuel economy. Middlebury supported their trek with a $10,000 grant and a send-off during which the team offered tours of their bus, whose engine they had converted themselves by following instructions in a library book.

The BioBus team revved up media coverage wherever they went. Once back on campus, they rejoined Sunday Night Group. The enthusiasm, collegiality, and weekly potlucks of the group attracted ever larger numbers of students, faculty, and townspeople. It grew into the largest organization on campus and the largest of its kind in the country.[10]

Although what had attracted May to Middlebury was its environmental studies program, she declared political science as her major. Her logical focus became climate activism. She and her friends invited their fellow students to think beyond their classes, beyond athletics and extracurriculars, even beyond getting the most out of a college as stimulating and supportive as Middlebury. It was, in short, an invitation to think beyond themselves and the present hour to the world we all inhabit, and its future, and all life with which we share it.

53

May ordered a wedge of strawberry-rhubarb pie and I had the cherry with a lattice crust. Behind her on the wall hung a large American flag. In 1872, when Tom Russell came through here with the Yale expedition, the American flag had thirty-seven stars.[11]

A slice of pie, the flag, and my daughter—the tableau before me offered up a large helping of irony. On her cross-country trip with the BioBus, May had been impressed to find progressive thinkers wherever she went. It was apparent, however, that at this moment we were in a stronghold of patriotism defined very differently from ours. I now realized why she had been so quiet.

Seeing May framed by the flag, I thought of my great-great-grandfather, whose spirit I felt my daughter had inherited. Gen. William H. Russell was called "a patriot whose counsels and labors throughout the war for the Union effected much for his country and for the citizen soldiers of his state."[12] That's what his friends said, but to citizens of the Confederacy he was an enemy. My idea of a patriot was sitting across the table from me.

One day while walking to class, May passed Bill McKibben, then a scholar in residence at Middlebury and one of the first authors to write about global warming for a general audience. Each recognizing the other from Sunday Night Group, they agreed to meet for coffee.

Meanwhile, graduation was on the horizon. A couple of May's schoolmates began researching where the superfriends, as one interviewer would later dub them, might move as a group and continue working together. The city would need to have a pressing environmental issue, a college, and a craft beer scene.

McKibben put a question to them: If he could find someone to provide them with a modest living allowance, would they consider staying in New England? He was once asked why he was working with these college kids. "If you knew five people who were seven feet tall," he said, "wouldn't you start a basketball team?"

The 2008 presidential election was but a year away, and the candidates had not yet demonstrated they were taking the climate issue seriously. Soon they would be campaigning close by in the key primary state of New Hampshire. What if the six friends moved there, got to know the candidates in town halls and cafes where they were meeting voters, and offered to help them define their positions on energy and the environment? What if one of these candidates were to win the Democratic nomination and these positions made it into the party platform? What if the candidate were elected president?

When May came home on break, we talked about it. I admired what she and her friends were doing. Their emerging plan would mean that she would not be coming home to California. I wished it could be otherwise, though I did not say it and probably did not need to. I did not want to keep her from seeing where her wings could take her.

As May and I finished our pie, a way to thank Mike Everhart occurred to me. Norma brought out a cherry pie still warm from the oven, placed it in a white box, and tied it with string.

We made one final stop in Colorado, seventeen miles from the Kansas border, to buy gas. Here, at a Sinclair station in Cheyenne Wells, we saw our first dinosaur of the trip, a green *Brontosaurus* on a white canopy high above the gas pumps. Sinclair Oil has used Dino the Dinosaur in its advertising since the 1930s, when they linked the "thunder lizard" to the company's products, equating the two with power, endurance, and stamina.[13] Dino was an instant hit. Sinclair distributed hundreds of thousands of materials about geology to schools and libraries. At one time they financed paleontological expeditions of the American Museum of Natural History. Later they turned to Dr. John H. Ostrom of the Peabody Museum at Yale, who served as a consultant on the company's dinosaur exhibit at the 1964 New York World's Fair.[14]

Fossil fuels, a daughter working to keep coal, oil, and gas in the ground, and an ancestor who discovered a prehistoric fossil. This was an intersection you can't find on a map.

54

May graduated in February 2007 and moved to New Hampshire. With her friends and Bill McKibben, she spent the spring and summer talking with Democratic presidential candidates, including Hillary Clinton, John Edwards, and Barack Obama. They organized public events to raise awareness of energy issues, mobilizing millennials like themselves. Their success led the six friends to ask what else they could do.

With the help of multilingual volunteers from the Monterey Language Institute, affiliated with Middlebury, they contacted thousands of social-change organizations around the world, which the non-profit Wiser Earth had recently catalogued. Hundreds of these organizations responded to an invitation to join forces in addressing the climate crisis. May and her colleagues also attended United Nations conferences, where they met leaders of emerging youth climate networks and international NGOs. Their method was to build coalitions. It reflected the very foundation of their work, namely friendship.

They wrote a book with McKibben about community organizing, called *Fight Global Warming Now*. "When we need help with something, we turn first to our friends," May wrote in her chapter on collaboration, "then to a wider circle of people who are still within our comfort zone. Though it's understandable to feel shy with strangers, much can be gained from reaching out." The team had come to realize, she said, "We weren't just brokering partnerships but starting friendships, cross-fertilizing different pools of volunteers and resources, sometimes even combining very different worldviews."[15]

It was time, they felt, for a bigger vision and reach. In deciding what to call themselves, they wanted a name that would translate into as many of the world's four thousand languages as possible. They settled not on a name but a number that represents the safe threshold of parts-per-million of carbon dioxide in the atmosphere. Launching their global climate movement in 2009, they called it 350.org.

For almost a year before May and I went to Kansas, she had been wrestling with ending a relationship with one of her 350 cofounders. They had been romantic partners and teammates for seven years. The work had always come first. Eventually May reached a point when she wanted to keep growing but no longer felt that the romantic relationship was the way to do it. Now it had ended. They had not told their teammates. May was troubled about how their work might change, because they had invested so much in building 350 together. She didn't know what to tell the team, or how.

To complicate matters, the burden May was carrying was even heavier. She had ended a relationship, and in doing that she was afraid she would damage the organization she had helped bring into being. She was 350's nurturing parent and now was risking breaking up something like a family. She was experiencing for herself what I had done to our family of three and in a sense reliving the sadness of it.

As I listened to May and observed her in the pain of upheaval, I saw my part in it. She was the most important person in my life, but when my marriage to her father ended, I had failed to give her what she wanted most. She just wanted her family to remain intact. It was natural, I knew, but for my own well-being I could not do it. I didn't feel guilty about creating a new life for myself, but I didn't feel good about hurting May, either.

Here we were on the Great Plains, both together and alone with our thoughts, two women asking questions about our past and future.

~ 55 ~

It was noon when we met up with Mike Everhart. He was a man in his fifties, sturdily built, wearing blue jeans and a black polo shirt. We climbed into his Chevy van, the back of which was crammed with tools of the fossil-hunting trade, complete with an Indiana

Jones–style fedora. A second hat lay on the top of the dashboard and stayed there both days we spent with him.

We stopped first at a museum in Wallace. As May and I looked at exhibits with military relics and uniforms, Mike showed pictures of Tom Russell and *Hesperornis regalis* to a friend who was a museum volunteer.

We bumped along county roads to the old cemetery on the grounds of the original Fort Wallace, where soldiers who died there were buried. In 1867 the men erected a cenotaph from locally quarried stone to honor the fallen. After the fort was decommissioned, in 1886, the bodies of eighty-eight soldiers were exhumed and moved to Fort Leavenworth, despite fear that the remains of those who died from cholera were dangerous. Civilians were also buried here, including John and Lydia German and their children Joanna, Rebecca, and Stephen.

The chalk outcroppings we passed on the road shone golden-yellow in the early-afternoon sunshine. One resembled nothing so much as a colossal bar of gold bullion. We stopped at a place where the road bisected a hill. Where the cut had been made, layers of sediment were exposed. We spent an hour looking for bones. I picked up a fragment of what Mike said was a deer jawbone. Nothing of interest, in other words.

Mike has done extensive research on the stratigraphy of the terrain in Logan and Wallace Counties and the fossil record of the Late Cretaceous. From this he had concluded that the most probable locality where Tom found his *Hesperornis regalis* specimen was a large exposure of gray chalk about a mile from Russell Springs.[16] Among the town's two dozen residents this exposure goes by several names, including Hell's Half Acre, the Buttes, the Rocks, Garden of the Gods, and most often—and aptly for the approaching Halloween weekend—Goblin Hollow. According to a paper Mike would publish after our visit, it is "the only substantial exposure of gray chalk on the south side of the Smoky Hill River within several miles." The locality, he determined, is "stratigraphically equivalent" to nearby sites where *Hesperornis regalis* specimens were collected in 1931, 1948, 1952, and 1958.[17]

Cautioning us against disappointment, Mike said he was unable to reach the property owner, and we would not be able to get onto the site. We could only park alongside and look in. When we reached Goblin Hollow, however, the gate was wide open. Without hesitating I stepped out of the car and walked down into the gray chalk. It was crumbly and soft underfoot, and with every step my boots sank enough to leave an impression. Erosion had created shallow, fingerlike canyons across many acres. In these canyons, dozens of waist- and shoulder-high mini-buttes showed what water and wind had wrought over eons. The landscape looked barren but not exactly spooky, only mysterious in its strangeness and silence. May, too, was walking among the formations. Mike, meanwhile, had also left the car and was studying the strata. I hadn't forgotten that we did not have permission to walk here, so I let go of my desire to linger and soon we were back on the road.

Our sightseeing route crisscrossed the Smoky Hill River, where riparian grasses swayed in the breeze. I tried to picture Sibley tents pitched along the bank. When we stopped occasionally and got out of the car, the squeak of spinning windmill blades was the only sound until a pickup or horse trailer approached. The drivers waved as they passed us. The Smoky Hill Trail had once been the most dangerous route for whites traveling from Atchison, Kansas, to Denver. Today there was almost nothing to fear.

— 56 —

"The Prairie Rattlesnake is an abundant inhabitant of Wallace and Logan Counties," Travis Taggart's email said. Travis is a research associate and herpetology expert at the Sternberg Museum in Hays, Kansas. I had written him to ask if there were venomous snakes in the area May and I would be visiting.

"At the time of your visit, they should have made it back to those places where they will spend the winter," he continued. "They congregate in rocky canyons and the few prairie dog towns that still exist. If you walk through these areas on a warm, sunny day you stand a decent chance of seeing a few as they catch the season's last rays before retreating for the winter. Let me know if you need more specific information. I couldn't tell from your message if you were interested in seeing or avoiding them."

I was interested in avoiding them. The fact that the Yale expedition members saw so many rattlesnakes had made an impression on me. I hate snakes and so does May. When people say snakes are more afraid of us than we are of them, I say they are wrong.

What is the best way, I asked Travis, to avoid rattlers? Is it possible to outrun them?

"If the weather is cool, you're not likely to see any snakes," he told me. "That is your best bet for avoiding them. If you're going to spend much time in the chalk looking at the fossil-bearing strata, you're also not likely to see any, as it's a pretty barren landscape with few places for rattlesnakes to hide. If they are present, you won't hear them until you are a few feet away. And yes, if it comes down to it, you can easily outrun them."[18]

May and I wore high boots in Kansas. As we walked in the grass and the canyons we stepped carefully. Before we reached for an interesting rock, we looked carefully. Fortunately we would encounter not one snake.

— 57 —

We stopped in Russell Springs. The town is not named for anyone I am related to but for Avra P. Russell, originally of Marion, New York, who served in the Second Regiment of Kansas Volunteer Cavalry. In 1862 he was mortally wounded at the Battle of Prairie

Grove, in Arkansas. Two of Russell Springs's few buildings are the old courthouse, which is now the Butterfield Trail Museum, and a wood-frame Episcopal church. Both were locked. There was not a person in sight. We decided to return in the morning.

After giving Mike his cherry pie and adjourning for the evening in Sharon Springs, May and I decided to observe the cocktail hour. Finding no bar, we settled for a liquor store run by a friendly woman with a nagging boy who pulled on her sleeve while we chatted. May studied a bottle of Kansas vodka as a possible souvenir. We left with a couple of bottled margaritas and drove to the edge of town to watch the sun set. May talked about work and a situation she was navigating with a partner organization. As we sipped our drinks, we reflected on the day. May noted that Mike had not asked either of us about ourselves. We wondered why. Was he perhaps uncomfortable, or shy, or sexist, or simply polite in a midwestern none-of-my-business way? He had been very generous, we agreed, and on our own we could never have found the places he showed us. The colors of the sky shifted and blended like watered silk, a moiré of lavender, coral, and gold. As Venus—what the ancient Greeks called Hesperus, the evening "star," father of the Nymphs of the Sunset and Daughters of Evening—rose in the sky, it was time to go. We returned to our motel, ate a light dinner, and watched an old James Bond movie.

"You can tell I'm from California, because I ask about the food," I told Mike over breakfast the next morning. I had just quizzed our waitress about the sausage versus the bacon. I explained to Mike that I had written about food and wine before I published a book about the Vietnam War and my family. He became more conversational. We were close in age, and he was a Vietnam veteran. He asked May what she did for a living, and she talked about her climate work.

Following behind Mike in our rental car, we tore along dirt roads listening to a country swing program on High Plains Public Radio. We stopped again at the museum in Russell Springs, which was still closed, and walked around the grounds. Seeing a rope coiled next to the sidewalk, I took hold and rang the bell attached to it. From the promontory where we stood, the cottonwoods that line the Smoky Hill River were showing their autumn yellows and golds. At our feet lay desiccated pods of locust trees. A dozen wild turkeys walked across a clearing. At the foot of the hill was a pretty glade with a spring, one of many in the area. The glade was supposedly a favorite campsite of George Armstrong Custer when he was stationed at Fort Wallace and patrolled this area.

I looked around at this place where my great-grandfather's curiosity about the West and mine about him intersected. There was no artifact to be found, no antique spoon half-buried in the dirt, no brass bullet casing waiting to be picked up. My desire to see where Tom Russell found a dinosaur fossil had led here without raising goosebumps or conjuring a whisper in the wind. Something had happened here and nothing was happening here. That was that. There was nothing more, it seemed, but for me to return to Sonoma and reenter the life that was familiar to me.

We drove to the castellated chalk pillars called Monument Rocks, an hour east of Russell Springs. One minute you are driving on land as flat as flat can be, and the next you are standing beside seventy-foot-high, near-blindingly white rocks that jut up from the plain. Formed 85 million years ago when an ocean teeming with mosasaurs and birds with teeth covered all this, the formation also goes by the name the Chalk Pyramids. The U.S. Department of the Interior has designated them a National Natural Landmark. Kansas voters named them, together with Castle Rock, one of the Eight Wonders of Kansas. Although they are on private land, the owner permits visitors to drive up to them and walk around.

Swallows had built nests high up on the rocks' eastern side, but birds were not in evidence this day. A few unfenced cows ambled toward us. May climbed to the top of a rock and stared into the distance. She looked sad and alone with her burden. But beyond inviting her to come with me to a place where she could absorb what the writer Gretel Ehrlich calls the solace of open spaces, could I do more?

– 58 –

We continued on to a truck stop for a last lunch with Mike and then parted ways with him. May wanted to see a college town in rural Kansas, so we headed east to Hays. At Fort Hays State Historic Site we walked around the buildings and grounds and imagined a soldier's life there. In the gift shop May bought two raffle tickets for a reproduction of an antique rifle as a birthday present for me.

Sharon Springs, Kansas, where we had spent the night, is in one time zone and Hays in another. We had forgotten about losing an hour when we arrived at the Sternberg Museum of Natural History thirty minutes before closing time. Mike had told us the Sternberg collections included a *Hesperornis regalis* specimen we should see. It was the day before Halloween, and as we walked briskly through the galleries, we passed a few staff members dressed in costumes. They were talking about a party the museum was hosting that evening.

I pointed to a sign and read it aloud: "'Cretaceous.' This way."

Hearing us, one of the staff approached. "You two seem to know what you're looking for," he said. "Can I help you?"

May responded with the urgency of Robert Donat's character in the climactic moment of the Hitchcock thriller *The Thirty-Nine Steps*. "What are the thirty-nine steps?" he shouts to Mr. Memory in a crowded theater.

"Where is your *Hesperornis regalis*?"

He led us to a glass case where the skeleton was mounted head-down in a diving position. This was his favorite exhibit in the museum because, as he put it, "It is the missing link, but not that many people know about it." May told him we were Thomas H. Russell's descendants. "Stay as long as you like," he offered. It was his turn to close the museum that evening, and we could take our time.

On the drive back to Sharon Springs, we talked about 350.org and where it seemed to be headed. We talked about May's new roommate, Jodie. They were going to a Halloween party the next night. Jodie was somehow making herself a *Hesperornis regalis* costume.

Our return to Denver the next morning would have been uneventful were it not for the speeding ticket I received outside of Cheyenne Wells, Colorado, the same town where we had bought gas at the Sinclair station with Dino the Dinosaur. According to the town's website, this was once a regular stop on the stagecoach line between Kansas City and Denver. Now it is the county seat. Two buildings stand out architecturally: the Georgian Revival courthouse and the whiter-than-white jail. Leaving Cheyenne County without seeing the interior of either building, I felt I had gotten away with something after the grizzled badass who pulled me over chewed me out with his hand resting on his holstered pistol.

May and I flew back to San Francisco. I left her at her apartment and drove home to Sonoma. An hour later I unlocked the door of the house where I had lived for twenty years. It seemed at rest. It smelled of antiques, like the old houses of my Connecticut relatives, and lavender from my garden. It was a good place to come home to.

Bedtime was approaching as I unpacked my suitcase. When I reached to turn back the covers, something on the floor caught my eye. It was a large insect, and I started at the sight of it. I bent down to see in the shadows the lifeless body of a dragonfly. This was no dainty blue skimmer like the ones that dart around ponds and birdbaths. This was the largest dragonfly I had ever seen anywhere, let alone indoors and in my bedroom. Its transparent double wings were perfectly intact. I picked it up carefully and placed it in a wastebasket.

In the morning I thought better of throwing away my winged visitor. I lifted it out of the wastebasket and set it on a table. Its glassy wings measured four inches across. The body was almost three inches long. It weighed less than an ounce. The brown exoskeleton looked utterly primitive, and in fact the dragonfly is an ancient creature. Fossil remains of these members of the order Odonata have been dated back 350 million years. Many eons before dinosaurs roamed on land and mosasaurs populated the seas, dragonflies were flitting over the fresh waters of the earth. Evidence of Permian-era dragonflies has turned up in Kansas. Regional folklore there has it that a dragonfly can sew up the mouth of a scold.[19]

Because dragonflies are among the largest insects on earth and prey on insects both smaller and bigger than themselves, some people believe that the appearance of one means your troubles will be devoured. Contrary to a superstition that dragonflies are poisonous, if one lands on you, some say good news or a change is coming.

From my bookshelves I pulled down a slim volume about the meaning of animals and insects according to American Indian teachings. Of all the earth's winged creatures, it said, the dragonfly is the most maneuverable, able to hover and to fly up, down, forward, backward, and sideways.[20] Even if the food supply in its natural home is exhausted, it tends to keep looking there for food. I took the meaning of my dragonfly's visit to be *Don't stop looking, learning, and adapting. Be prepared to go in a new direction.* I placed the dragonfly in a wooden box and set it on the mantel.

Two weeks later I met the man whom I would marry in a little more than a year. May told the 350.org team that she and her partner were no longer a couple. She assured them, and him, that she would remain his friend and do everything she could to minimize damage to the team.

— 59 —

What was the meaning of our time in Kansas? We had seen no evidence of our ancestor, but we had imagined what he felt when he looked around. We understood how foreign this place must have seemed to him. We had stood beside the old railroad tracks where Tom and the other expedition members disembarked from the train. We had seen a fascinating new landscape and sipped margaritas and laughed while the sun set. We had climbed onto rocks, looked at the far horizon, and seen the Smoky Hill country in its autumn goldenness. The value to us turned out to be our own experience, not our ancestor's.

This had been for both of us a pause, a retreat from routine and the clamor of texts and emails, and a journey somewhere new. We had found a place where one can breathe deeply in a way that the American West uniquely inspires. As we were to advance into the future, May with 350.org and the transition from a romantic relationship to a collegial one, and me toward I knew not what, our trip had been a step back in order to make a better leap forward, a *reculer pour mieux sauter*.

The expansion and global reach of 350 continued. May became its executive director and continued working with her friends, including her former college boyfriend. On September 21, 2014, the organization coordinated the largest climate-change gathering in history, the People's Climate March in New York City. Four hundred thousand people participated in a peaceful demonstration of support for political action. In 156 countries, thousands more held events in solidarity. Since then, many more actions have followed, such as efforts to stop construction of the Keystone XL Pipeline through tribal lands and coordination of the September 2019 demonstrations joined by millions of climate activists, such as Greta Thunberg, around the world. Like all of life itself, 350.org and the climate movement continue to evolve.

Now and then I wonder what my great-granddad Tom would say if he could know that two of his descendants followed him to Kansas. I hope that when he got back to New Haven, he found a way to keep the memory of his adventure tucked into his pocket. When I look at his portrait in my house, I wish I could ask him about it. I wish he could speak to me, though in a way he already does.

Part V

Diaspora

– 60 –

Tom Russell returned to New Haven with his classmate Charles Hill and Professor Marsh on December 7, 1872. On December 12 the *Hartford Daily Courant* reported as front-page news that the Yale expedition Marsh led had returned from their "trip to the Rocky Mountains in good health and success."[1]

One week later Tom turned twenty-one. The same month, he began his postgraduate studies at Yale Medical School. He lived at the family home on Wooster Place and supported himself by teaching mathematics and natural science at his father's Russell School. Within a few months of starting medical studies he also became an assistant to surgery professor Francis Bacon, working with him for six or eight years. In this period he also assisted Marsh in his lab. Marsh asked him to return with him to the West in 1873, but Tom declined.[2]

In January 1875 he submitted his graduate thesis on the congenital malformation *talipes equinus*, "so called from the position of the foot resembling the hoof of a horse," he wrote.[3] He received his MD the following month. He did a surgical residency at New Haven Hospital and served for a number of years at the New Haven Dispensary.[4] The clinic's purpose was to provide medical advice, medicines, and assistance to "such as may be sick and needy in New Haven and its vicinity," primarily working-class patients.[5]

In 1883, he was promoted to professor. He was assigned to the chair of materia medica and therapeutics. "Coming after only eight years in the practice of surgery, his appointment marks a career of unusual brilliancy," the *New Haven Evening Register* said.[6] In 1891 he was named professor of clinical surgery and taught surgical anatomy. At New Haven Hospital he served as attending surgeon for thirty years and consulting surgeon for eight. He established an extensive practice in Connecticut and, according to a fellow physician, "operated in nearly every town."[7]

Almost exactly ten years after returning from the West with Marsh, Tom married Mary Katherine Munson, who had attended European and American boarding schools but not college. As a young woman she'd had other admirers. Among them was supposedly William Howard Taft, whose letters a relative claimed he saw when my great-aunt's estate was settled.

Mary's father, Lyman Ezra Munson, was, like Tom's father, an abolitionist, a Republican, and a Yale graduate. In March 1865 President Lincoln appointed him to the first supreme court of territorial Montana. After returning to New Haven three years later, Judge Munson lectured and wrote about his years in the awe-inspiring region. Which man told the more riveting stories about the American West, Mary's father or her husband?

Tom and Mary Russell had three sons and two daughters. A biographical article written about Tom during his lifetime stated, "He owes much to the help and companionship of his good wife, who has been all that a Christian wife and mother could be, who never tires of doing good, and has always had perfect health, sound common sense, and all the most lovable qualities of mind and heart."[8] In 1880, not yet married, Tom moved his residence and office from 156 to 137 Elm Street after another professor vacated the house opposite the Peabody Museum (then located on the corner of Elm and High Streets). In 1910 the family moved to a house on the corner of Temple and Trumbull streets.

Tom's published work includes articles in the Connecticut Medical Society journal, ranging from prostate illness to the treatment of syphilis, beginning in the 1890s. He advocated careful hand washing before it was universally accepted among doctors. He advocated an approach to treating kidney stones that dismissed unscientific remedies and wrote an encyclopedia entry on skull fractures.

When Tom died, his colleague of twenty-eight years on the surgical staff of New Haven Hospital, Dr. William Whitney Hawkes, wrote about the difficult cases he was brought in on. They were beyond the skill of most surgeons, "which furthermore prompted him to carry about with him an armamentarium that would often have sufficed for a surgical display," he said. "His formal approach to a private residence was notable of the cautious and painstaking doctor that he was."[9] I remember my grandmother talking about a house call her father-in-law made. He instructed the family to clear the kitchen table, and he operated there.

Dr. Hawkes, who left the most detailed description of Tom Russell that exists anywhere, also said this:

> His methodical thoroughness, his sober seriousness of purpose, his conspicuously quiet and sympathetic manner, all won for him the confidence and lasting gratitude of his patients. So, too, his ability in concentration, his analytical habit of mind, his poise in judgment, unvarying courtesy, soundness of opinion, grasp and interpretation of symptoms and his skill in operating, begat and held the respect of his associates.
>
> In private practice, also, he never seemed to hurry. [. . .]
>
> He was generous minded, was a stalwart in friendship, seldom spoke disparagingly of anybody; and, in those rare instances, mentioned glaring facts alone, leaving the judgment for the hearer to form. With all his seriousness he was hopeful and cheerful; and had a fine, often resembling a sub-conscious, sense of humor.[10]

Newspapers carried reports of Tom's cases. In 1894 the *New York Times* reported that Dr. Russell was called in to consult on the case of a man thought to have died from Asiatic cholera. Tom concluded that nothing in the man's symptoms indicated more than a lethal attack of "summer complaint," otherwise known as acute diarrhea.[11]

An article in the *Boston Post* in 1896 told of Dr. Russell removing pieces of steel from a man's hand using X-rays. There had been an explosion in a gun factory where the patient worked. "The hand will now heal and amputation will be avoided," the article concluded.[12]

In 1897 a twenty-four-year-old woman came to New Haven on the pretense of attending a friend's wedding. She had come for an abortion, which a local doctor performed in his home. When she fell ill, the family with whom she was staying called their physician, who determined that the young woman was suffering from the effects of an illegal operation. Dr. Russell was summoned. The dying patient told Tom the name of the doctor who had operated on her. He was arrested for murder.[13]

In 1899 Dr. Russell diagnosed the cause of a young woman's illness and subsequent death as typhoid fever. She, her sisters, and a brother had drunk water that had not been boiled. It came from a brook that property owners had been warned not to empty drains into. Sewage had also been deposited in the brook.[14]

Several newspapers reported in late July 1902 on a dangerous surgery Dr. Russell performed on a sixteen-year-old athlete, John Nichols Jr., from northern New Jersey. The six-foot-two, 180-pound teenager was walking on a cliff near his mother's vacation cottage at Guilford, Connecticut, on the coast of Long Island Sound, when he called to his younger brother to watch him dive. The brother answered that the water was too shallow. That wasn't enough to stop the older brother from plunging headlong into eighteen inches of water. Landing on his neck, he fractured his sixth vertebra. The broken bones pressed on young Nichols's spine, paralyzing him from the neck down. He would never walk again.[15] "Not half a dozen persons are on record who have escaped alive under similar conditions," the *Scranton Republican* reported, "and of those whose necks have been broken, only one is recorded to have been saved."[16]

Nichols showed some improvement after he was taken inside his mother's cottage, but his condition declined rapidly. Dr. Russell was called in. The decision was taken that the only chance of saving the young man's life was to relieve the pressure on his spinal column by removing the broken vertebra.[17]

Tom performed the operation with his colleague Alfred Nadler, also of the Yale Medical School. Afterward he said the operation was without parallel in medical history.[18] "Nichols was instantly relieved," a newspaper in Rochester, New York, reported. "The symptoms are all favorable, and the operation appears to have been thoroughly successful."[19] There was hope he would at least live. The *Baltimore Sun* reported that the young man's life had been saved.[20]

Sadly, John Nichols did not live long. On August 2 the *Hartford Daily Courant* reported that he had died following the surgery that had given him "the only chance of life."[21] His death resulted from the combination of a concussion from the blow to his head and lung congestion as a result of the accident and the operation.

A little more than a year later, in 1903, Tom was the attending physician at the Yale Infirmary when he witnessed the outcome of another tragic accident. A young man had plummeted from a ledge on West Rock, near New Haven, a popular climbing spot then and now.[22] Eighteen-year-old George Sherman, a grandson of the Union general William Tecumseh Sherman, was climbing with two college classmates when he either dislodged or was struck by a rock and fell ten feet. His head hit a projecting rock, causing the young man to fall another forty or fifty feet. The present-day observation area at West Rock is at an elevation of about four hundred feet; a newspaper at the time of the accident reported that the young men's climbing goal was two hundred feet above the road where they started.

Sherman's two companions, who were ahead of him, heard his scream and saw him falling. They descended, carried him to the road, and called for help. An ambulance took Sherman first to the hospital and then to the college infirmary. Dr. Russell said the cause of death was cerebral hemorrhages, plural.

In 1916, when the end came for Tom Russell, he was sixty-four. It was February, and he had come down with influenza or another virus, then commonly called "the grippe." His family, including his son Dr. Thomas H. Russell Jr., urged him to rest, but he continued working. He returned home after going on a case in Guilford, Connecticut, and took a chill. Pneumonia followed. He had what the *Boston Morning Herald* termed a sinking spell, and prayers were said for him at Center Church on the New Haven Green.[23] He regained strength briefly before breathing his last on February 2 at his home on Trumbull Street.

Tom never lived more than a short walk from his famous fossil once it came to live in the city where he spent his entire life. He was alive when the specimen was mounted, from 1914 to 1915, in New York City. Whether he ever saw it when it went on exhibit at the Yale Peabody Museum is not known.

Newspapers at the time of Tom's death referred to him as a distinguished local physician and even a famous surgeon.[24] Respected in his lifetime for his work as a doctor, he is hardly remembered today, except by his descendants, as either a medical man or the discoverer of one of the most important, if least known, finds from the Age of Dinosaurs. In this sense he led what the author Akiko Busch has called an inconspicuous life. It is time, she suggests, to reevaluate the merit of an unseen life, which may be "a sign of decency and self-assurance," and to appreciate that it can be "something interior, private, and self-contained. We can gain, rather than suffer, from deep reserve."[25] Tom Russell does not need to be rescued from obscurity. His life was enough.

To me, Tom Russell was of a type George Eliot described in the last sentence of *Middlemarch:* "For the growing good of the world is partly dependent on unhistoric acts; and that things are not so ill with you and me as they might have been, is half owing to the number who lived faithfully a hidden life, and rest in unvisited tombs." Tom rests in New Haven's Grove Street Cemetery in a mostly unvisited plot, unless you count the Yale students soaking up the sunshine and reading a book there in springtime.

Soon after Marsh, Tom, and the others returned from the 1872 Yale College Scientific Expedition, word began circulating that remains of a nearly complete fossil of *Hesperornis regalis* had been found in western Kansas. Unlike the previous year's find, described and collected by Marsh, this specimen had the all-important skull and teeth.

Marsh has been dismissed as an "armchair paleontologist" for doing limited work in the field.[26] He has been described as a lesser theoretician than his archrival Edward D. Cope, who branded him "a scientifico-political adventurer."[27] He has also been called "the greatest American paleontologist of the nineteenth century."[28] According to his principal biographers, Marsh established 228 genera.[29] He also compiled a bibliography of about three hundred titles between 1861 and 1899.[30] His indefatigable work for and at Yale, his service to the National Academy of Sciences and the U.S. Geological Survey, and his collections deeded to the Yale Peabody Museum and National Museum (the Smithsonian) are the subjects of hundreds of books and articles. So thoroughly, in fact, have scientists and historians of science covered the life and contributions of O. C. Marsh that to present even a brief biography would overwhelm the story of Tom Russell, his toothed bird, and the two descendants who picked up his trail in Kansas.

Consider, however, that while Marsh was not attached to people, as George Grinnell said of him, he attached himself to the cause and person of Red Cloud, the eminent Oglala Sioux chief. His doing so sheds such light on Marsh's character that it is important to cover here. As a descendant of one of his intimate friends, to me this attachment reveals why, in spite of the contradictory opinions about Marsh, he could make enduring friendships.

In 1874, following an expedition led by Custer that found gold in the Black Hills, Marsh received word that fossils had been found in badlands several miles southeast of there, near the Red Cloud Agency (now the Pine Ridge Reservation). He left New Haven in

October without assistants, unlike his expeditions of the previous four years. An 1868 treaty still in effect required whites to obtain consent before entering Sioux lands. Some twelve thousand Sioux were in the area when Marsh arrived at the Red Cloud Agency in November 1874. Although the fossil bed Marsh intended to visit was not on reservation land, the Indian agent, Dr. J. J. Saville, advised convening a council of chiefs to inform them of Marsh's intentions and to arrange for guards to accompany him.

Marsh explained to the assembled group that he sought only bones, not gold. He said that he would pay the Indians who served as guards and helped collect fossils and would make known any grievances they had to officials in Washington, D.C. The council consented and selected a group of young men to guard the expedition.

When Marsh and his military detail came to collect their guard, armed and unwilling Sioux surrounded them. Marsh asked Red Cloud to explain the reversal. Red Cloud stated that his people believed Marsh intended to look for gold.

Agent Saville urged Marsh to win back the Sioux's goodwill by hosting a banquet in the chiefs' honor and presenting them with gifts. He grudgingly consented. Still the Indians did not relent. That midnight, Marsh and a detail of soldiers left the agency and crept past the Indian lodges. When they arrived safely at the first fossil bed and with winter fast approaching, they wasted no time and began collecting right away. After only two or three weeks, the expedition returned to the agency and the bones were packed. Less than twenty-four hours later a large war party, about which Red Cloud had sent Marsh a warning through messengers, came looking for him.

Before Marsh left to return east, Red Cloud stated his grievances about the shoddy provisions given his people, including substandard food and blankets. Convinced, Marsh left with samples.

The following spring, in 1875, after attending meetings of the National Academy of Sciences in Washington, Marsh showed some of the samples to the commissioner of Indian Affairs. Unsatisfied that adequate measures would be taken to correct the injustice, Marsh, together with Postmaster General Marshall Jewell (formerly the governor of Connecticut), went to see President Grant the next day.

Subsequent meetings were held, and accusations and counter-accusations accumulated over several months. Marsh was drawn deeply into an investigation that at times sidestepped the issue and devolved into personal criticism of himself. He was a scientist and professor, not a politician, and this was far from his line of work, but he was also by now one of the most famous individuals in the United States, and he did not let up.[31] In the fall of 1875 President Grant accepted the resignation of the secretary of the interior.[32]

In 1877 Marsh received a package from Fort Robinson, near the Red Cloud Agency. Red Cloud had gone there and asked that his peace pipe be sent to Marsh with a message: "I remember the wise chief. He came here and I asked him to tell the Great Father something. He promised to do so, and I thought he would do like all white men, and forget me when he went away. But he did not. He told the Great Father everything just as he promised he would, and I think he is the best white man I ever saw. I like him. I want you to tell him this."[33]

Red Cloud and Marsh met again, in 1883, when the distinguished chief came to New Haven for a visit. Marsh and hundreds of interested citizens met his arriving train. Tall, dignified, dressed in a suit, and about sixty years old, Red Cloud conversed with Marsh, who was then fifty-two, through an interpreter. Though he may have understood English, speaking it would have been beneath the man whom Marsh called "the greatest Indian of these times."[34] No other chief, he said, equaled him as a warrior and orator.

Marsh showed Red Cloud bones he had collected from his homelands and now displayed at the Peabody Museum. They evoked in him no expression. Another day, shown a group of rifles at the Winchester Repeating Arms Factory, also in New Haven, Red Cloud smiled soberly. At a fire station, however, the sight of men sliding down a pole elicited a laugh. Professor Marsh opened his home to more than a hundred guests eager to meet the famous visitor. Tom Russell might have been among them.

Marsh's work, along with that of Charles Darwin and others, helped to reshape the conception of time. No longer could an educated person accept the book of Genesis as a historically credible account of the creation of the earth and life on earth. The word *paleontology* came into use in the mid-1800s. In the same century, Marsh brought the new science forward and into the public discourse with his discoveries of prehistoric life in the American West.

In February 1899 he attended a meeting in Washington and stayed over in New York City after attending a dinner in honor of a friend. The next morning he took the train to New Haven and then set out on foot for home. It was raining heavily, and Marsh stopped at the New Haven House across from the city's green to summon help. His assistants found him soaking wet and cold. He was taken to his house on Prospect Street but continued going into the museum, even though he was not feeling well. Pneumonia followed, and Marsh's old friend, Dr. Russell, attended him. A week later, on March 18, 1899, Marsh died. He is buried in the Grove Street Cemetery across from Yale. Less than a year after his death, the last of four shipments to the Smithsonian of 259 boxes of bones he collected for the national museum and the American people filled five freight cars.

James Pope served on the active list of the army for more than forty-five years. He participated in an expedition to Indian Territory (present-day Oklahoma) in 1874–75 and, after the Battle of Little Bighorn, or Greasy Grass, he volunteered for service as a scout in Montana. He was detailed for duty at the military prison at Fort Leavenworth and later served as its commandant, advocating for reforms in the interest of the prisoners. In 1880 he married

Mary E. Lynch and with her had two children. He served as chief quartermaster supplying the Army of the Philippines under General Wesley Merritt. He wrote articles on military subjects, retired in 1910 as a colonel, and was elevated to the rank of brigadier general by an act of Congress in 1916. In 1919 he died at age seventy-three in Denver and is buried at Arlington National Cemetery.

Benjamin Hoppin, the Phi Beta Kappa Yale graduate who won three composition prizes as an undergraduate and whose ambition was to be a writer, suffered a mental breakdown and was not able to sustain a career. He settled in Baddeck, Nova Scotia, in a house purchased by his mother and staffed by husband-and-wife caretakers. He studied, on his own, Asian languages and history and made three trips to the Arctic, writing a detailed account of the final one. He translated, from German, a book about legendary Greek heroes. Hoppin never lost his interest in fossils and geology and donated his collection of indigenous artifacts—including a polar bear skin, harpoons, a kayak, trousers, a sealskin parka, and fur-lined boots—to the Peabody Museum. He died in 1922 and is buried in the Yale plot with his parents in the Grove Street Cemetery, within a few steps of O. C. Marsh's grave. He never married.

After two years at Rensselaer Polytechnic Institute and training at other schools, James MacNaughton became a civil engineer and engaged in survey work, railroad construction, and exploration of the Hudson Bay region for the British government. At the time of his death he was president of Macintyre Iron Works, a mining company and manufacturer of iron and steel products in upstate New York. MacNaughton served as an officer with the Association for the

Protection of the Adirondacks. MacNaughton Mountain, a peak in the Street Range described by present-day hikers as an "obscure and very demanding" climb, is named for him.[35] He died of pneumonia at his apartments on Central Park West, in Manhattan, in 1905. He was unmarried.

After the Yale expedition, Charles D. Hill returned to his home in Calais, Maine, and worked as a clerk in the Calais National Bank for four years. In 1887 he, along with partners, bought the business of Willard B. King, an importer with whom he worked after clerking at the bank, and changed the firm's name to C. D. Hill & Co. The firm dissolved in 1894. Hill went into business with W. H. Pike and purchased a store that had opened in Calais as a branch of C. D. Hill & Co. The firm name became Hill, Pike, & Co. It was a large wholesale grocery business and an importer of goods from the Caribbean. Hill married Elmira King, the daughter of his late business partner. He died April 30, 1898, when a revolver he was handling discharged, killing him. Following an inquest, the coroner ruled the death accidental.[36]

Born in Pennsylvania in 1847, Edward Smith Lane enlisted in the army at the age of eighteen. He was twenty-six when he signed on to scout for the 1872 Yale expedition. Marsh called him "the famous 'Ned Lane,' known over that whole region for his knowledge of the country, especially of the Indians."[37] The following year he accompanied the last of Marsh's four Yale expeditions. In 1875 he married a woman named Narsona, who may have been a Cherokee Indian. According to the 1880 federal census, the couple had two children. In later years he stated his occupation as farmer. In 1900 he was enrolled as "Cherokee by Blood" at Muskogee, Indian Territory, at age fifty-four when he applied for enrollment in the Five Tribes, consisting of the Cherokee, Choctaw, Muscogee (Creek), Chickasaw, and Seminole nations. He was granted a pension. A census of Craig County, Oklahoma, in 1920 shows that at age seventy-three he was living in that county in eastern Oklahoma. He is buried in Oak Hill Cemetery, Labette County, Kansas.

The four Yale graduates who accompanied Marsh in 1872 were around twenty years old at the time of their great western adventure. What was it like to have experienced such a thrill so young? In *The Sound and the Fury*, Quentin Compson the father says that the saddest word is *was*. His son Quentin believes it is *again*, because the past cannot be repeated.

Sally Ride, the first female American astronaut, was thirty-two in 1983, when she went into space as a crew member on the space shuttle *Challenger*. She said of her experience, "The thing that I'll remember most about the flight is that it was fun. In fact, I'm sure it was the most fun I'll ever have in my life."[38] She went on to distinguish herself both in her career and as a role model, inspiring girls and women to pursue careers in science, technology, engineering, and mathematics.

If you think the most fun of your life or the most exciting experience is one you had around the age of twenty or even thirty-two, does it hinder you because you think you can never repeat it? Or does it build confidence: *I did that! What else can I do?*

– 62 –

Wrapped in muslin and freed from its sepulcher in Goblin Hollow, Kansas, Tom Russell's *Hesperornis regalis* specimen made the journey to New Haven, a distance of about seventeen hundred miles. As a reporter for the *New York Tribune* said after another Marsh expedition, "There was doubtless the usual amount of profanity expended over the heavy boxes in their long transits by stage and rail."[39]

After a stretch of work in the field, Marsh and his assistants crated and shipped fossils east, sometimes more than a ton a week.[40] From 1870 to 1892 the continual flow of shipments to New Haven resulted in about three thousand entries into the museum accession books.[41]

Russell's bird, still in its chalk matrix, reached Yale on November 29, 1872, in one of six large boxes of fossils. It was later assigned the catalog number by which it is still known in the scientific literature, YPM VP.001206—YPM meaning Yale Peabody Museum and VP meaning vertebrate paleontology. Marsh did not report the discovery of this fossil until 1875. The reason, according to Mike Everhart, is that he was apparently also focused on the smaller bird with teeth from Kansas, *Ichthyornis dispar*. Marsh's publications for the next two years indicate that he was absorbed, additionally, with other kinds of fossil vertebrates from the West.[42] In 1880 he published his monumental, lavishly illustrated study of birds with teeth, *Odontornithes*, published under the auspices of the federal government in Clarence King's seven-volume *Report of the Geological Exploration of the Fortieth Parallel*. With this, the 83-million-year-old *Hesperornis regalis* VP.001206 began life anew as a celebrity fossil.

It was years before the skull and bones were removed from the rock in which they were found, and for that reason the bones were initially cleaned on only one side. Paleontologist Philip D. Gingerich noted in a 1975 article that the chalk matrix containing the skull had been placed on view for many years but had only recently been made available for study.[43] By 2011 the skull elements had been fully prepared by dissolving or otherwise cleaning away the matrix for even further study.[44] The catalogued *Hesperornis* material at the Yale Peabody Museum currently numbers sixty-three specimens.

Meanwhile, construction of the first museum building began in 1874 on the corner of Elm and High Streets. It was completed in 1876. In 1880 Tom Russell moved his residence and office to a house directly across the street. Marriage was still two years away, and in this time he may still have been assisting Marsh. Marsh biographers Schuchert and LeVene explained the rules of procedure in the laboratory. "Marsh's method of work was to assign to each assistant a certain series of fossil bones. [. . .] He then gave instructions as to what he wanted done, which usually was to have the nearest affinities of these animals sought for, either in the literature, in his own fossil collections, or in his large amount of osteological material. In due time he would sit down with each man, asking questions, discussing conclusions arrived at, and all the while making notes in regard to what he heard and what he saw in the assembled material.[45]

Arthur Lakes, one of Marsh's first hired collectors, visited the museum in 1879 and recorded his observations:

Passing into the basement we find lying in state awaiting cleaning and arrangement, the huge fossil bones from Colorado. [. . .] Three or four assistants are at work chopping and cutting off the clay whilst others are engaged in the more tedious business of fitting little fragments of bone together like a Chinese puzzle. Professor Marsh is among them, watching with a scientist's interest, as some of his pet bones begin to take shape from out of chaos. [. . .] In the second story we enter an elegant room with cases in which are the bones of the celebrated Odontornithes, birds with teeth, lying on the chalk as they were exhumed from the bluffs of Kansas. One of these, the *Hesperornis*, resembled our modern loon, but stood from four to five feet in height.[46]

Marsh's assistant Samuel W. Williston presented a slightly different picture of Marsh's involvement, claiming he came to work at the museum in the afternoon and stayed only an hour or two, "devoting his time chiefly to the most absurd details and old maid crotchets."[47]

It was not unusual at this time to keep fossil specimens in drawers or on shelves. They were not commonly mounted as we see them today in natural history museums. It was important for paleontologists to be able to study them and handle them. Moreover, with the Civil War only a decade in the past, as one writer of the period pointed out, it was as important to reconstruct a fossil specimen correctly as to reconstruct the postwar South. "It were better to postpone the announcement of new animals, new species, and new principles in zoology for a few months or even for years, than to rush into print with a quadruped, like our Southern States, too hastily reconstructed."[48]

To correctly articulate a skeleton requires scientific knowledge, imagination, and patience. Scientists could get it wrong, as an early drawing of a *Stegosaurus* proves. The four-footed dinosaur so well known today for the upright plates along its back was misunderstood as a creature that walked on two feet and had not only plates but also long, sharp spikes on its body and tail.[49] Another example is the *Brontosaurus excelsus*, "helped to its feet by wood, steel, and hearty Peabody Museum staff" in 1931 "to stand on Earth for the first time in 150 million years."[50] The fossil was disassembled in 2020 in preparation for a major renovation. David Skelly, the museum's director, explained that the dinosaur in the reopened museum would look different: "The tail on the *Brontosaurus* as it is mounted right now is about 30 feet shorter than we know it would have been, so the animal is going to be longer. The tail will be held up in the air."[51]

In 1914 and 1915 two *Hesperornis* skeletons, one standing (species *H. regalis*) and one diving (species *H. crassipes*), were mounted under the direction of Peabody curator and paleontologist Richard Swann Lull. By then Marsh had been gone some fifteen years. Tom Russell was still practicing medicine.

For both the standing and diving skeletons, a model was made from the uncrushed skull of a different *Hesperornis* individual, because the skull of Russell's bird, VP.001206, was still imbedded in the original chalk matrix from Kansas. The standing skeleton was mounted in this pose for two reasons. First, for a lithograph in his *Odontornithes* monograph, Marsh had it drawn in that position. Second, the standing position was and is considered, according to Dan Brinkman, "the easiest, most straightforward, and practical way to mount a fossil skeleton for display."[52] Marsh knew that *Hesperornis* was a diving bird, but he also knew that to lay its eggs and raise its hatchlings it had to have moved on land, even if awkwardly.

What else did he know about this reptilian bird that has been called the missing link, an ancient water bird, a feathered dinosaur, and "an extraordinarily significant but surprisingly little known fossil bird"?[53]

Standing, it would have been a little taller than three feet. Fully extended while diving for a meal of fish, it would have measured about five feet from the tip of its bill to the end of its feet. *Hesperornis* laid its eggs on islands in the Western Interior Seaway, islands that today are the Rocky Mountains. As it became increasingly aquatic, the legs and feet grew larger. The wings, once effective for underwater propulsion, were used less and less. They evolved, as Marsh wrote, similarly to ocean-going vessels, as their method of propulsion transitioned from side wheels to propellers.[54]

Because the wings were not advantageous for diving, they all but disappeared, according to Marsh: "We may imagine, among the reasons for the gradual loss of wings, the fact that they were too weak to be of much service under water, while from their position they added greatly to the resistance, especially during rapid diving. To diminish this resistance, they would naturally be applied closely to the side, and from such disuse, would gradually suffer atrophy."[55]

Hesperornis was a strong diver with a tail useful for swimming. With its long, flexible neck, elongated jaws, and teeth, it was well equipped to catch and hold onto its prey of fish. The lower jaws were connected with cartilage, like those of snakes. With these jaws that "admitted of some motion, the power of swallowing was doubtless equal to almost any emergency."[56]

Understanding a creature 83 million years old, almost as distant from us in time as the Earth is distant in space from the sun, requires imagination. Georges Cuvier, the French scientist of the late eighteenth and early nineteenth century who has been called the founding father of paleontology, is said to have had "an almost magical ability" to "reconstruct an entire prehistoric species from a bone fragment."[57]

To connect the fossil of an extinct bird back to its reptilian ancestors, and from there to assert that all birds evolved from theropod dinosaurs—namely, the "hand-snatcher" maniraptorans such as *Deinonychus* and *Velociraptor*—takes more than ordinary imagination. If we lack the knowledge and imagination ourselves to make leaps like these, we can turn to pioneering thinkers such as Cuvier and Marsh and to the great minds of today, for whom science is only another name for truth.

– 63 –

In the late nineteenth century, news of prehistoric animals discovered in the American West traveled throughout the scientific community and into the public conversation. Scientists like O. C. Marsh relied on scientific journals and books, such as his *Odontornithes* monograph with its exquisite woodcuts and unfolding pages of lithographs, to make their work known among peers. As academic publications and newspaper articles disseminated information, another form of publishing, plaster-cast reproductions of fossils, came into widespread use.[58] It was not a new technique, but during this first Golden Age of Paleontology the plaster casts came to be regarded as superior even to artists' renderings. They were seen as "authoritative stand-ins" for the real thing.[59]

In April and May 1881 Marsh contracted to have plaster-cast replicas of *Hesperornis regalis* manufactured. To encourage the study of his famous fossil, he sent these replicas to twenty-nine universities and museums, seventeen in North America and twelve in northern Europe. The Yale alumni society reported in June 1881 on the condition of various departments of the university. It stated that the paleontology department had distributed casts of the more important birds with teeth to various institutions, and casts of other vertebrates were being made and would be distributed.[60]

Real fossils were too rare, too hard to come by, too large, or, particularly in the case of birds, too fragile to circulate among scientists for examination and repeated handling. Travel to museums with important collections could be prohibitively expensive. Photographs of the objects were also of limited value. They were only two-dimensional, and imperfect lighting, shadows, or even a photographer's effort to correct these could affect a scientist's interpretation of the fossil under study. How then could a scientist, student, or researcher be brought closer to the prehistoric evidence?

Plaster casts were a practicable solution and medium. They could be fabricated reasonably inexpensively and in quantity. They emerged as such a good alternative to irreplaceable actual fossils that, according to the historian of science Lukas Rieppel, they "came to function as a kind of publication in their own right."[61]

Before circulating plaster casts, Marsh wanted to see descriptions of his findings in print. Once his *Odontornithes* volume was close to publication, he engaged Tobias Kappeler, a Swiss sculptor living in New Haven, to produce casts of *Hesperornis regalis* bones. A receipt dated April 5, 1881, shows that Kappeler charged Marsh $150 for ten sets of casts. Each set contained twenty-six bones.[62]

In April 1881 Marsh sent these first ten sets to the Smithsonian; to Princeton, Wesleyan, and McGill (in Montreal) universities; and to natural history museums in New York, Philadelphia, and Salem, Boston, and Cambridge (two sets), Massachusetts.

A month later he sent casts to Amherst and Williams colleges, Cornell and the universities of Virginia and Michigan, the state geological collection of New York, and the Chicago Academy of Sciences. He also sent casts to twelve museums and academic institutions in northern Europe: in Great Britain, to the British Museum; the Royal College of Surgeons, in London; the Owens College Museum, in Manchester; the Oxford Museum; the Woodwardian Museum, in Cambridge; and to Trinity College Dublin. On the continent, casts went to museums in Munich, Berlin, Vienna, Paris, and Breslau (then in Prussia). Kappeler produced thirty sets in all. Marsh kept one for the Peabody Museum collections.

I wrote to all twenty-nine institutions still in existence. Many were closed entirely or partially because of the COVID-19 outbreak. Several replied that the casts, paperwork, or correspondence with Marsh, or all three, could not be located. In some cases, casts had passed from one institution to another as the recipient institution's name or location changed and the 140-year-old plaster casts dispersed. Geology or paleontology collections and instruction sometimes had been subsumed under the department of Environmental Sciences. Or, because the plaster casts were no longer teaching aids but relics, they had found a home in the history department. The collection manager in a Virginia state geology office inherited a few fossil replicas. They were obtained not from Marsh but from Henry Ward, whom Marsh later permitted to fabricate, sell, and distribute casts of his fossils. These hand-me-downs in Charlottesville were "in a bad state of non-curation" by the time the geology office received them and later placed them on three shelves in a cabinet.[63] With time, collections once considered valuable, along with records pertaining to them, may be discarded instead of archived.

Marsh's investment in plaster casts may have once heightened scholarly interest in prehistoric birds, even if we don't know how the fossil replicas were used at the museums and universities that received them. The fact that several institutions took care to archive and preserve their *Hesperornis* reproductions suggests the value placed on them. Paleontologists, archivists, and collections managers at the Sedgwick (formerly Woodwardian) Museum, in Cambridge; the National

Museums of Scotland; the National History Museum, in London; the Oxford University Museum of Natural History; the Chicago Academy of Sciences; the Bentley Historical Library, at the University of Michigan; and Wesleyan University all confirmed plaster casts or records of their receipt in the collections. Inevitably, war intervened in one case, when the Royal College of Surgeons, in London, was bombed in 1941. Collections were destroyed then or, in some cases, transferred later to another institution, with record-keeping suffering.

The oldest museum of its kind in the Western Hemisphere, the Academy of Natural Sciences of Drexel University, holds the most complete record of Marsh's singular method of publishing the famous find from the Cretaceous of Kansas. In a letter accompanying the shipment from New Haven in 1881, Marsh wrote to the distinguished scientist Joseph Leidy, then head of the academy:

> Yale College Museum
> New Haven, Conn.
>
> My dear Leidy,
>
> I send today by express a small box containing a series of casts of Hesperornis, a present to the Academy. With them are printed labels. Please see that they have a good place somewhere in the Museum, as I have only a few sets to distribute.
>
> Yours very truly,
> O. C. Marsh[64]

I visited one of the institutions on Marsh's list, the Redpath Museum at McGill University, in Montreal. The collections manager, Anthony Howell, showed me the plaster replica of the *Hesperornis regalis* pelvic girdle. Though clearly avian, the pelvic bones of *Hesperornis* exhibit distinct reptilian features.

Howell did not know much about the cast's backstory, such as how the museum had acquired it or how it had been used for study or teaching in the nineteenth century. His unfamiliarity does not, however, reflect badly on the museum. It shows only that plaster-cast models are an example of how teaching aids have evolved. Just as slate blackboards and chalk gave way to erasable whiteboards and dry-erase markers, the objects used in a classroom change. Yesterday's handheld calculator is today's iPad or smartphone.

Posters of prehistoric bones and extinct toothed birds like those in the original lecture room of the first Yale Peabody Museum have gone the way of pull-down maps, once the pride of geography teachers. Computer apps now allow teachers and students to create models of dinosaur fossils they can assemble and paint, from *Velociraptor* skulls to a necklace of dinosaur bones to chess pieces to "transforming" articulated dinosaur models.[65]

Computer-animated images and 3-D printed parts of partial or entire dinosaurs, such as those fabricated by the Dinosaur Resource Center in Woodland Park, Colorado, have long since replaced Marsh's plaster-cast replicas. To create 3-D printed parts, fabricators lay down many layers of material, like miniature layers of sediment forming geological strata.[66]

From the circulation of plaster-cast replicas to representations of dinosaurs that anyone with a computer can generate, the number of hesperornithiform individuals has proliferated beyond anything Marsh could have imagined, especially considering that he believed *Hesperornis* could be found only in the Cretaceous beds of Kansas.[67] In fact, numerous related specimens have been discovered, and in many locations. Within the genus *Hesperornis*, birds only half the size of *Hesperornis regalis* and as large as an emperor penguin have been found. As of 2015 twenty-nine *Hesperornis* species in thirteen genera and four families of hesperornithiforms have been described. The relationships between these foot-propelled divers are not yet understood and are a matter of present-day study.[68]

As to their distribution, hesperornithiforms have been found in the central United States and Canada, in the Arctic and far northern Europe, and in China and Kazakhstan. In a sense, the bird that could not fly did, after all, take wing.

Twenty-four-year-old Viktor Schreckengost reached into the job jar at the Cowan Pottery Studio in Rock River, a suburb of Cleveland, for his next assignment.[69] The job jar contained descriptions of commissions that the company's ceramicists were to design and fabricate. It was 1930, and the Great Depression was underway. Later that year, financial troubles would force the company into receivership.

The instructions Viktor drew from the jar left much to a designer's imagination: make a punch bowl with a New York City theme. The client was an unidentified New York housewife.

Viktor came from a family of accomplished potters. He had studied at the Cleveland School of Art and, after graduation, in Vienna.

As inspiration for the punch bowl commission, he returned in his memory to a New Year's Eve he had spent in Manhattan. The sights he saw—such as his stops at Radio City Music Hall and the Cotton Club, where he heard Cab Calloway perform—transformed into sketches of skyscrapers, streetlamps, neon signs, lit cigarettes, and champagne and cocktail glasses. Viktor's technique in fabricating the bowl was as striking as the scene he brought to life. He covered the bowl with loose clay mixed with glaze. He then scratched his design onto the bowl's surface and covered it with a glaze of Egyptian Blue, a pigment of intense color known since ancient times. The effect evoked the merriment and excitement of Manhattan nightlife. He called it *The Jazz Bowl*. The witty, exuberant style and the vivid blue that seemed lit from within would lead to Viktor's masterpiece earning the reputation as one of the most famous examples of American Art Deco.

The "housewife" who commissioned it turned out to be Eleanor Roosevelt, then the First Lady of the state of New York—soon, of the United States. She was so pleased with the bowl that she ordered two more. In 2004 a punch bowl from the *Jazz Bowl* series hammered down at Sotheby's for $254,400.[70]

Thus was ushered in a seventy-year-long career for Schreckengost in ceramics, industrial design, painting, and sculpture. Today, additional versions of the *Jazz Bowl*, along with bicycles, dinner-ware, and furniture of his design, can be found in collections across the United States, such as those of the National Museum of American Art/Smithsonian Institution, the Metropolitan Museum of Art, the Wadsworth Athenaeum, the Art Institute of Chicago, and the Cleveland Institute of Art. He designed children's toys, including a bicycle that looks ready to speed away even before a rider takes the seat, and an airplane with foot pedals and stubby wings short enough for a child to career through doorways.[71] His students at the Cleveland Institute of Art, where he founded the industrial design program, went on to become designers of the 1964 Ford Mustang, International Harvester equipment, and Chris-Craft boats. A good design, one of his protégés said, should in addition to everything else establish an emotional connection with the end user.[72]

Viktor Schreckengost has been called the "American da Vinci." He also "may be the most prolific designer you've never heard of."[73]

In 1948 the noted Cleveland architect J. Byers Hays, a friend of Viktor and his wife and the designer of their home, was commissioned to create a plan for the city's zoo. Cleveland was proud of its citizens' history as birders. In 1874 the Cleveland Academy of Natural Science boasted one of the best collections of ornithology in the country.[74] After Hays completed his general plan, he was asked to add structures for birds and pachyderms. For the bird house he proposed a tall tower. He turned to Viktor, and together they designed a tower faced with brightly colored ceramic tiles, creating a totem-pole appearance.[75]

The tiles would depict the history of birds. The choice of birds was left to Viktor, so he turned to his nephew Don Eckelberry, an ornithologist and author of four Audubon guides. Together they came up with five extinct or endangered candidates. First would come the earliest-known bird, the toothed carnivore *Archaeopteryx* of 140 million years ago. Next came *Hesperornis*, which Schreckengost envisioned as having large, red webbed feet. The giant, flightless *Diatryma* followed, then the dodo. Topmost on the tower would be the bald eagle.

Each plaque would be five feet by eight feet and weigh about a ton. They were too large for Viktor to model in his own studio, so the models were produced at another location in Cleveland. Because they were also too large to fire whole, they were cut into smaller sections for this step. To allow visitors to see the details on the top panel with the bald eagle as well as they could see the *Archaeopteryx* at the base, Viktor increased the relief of the higher panels proportionally.

The panels were both spray- and hand-painted in almost two dozen colors to create gradations of plumage. Then they were fired. The bird building with its tower was dedicated on October 19, 1950. Viktor had agreed to replace the tiles if the tower did not last twenty-five years. The terracotta on the tower showed wear and tear over time, but the colorful tiles remained in perfect condition until they were taken down and a new building was constructed.[76] Viktor outlasted the contract by thirty-three years and lived to the age of 101.

In 2006 Viktor Schreckengost, one of the twentieth century's most gifted and prolific artists, was awarded the National Medal of Arts in a ceremony at the White House as the guest of George W. Bush and First Lady Laura Bush.

Viktor saw no division between fine arts and applied arts and believed neither was superior to the other.[77] Neither is art or science on a plane higher than the other. When an artist chooses a bird for a subject and examines it closely, as John James Audubon did, we see the animal from a different perspective than an ornithologist's, that is all. Art can increase our appreciation and understanding of the natural world. Science can inspire and inform art.

When I asked staff at the Cleveland Metroparks Zoo and Cleveland Zoological Society about the whereabouts of the bird tiles, hoping I might see them in person, they could not say precisely where they are stored. Perhaps Schreckengost's beautiful *Hesperornis* tile will someday be placed before the world again, to honor the man and the bird.

Part VI
I Return to Kansas

– 65 –

I made two more trips to Russell Springs. The first was to show my husband the place that had come to mean so much to me that every morning I check the weather there. On the second trip we attended a history conference in nearby Wallace. Afterward we drove to Wabaunsee, in eastern Kansas, to pay tribute to the New Haven abolitionists who established a settlement there in 1856.

In Russell Springs we stayed in a former hotel, the town's only lodging, which was vacant but for us. One morning I answered a knock at the door to find standing on the porch the owner of Goblin Hollow, the fossil bed where Tom Russell found his *Hesperornis regalis*. We drank coffee and shot the breeze. When I asked if we could walk on his property, he said yes, and would we just close the gate so the cattle couldn't get out. That day, I explored the mini-buttes and walked in the soft gray chalk at my leisure.

A volunteer opened the Butterfield Trail Museum, formerly the county courthouse, for us and phoned a second woman who came up the hill to join our conversation. Their town's early white settlers and the railroad's history were familiar ground to them. They were less conversant with the natural history that has drawn paleontologists to the Smoky Hill country for a century and a half.

I was standing on the main street, Broadway, near a cluster of mailboxes when a man in a pickup stopped to see if he had any mail. He didn't, but we introduced ourselves and made small talk for fifteen minutes. The rattlesnake situation was bad, he said. A dog was bitten recently and a new couple in town found rattlers in the house they moved into, which had sat unoccupied awhile. Apart from the newcomers, nothing seemed to have changed since May and I were there.

The next morning my husband and I drove east across Kansas. Visibility was about forty miles. The distant horizon was a blue-gray blur of land and sky. I thought about O. C. Marsh seeing this landscape for the first time and thinking it looked like the ocean. What was once in fact a great, shallow sea is still a largely blank vista, though not a desolate one. Thunderstorms were holding up the harvest intermittently that summer, but green combines here and there were moving through fields of semi-dwarf wheat, a variety developed to resist lodging, or being blown down by wind and rain. On county roads in the distance, vehicles sent up billows of dust.

A few hours later we made Wabaunsee, about a hundred miles west of the border with Missouri. The abolitionists who came here in 1856, to what some called "the New Haven of the West," named their town for a Potawatomi Indian leader, not because he had lived here but because his name means "dawn of day." It suited their hopeful mission of bringing Kansas into the Union by popular sovereignty as a free state. Like settlers everywhere, they named streets after the ones back home. The resemblance to New Haven ended there.

At the intersection of Elm and Chapel streets, half a mile south of the Kansas River, sits the Beecher Bible and Rifle Church. After the intrepid New Haven men passed their first winter here in tents, their families joined them and helped organize a Congregational church. Stone for the building was hauled from a nearby quarry. In the churchyard they planted lilacs and installed hitching posts. When the Civil War began, some of the settlers left, never to return. Wabaunsee did not become the bustling city that Henry Ward Beecher, the abolitionist clergyman, once predicted. He wrote a letter to encourage the pioneer men. "There are times when self-defense is a religious duty," he said. "If that duty was ever imperative, it is now, and in Kansas."[1]

Services are still conducted at the Beecher Bible and Rifle Church on Sundays, but on this Wednesday only calling birds and buzzing insects interrupted the silence. A breeze stirred tufted weeds growing alongside the road. Across the way stood a field of corn, hip high in early July. I startled a bluebird from a shrub as I walked past, and caught the red flash of a low-flying cardinal. A mourning dove cooed from its perch on a cable as a hawk circled high overhead. Singers praise the color of the skies in Seattle and artists love the light in Santa Fe, but when I think of sheer blue brilliance, I think of Kansas.

Three weeks after the settlers reached Wabaunsee, violence broke out among pro- and antislavery factions in the territory. The city of Lawrence, founded by other abolitionist settlers, was burned. When the New Haven men went there to defend their compatriots and were fired upon, they were drawn into the conflict. Wabaunsee became a station on the Underground Railroad, helping passengers skirt the slave state of Missouri on their way to freedom.

Sixteen years later, when Tom Russell came through here with Professor Marsh, their westbound train passed within a few miles of Wabaunsee. Tom surely knew this as he looked out on the prairie from a railroad car, just as he knew his father had grasped the strategic role Kansas must play in abolishing slavery in the United States.

A short distance from the church, my husband and I stopped to read the words on a memorial. I pulled a notebook and pen from my pocket and took down the words: "In memory of the Beecher Bible and Rifle Colony, which settled this area in 1856 and helped make Kansas a free state. May future generations forever pay them tribute." For this purpose I had come to Wabaunsee, to pay my respects to those who had left home and accepted an uncertain future in the hope of helping the United States break the chokehold of slavery.

My husband had moved a short distance away to take pictures when a man on a bicycle braked to a stop beside me and interrupted my reverie.

"Where're you from?"

"Pasadena, California," I said. I explained that we had just come from the church and my ancestor had contributed a rifle for the Wabaunsee settlers' self-defense.

His relatives had homesteaded in the western part of the state. He was riding a forty-mile course starting from Manhattan, Kansas, where he worked. He did not get off his bike, introduce himself, or ask if we were enjoying our time in Kansas.

"I have a question for you," he said. "What happened to all the buffalo? How did they die?"

The near-extinction of *Bison bison* and the suppression of American Indian culture were subjects I had given a good deal of thought, but sensing this man might be baiting me, I demurred. Later I wondered if he had stereotyped me when I identified myself as a Californian and an abolitionist's descendant, or if my being a small woman had quickened in him an urge to dominate. My husband, who had been photographing vultures in a dead tree across the street, now joined us.

"Brucellosis," the man said. The buffalo were killed off by an infectious disease endemic to buffalo and cattle, he asserted. Whites were not responsible. Anyway, he said, there weren't enough bullets to kill them off.

What I was hearing now were not words but a tone. Carl Sandburg's poem "Buffalo Dusk," about bison and those who had seen them in great numbers, came to my mind. I thought about Tom Russell seeing a herd of almost a hundred thousand.

He cocked and aimed. "Here's another question for you. How did the Indians die?"

Mansplainer, I wrote in my notebook as I edged toward our car, leaving my genial husband listening incredulously to a theory about Indian populations declining because they interbred with Spanish explorers.

On we went to the Wabaunsee County Historical Society and Museum, in Alma. I had been told their collections included something I very much wanted to see: one of the twenty-seven Sharps rifles that New Haven residents, including my great-great-grandfather William Russell, pledged to the Kansas cause. Henry Ward Beecher was widely quoted as saying that "the Sharps rifle was a truly moral agency, and there was more moral power in one of those instruments than in a hundred Bibles."

These Beecher's Bibles, as they became known, were Model 1853 single-shot, breech-loading carbines, designed by Christian Sharps and manufactured by the Sharps Rifle Manufacturing Company in Hartford, Connecticut. The gun used a paper cartridge and shot a .52-caliber bullet from a barrel 21.5 inches long. It could fire eight to ten rounds a minute. The rifle had a long range—five hundred yards—and was known for its accuracy.[2] Ultimately about nine hundred of these rifles were shipped to Free Soilers in Kansas.[3]

The historical museum was staffed that day by a single volunteer who led me to a case containing the Sharps rifle. My husband and I were the only visitors, so I asked her if she could take out the rifle. She unlocked the case and lifted the gun onto the glass top. It was heavy for her. We guessed at the strength it would take to lift a crate filled with rifles and Bibles.

Picking up the gun, I judged its weight to be about the same as a couple of bags of sugar. The black walnut stock and brass carried the beautiful patina of age. The brass was engraved "Weston Ferris." Ferris, a New Haven resident, served with the First Connecticut Cavalry Regiment during the Civil War. Whether his gun stayed in Kansas when he left for the war or made its way back afterward is not known.

My husband and I took our time looking around the museum. Upstairs we came upon a pump organ on which lay a piece of sheet music called "Beautiful Lake Wabaunsee." It was a waltz composed by Marshall Harkness. We picked up the music and sight-read the song.

We rounded a large piece of furniture and came upon five women seated in silence, quilting. They invited me to take a few stitches with them. I had nearly flunked eighth-grade home economics because I sewed poorly, but I sat down and picked up a needle.

"Would you like to buy a raffle ticket?" one of the women asked me. "They're two dollars each or five dollars for six."

They called the quilt they were working on a kaleidoscope design. It was the raffle prize for a fund-raiser for the museum. I bought twenty-four tickets and filled out my contact information on each one. My daughter was engaged, I told the women, and I would love nothing more than to give her a handmade quilt from Kansas as a wedding present.

Back home three months later, the phone rang and a voice told me I had won the raffle.

"Are you the woman whose daughter is getting married?" the caller asked. "And you hoped you could give her the quilt for a wedding present?"

"I am," I said. "Are you the woman who took the rifle out of the case and let me hold it?" She was.

A year later, May married a man who was not with 350.org and did not work in the climate movement. My husband and I gave them the quilt as a wedding present.

After May and I visited Fort Hays seven years earlier, I had not won the raffle for the replica of a rifle. A rifle might have connected me to Tom Russell and William Russell, but a quilt connected me to my daughter and the future. Stitched by many hands from many pieces of fabric, could there be a better metaphor than a quilt for a story that brings together a mother and daughter, an abolitionist, a fossil hunter, and so many others?

How do you reconstruct the story of someone's life or construct a life for yourself? You begin with what you have. A conversation in a doctor's office, a question, an inkling. You set your intention, apply yourself to it, plunge in, go places, talk to people, and learn as you go. It's not unlike finding a fossil. You hold a fragment in your hands and ask yourself how this piece fits with that until enough pieces come together to form a skull, a skeleton, a picture in your mind. With time comes clarity and some imponderables, too. What you have reconstructed or created—a creature from eons past, a life for yourself—and what it means to you or the generations to come, that is a question for the ages.

Acknowledgments

This book is dedicated to my husband, Bob Aicher, with everlasting appreciation. Together we walked the streets of my ancestors in New Haven and Middletown, Connecticut. We tromped through old cemeteries in the rain to find headstones. We drove on county roads so muddy that clumps of Kansas earth were still dropping from our car's undercarriage years later in the car wash. There was more, much more, and through it all Bob was my cheerful, devoted, ideal companion.

Thank you, May Boeve, for permitting me to write about you and offering your support.

Thank you, May, Dan Brinkman, Jack Chambers, Colleen Daly, Lynn Downey, Mike Everhart, Lis Harris, Leo Oliva, and Debby Shapiro for reading portions of the manuscript early on, and to Bob for listening to chapters as I wrote them. Your suggestions were invaluable.

Many thanks most especially to Kent Calder, for bringing me into the fold of the University of Oklahoma Press and guiding this book from the beginning; and sincere appreciation to OU Press's entire team, including Steven Baker, Katie Baker, and Amy Hernandez, as well as freelance copyeditor Leslie Tingle.

Thank you, Henry Adams, Marianne Berardi, Peter Blodgett, Mark Brokering, Tom Eggebeen, Steve Graydon, Erin Gredell, and Zyrel Rojo for your special assistance, and my dear cousins Mary (Molly) Russell Stone, Steve Joyce, and Jane Russell Bate for generously sharing family photos and mementos.

Thank you, helpful and expert archivists, librarians, and staff of the following institutions and organizations who more than came through, even as you worked under the constraints of the COVID-19 pandemic: Peabody Museum of Natural History at Yale University; Manuscripts and Archives, Yale University; Whitney Library and

215

New Haven Museum and Historical Society; New Haven Free Public Library; Grove Street Cemetery; Middlesex County Historical Society; Olin Memorial Library, Wesleyan University; United States Military Academy at West Point; Fort Wallace Museum; Sternberg Museum of Natural History; Butterfield Trail Museum; Wabaunsee County Historical Society and Museum; Smithsonian Museum of the American Indian; Smithsonian Institution Archives; National Archives and Records Administration; Mi'kmaq Resource Centre, Unama'ki College, Cape Breton University; Beaton Institute at Cape Breton University; Church History Library Reference Department, The Church of Jesus Christ of Latter-Day Saints; Denver Art Museum; Cleveland Metroparks Zoo; Western Costume Company; Pasadena Public Library; The Huntington Library; University of Nebraska–Lincoln Libraries; Brigham Young Collection, Princeton University; Seeley G. Mudd Manuscript Library, Princeton University; Sedgwick Museum, Cambridge, England; The National Museums of Scotland; National History Museum, London; Oxford University Museum of Natural History; Royal College of Surgeons, London; Redpath Museum at McGill University; Academy of Natural Sciences of Drexel University; Wesleyan University; The University of Virginia, Charlottesville; Chicago Academy of Sciences; Bentley Historical Library at the University of Michigan; and the Virginia Department of Mines, Minerals and Energy, Division of Geology and Mineral Resources.

NOTES

Note on the text: Ellipses in brackets signify an omission made by the author. These brackets distinguish the author's omissions from ellipses used in original quoted material.

Prologue

1. Reimagined and retold by the author, based on O. C. Marsh's manuscript "A Ride for Life in a Herd of Buffalo," in the Othniel Charles Marsh Papers, Manuscripts and Archives, Yale University Library. (Marsh's papers in the Yale collection are hereafter cited as Marsh Papers, Yale University Library.) The account also appears in Charles Schuchert and Clara Mae LeVene, *O. C. Marsh: Pioneer in Paleontology* (New Haven, Conn: Yale University Press, 1940), 127–32.

Part I: Origins

1. "American Indians," "Natives," and "Native people" are used here unless the tribal name is known and appropriate in context. This usage is in accordance with a request made of the Oklahoma Historical Society by tribes in Oklahoma and with the policy of the Smithsonian National Museum of the American Indian. As the museum's education page states, the terms "American Indian," "Indian," "Native American," and "Native" are all acceptable: "The consensus, however, is that whenever possible, Native people prefer to be called by their specific tribal name. In the United States, Native American has been widely used but is falling out of favor with some groups, and the terms American Indian or indigenous American are preferred by many Native people." FAQ, "What Is the Correct Terminology?," National Museum of the American Indian, accessed April 13, 2021, https://americanindian.si.edu/nk360 /faq/did-you-know/.

2. George Bird Grinnell, "From Yale to the Wild West: An Old-Time Bone Hunt; An Account of the Expedition Undertaken by Prof. O. C. Marsh in 1870 to the Then Wild West," in *Pawnee, Blackfoot, and Cheyenne: History and Folklore of the Plains from the Writings of George Bird Grinnell* (New York: Charles Scribner's Sons, 1961), 4. In their biography of Marsh, authors Schuchert and LeVene state that Marsh made it possible for one assistant, Oscar Harger, to join the 1871 and 1873 expeditions by paying his expenses of $950 (*O. C. Marsh*, 307). What other members of the four expeditions paid is not known.

3. William Tecumseh Sherman to O. C. Marsh, March 24, 1870, and June 24, 1871. O. C. Marsh Correspondence, box 29, folder 1247, Peabody Museum of Natural History, http://peabody.yale.edu/collections/vertebrate-paleontology /correspondence-o-c-marsh.

4. Charles Wyllys Betts, "The Yale College Expedition of 1870," *Harper's New Monthly Magazine* 257 (October 1871): 666.

5. "Gigantic swimming bird" is from "New and Remarkable Fossils," *College Courant: A Weekly Journal* 10, no. 24 (June 15, 1872): 283.

6. O. C. Marsh, "On the Odontornithes, or Birds with Teeth," *American Journal of Science*, ser. 3,10, no. 59 (1875): 403–8.

7. Michael J. Everhart, *Oceans of Kansas: A Natural History of the Western Interior Sea*, 2nd ed. (Bloomington: Indiana University Press, 2017), 314.

8. Charles Darwin to O. C. Marsh, August 31, 1880, O. C. Marsh Correspondence, Peabody Museum of Natural History, https://peabody.yale.edu/exhibits /fossil-fragments/history/darwins-letter-oc-marsh.

9. Elizabeth Sullivan, "From the Oldest Feather to the Largest Volcano," *Yale Alumni Magazine* 38, no. 5 (February 1975): 8–13; letter from Margaret R. Leavy '60 Law, "The Rough-Looking Character," *Yale Alumni Magazine* 38, no. 8 (May 1975): 6–7.

10. David C. Krakauer, John Lewis Gaddis, and Kenneth Pomeranz, eds., *History, Big History, and Metahistory* (Santa Fe, N.M.: Santa Fe Institute Press, 2017), i–vii.

11. "Thomas Hubbard Russell," in *Men of Mark in Connecticut: Ideals of American Life Told in Biographies and Autobiographies of Eminent Living Americans*, vol. 2, ed. Col. Norris Galpin Osborn (Hartford: William R. Goodspeed, 1906), 427.

12. Schuchert and LeVene, *O. C. Marsh*, 307. Marsh's staff were so discontented with him in the 1800s, according to the authors, that their unhappiness rose to "active dislike." They made public accusations against him in 1890. Had Tom Russell gone to work for Marsh, his salary might have been just $35 a month. Oscar Harger, a longtime paleontology assistant in the Yale Peabody Museum, was paid this sum when he went to work for Marsh in the fall of 1872, according to Schuchert and LeVene (299).

Part II: Strata

1. Franklin Benjamin Sanborn, ed., *Life and Letters of John Brown, Liberator of Kansas and Martyr of Virginia* (Boston: Roberts Brothers, 1885), 451, https://archive .org/stream/lifeandlettersofoosanbrich#page/n7/mode/2up. On Brown implying that friends in Boston and New Haven "trifled" with him, see page 467.

2. On Russell not knowing Brown's plans, see Reverdy Whitlock, "William Huntington Russell and the Collegiate and Commercial Institute," *Journal of the New Haven Colony Historical Society* 18, no. 4 (1969): 87.

3. Senate Report 278, 36th Cong., 1st sess., Senate Select Committee on the Harper's Ferry Invasion, *Report [of] the Select Committee of the Senate Appointed to Inquire into the Late Invasion and Seizure of the Public Property at Harpers Ferry* (Washington, D.C.: 1860), https://www.wvculture.org/history/jbexhibit /masonreport.html.

4. Abraham Lincoln, Cooper Union Speech, New York City, February 27, 1860, Abraham Lincoln Online, http://www.abrahamlincolnonline.org/lincoln /speeches/cooper.htm.

5. William Richard Cutter, Edward Henry Clement, Samuel Hart, Mary Kingsbury Talcott, Frederick Bostwick, Ezra Scollay Stearns, eds., "General William Huntington Russell," *Genealogical and Family History of the State of Connecticut: A Record of the Achievements of Her People in the Making of a Commonwealth and the Founding of a Nation*, vol. 1 (New York: Lewis Historical Publishing, 1911), 431.

6. Cutter et al., "General William Huntington Russell," 430.

7. Cutter et al., "General William Huntington Russell," 430.

8. Cutter et al., "General William Huntington Russell," 427.

9. Franklin Bowditch Dexter, "The Founding of Yale College," in *A Selection from the Miscellaneous Historical Papers of Fifty Years* (New Haven, Conn.: Tuttle, Morehouse, and Taylor Co., 1918), 82.

10. Perry Miller and Thomas Herbert Johnson, *The Puritans: A Sourcebook of Their Writings*, 2 vols. bound as 1 (Minneola, N.Y.: Dover Publications, 2001), 744.

11. Michael Sletcher, *New Haven: From Puritanism to the Age of Terror* (Charleston, S.C.: Arcadia Publishing, 2004), 52; William Chauncey Fowler, *The Historical Status of the Negro in Connecticut, A Paper Read before the New Haven Colony Historical Society (in 1873)* (Charleston, S.C.: Walker, Evans & Cogswell, 1901), 13, https://catalog.hathitrust.org/Record/000542885.

12. Mary H. Mitchell, "Slavery in Connecticut and Especially in New Haven," read April 9, 1934, *Papers of the New Haven Historical Society* 10 (1951): 292.

13. Fowler, *Historical Status of the Negro in Connecticut*, 19. Fowler refers to "Dr. Belknap," an American clergyman and historian (1744–98), https://catalog.hathitrust.org/Record/100338982.

14. Sletcher, *New Haven*, 21, 52, 53.

15. Sletcher, *New Haven*, 53.

16. On September 28, 2019, Middletown, Connecticut, held a Middle Passage ceremony and unveiled a plaque of remembrance after UNESCO designated the city as a Site of Memory because of its participation in the Atlantic slave trade. Deborah Shapiro, the Middletown municipal historian, presided at the ceremony.

17. J. B. Beers and Company and Henry B. Whittemore, *History of Middlesex County, Connecticut. 1635–1885: With Biographical Sketches of Its Prominent Men* (New York: J. B. Beers and Co., 1884), 135, https://archive.org/stream /cu31924097556595#page/n7/mode/2up.

18. From a photocopy provided by the Middlesex County [Connecticut] Historical Society of the *Daily Herald*, undated with unnumbered pages, "The Third Century, History of the First Church of Christ in this City, A Remarkable Record—Among the Oldest Churches in This State—Many Noted Men Have Occupied the Pulpits—Gentlemen of Culture Have Worshiped under the Administration of the Pastors." The article was evidently published in 1893, as it states that the church would soon commemorate the 225th anniversary of its organization on November 4, 1668. The same comment is attributed to "Whitfield" in Sherman Wolcott Adams, *Families of Ancient Wethersfield, Connecticut: Comprising the Present Towns of Wethersfield, Rocky Hill, and Newington, and of Glastonbury*

Prior to Its Incorporation in 1693: From Date of Earliest Settlement Until the Present Time, vol. 2, *Genealogies and Biographies* (New York: Grafton Press, 1904), 599, https://babel.hathitrust.org/cgi/pt?id=coo.31924096458595&view=image&seq=685&size=125.

19. King cited the sermon in a 1950 term paper written while a student at Crozer Theological Seminary. See "An Appraisal of the Great Awakening," November 17, 1950, the Martin Luther King Jr. Research and Education Institute, Stanford, https://kinginstitute.stanford.edu/king-papers/documents/appraisal-great-awakening.

20. Deborah Shapiro retired from her position as executive director of the Middlesex County Historical Society in 2019 and currently serves as the municipal historian of Middletown, Connecticut.

21. Sanborn, *Life and Letters of John Brown*, 467–68.

22. Edward Elias Atwater, ed., "Schools" and "William Huntington Russell," in *History of the City of New Haven to the Present Time* (New York: W. W. Munsell, 1887), 163–64, ebooksread.com, http://www.ebooksread.com/authors-eng/edward-e-edward-elias-atwater/history-of-the-city-of-new-haven-to-the-present-time-taw/page-44-history-of-the-city-of-new-haven-to-the-present-time-taw.shtml.

23. Letter of H. Whittelsey, January 11, 1841, to Ebenezer Jackson, in Mabel Cassine Holman, "Letters of Early American Warriors: Heirlooms of the Jacksons of Connecticut," in Harry Clemons, *Connecticut Magazine: An Illustrated Monthly* 11 (1907): 11.

24. Azel Washburn Hazen, *A Brief History of the First Church of Christ in Middletown, Connecticut, for Two Centuries and a Half, 1668–1918* (Middletown, Conn.: n.p., 1920), 52, https://archive.org/details/briefhistoryoffioohaze.

25. Angelika Krüger-Kahloula, "Tribute in Stone and Lapidary Lapses: Commemorating Black People in Eighteenth- and Nineteenth-century America," 60, *Markers VI: The Journal of the Association for Gravestone Studies* 11 (1993): 32–100, https://archive.org/details/markerso6asso.

26. Spreadsheet of pages 654–55 compiled from Ancestry.com, *Connecticut, Church Record Abstracts, 1630–1920* (Provo, Utah: 2013) based on original data in Connecticut, courtesy of Deborah Shapiro, from Church Records Index, Connecticut State Library, Hartford, Connecticut. Email from Deborah Shapiro, Municipal Historian, Middletown, to the author, December 3, 2019.

27. Email from Deborah Shapiro to the author, May 16, 2017.

28. Hazen, *Brief History of the First Church of Christ in Middletown*, 60.

29. Thomas Paine, "African Slavery in America," first essay (no page number) in *The Writings of Thomas Paine*, vol. 1 (1774–79), Online Library of Liberty, http://oll.libertyfund.org/titles/343.

30. Enoch Huntington's diary entry for May 30, 1806, is in Peter Hall, "Middletown: Streets, Commerce, and People, 1650–1981," in *Sesquicentennial Papers Number 8: A Pamphlet Written for the 150th Anniversary of Wesleyan University* (Middletown, Conn.: Wesleyan University, 1981), 16, passim.

31. Hall, "Middletown," 17.

32. Fowler, *Historical Status of the Negro in Connecticut*, 6–7.

33. Enoch Huntington, "A sermon, delivered at Middletown, July 20th, A.D. 1775, the day appointed by the Continental Congress, to be observed by the inhabitants of all the English colonies on this continent, as a day of public humiliation, fasting and prayer. Published at the request of the auditors," Evans Early Imprint Collection, accessed July 3, 2015, http://quod.lib.umich.edu/e/evans /n11153.0001.001/1?node=n11153.0001.001%3AN11153.0001.001&view=text.

34. William Cooper Nell, *The Colored Patriots of the American Revolution, to Which Is Added a Brief Survey of the Condition and Prospects of Colored Americans* (Boston: Robert F. Walcutt, 1855), 135.

35. Terry Tempest Williams, *When Women Were Birds: Fifty-Four Variations on Voice* (New York: Picador, 2012), 54.

36. Mitchell, "Slavery in Connecticut," 302.

37. For more about Enoch Huntington, his descendants in Middletown, and changes in the city's economy and culture, see Hall, "Middletown," especially 19–20 and 23–24. Wesleyan University was founded in 1831. Hall says of the town elders, "Having stomached an Alden Partridge, they were willing to make an offer to the once-despised Methodists who were, by the late 1820s, considering plans to open a college in New England that would do for their denomination what Harvard did for Unitarians, Yale for Congregationalists, Trinity for Episcopalians, and Brown for Baptists" (23).

38. American Literary, Scientific and Military Academy, "Catalogue of the Officers and Cadets: Together with the Prospectus and Internal Regulations of the American Literary, Scientific and Military Academy, at Middletown, Connecticut," book 4 (Middletown, Conn.: E & H Clark, 1827), 30–31, https:// digitalcollections.wesleyan.edu.

39. American Literary, Scientific and Military Academy, "Catalogue of the Officers and Cadets."

40. Stephen E. Ambrose, *Duty, Honor, Country: A History of West Point* (Baltimore: Johns Hopkins University Press, 1999), 90. Ambrose's chapter on Alden Partridge paints a vivid picture of the academy's superintendent and covers his tenure there. The chapters "Thayer's Curriculum and Faculty" and "The Jacksonians and the Academy" compare West Point to other educational institutions and provide context for understanding Partridge's influence on William Huntington Russell.

41. Ambrose, *Duty, Honor, Country*, 88–89.

42. Hall, "Middletown," 23.

43. David Alan Richards, "The Founding of Scull and Bone [*sic*], 1832–1842," in *Skulls and Keys: The Hidden History of Yale's Secret Societies*, 43–112 (New York: Pegasus Books, 2017), 60.

44. Ron Rosenbaum, "The Last Secrets of Skull and Bones," *Esquire* (September 1977): 85–89, 148–50.

45. Lyman Hotchkiss Bagg, *Four Years at Yale: By a Graduate of '69* (New Haven, Conn.: Charles C. Chatfield, 1871), 146, https://archive.org/stream/four yearsatyaleoobaggrich#page/n5/mode/2up. A lexicon of Yale terms on page 47 includes the definition of a "Russellite" as "a member of Gen. Russell's military school."

46. Joshua L. Chamberlain, Charles Henry Smith, et al., *Universities and Their Sons: History, Influence and Characteristics of American Universities* (Boston: R. Herndon, 1899), 567, http://catalog.hathitrust.org/Record/000775862.

47. Handwritten name on an illegible and unidentified newspaper clipping, "City Affairs: Russell's Collegiate School," May 10, 1856, Dana Scrapbook Collection, New Haven Museum. Used with permission.

48. "Old Russell School: Her Famous Graduates," unidentified newspaper clipping, undated, Dana Scrapbook Collection, New Haven Museum. Used with permission.

49. Reverdy Whitlock, "William Huntington Russell and the Collegiate and Commercial Institute," *Journal of the New Haven Colony Historical Society* 18, no. 4 (1969): 86.

50. Henry Holt, *Garrulities of an Octogenarian Editor: With Other Essays Somewhat Biographical and Autobiographical* (Boston: Houghton Mifflin, 1923), 32–33.

51. Letter from A. J. McNutt to William Huntington Russell, October 16, 1874. Collection of Jane Russell Bate, used with permission.

52. Donald Sutherland, "The Severe Winter of 1851–52," Digital Snow Museum, accessed April 15, 2021, http://wintercenter.homestead.com/files /1851–52.pdf.

53. Sutherland, "Severe Winter of 1851–52," 2, 3.

54. Edward Strong, *The Pulpit's Sphere and Urgencies: A Sermon Preached in the College Street Church, New Haven, December 14, 1851, on Occasion of the Ninth Anniversary of the Pastor's Ordination* (New Haven: J. H. Benham, 1852), accessed October 29, 2014, Google Books.

55. "Emigrants for Kansas," (Hartford) *Connecticut Courant* 94, no. 4810 (March 28, 1857): 2.

56. "Sharp's [*sic*] Rifles in New-Haven. Meeting in the North Church. Speech of Henry Ward Beecher. Weapons from the Church and Yale College. Prof. Silliman Bidding for Rifles. (From our own reporter)," *New York Daily Times* 10, no. 1407 (March 22, 1856), archives of the *New York Times*.

57. "Sharp's [*sic*] Rifles in New-Haven," *New York Daily Times*, March 22, 1856, 1.

58. "Departure of the Connecticut Colony for Kansas," *New York Tribune*, April 4, 1856, 5.

59. "Departure of the Connecticut Colony," *New York Tribune*, April 4, 1856, 5.

60. David S. Reynolds, *John Brown, Abolitionist: The Man Who Killed Slavery, Sparked the Civil War, and Seeded Civil Rights* (New York: Knopf, 2005), 212.

61. Sanborn, *Life and Letters of John Brown*, 385–86.

62. Sanborn, *Life and Letters of John Brown*, 385–86.

63. William Deverell, "After Antietam: Memory and Memorabilia in the Far West," in *Empire and Liberty: The Civil War and the West*, ed. Virginia Scharff (Oakland: University of California Press, 2015), 182.

64. Letter from John Brown Jr. to Horatio Nelson Rust, January 1, 1884, Horatio Nelson Rust Papers, RU 307, box 1, Huntington Library, San Marino, California.

65. Letter from John Brown Jr. to Horatio Nelson Rust, February 3, 1884, Rust Papers, RU 308, box 1, Huntington Library.

66. Jane Apostol, "Horatio Nelson Rust: Abolitionist, Archaeologist, Indian Agent," *California History* 57, no. 4 (Winter 1979/80): 305.

67. John M. Radebaugh, MD, "Pasadena as a Health Resort," in *A Southern California Paradise (in the Suburbs of Los Angeles)*, ed. R. W. C. Farnsworth, 102–4 (Pasadena, Calif.: R. W. C. Farnsworth, 1883), 103.

68. The author and historian William Deverell described Horatio Nelson Rust as a "one-man eBay" in a conversation with the author on July 24, 2019, at the Huntington Library.

69. Ambrose, *Duty, Honor, Country*, 171–72. Ambrose describes reactions at West Point to the attack on Fort Sumter and the early days of the Civil War, including the sendoff of Lieutenant Lee.

70. Resolution of David W. Sharpe, Post Commander, Admiral Foote Post, Department of Connecticut, Grand Army of the Republic, in "Old Russell School: Her Famous Graduates," undated, Dana Scrapbook Collection, New Haven Museum. Used with permission.

71. New Haven Sanitary Commission, "New Haven Women Act on Behalf of the Sick and Wounded, 1861," Cengage.com, accessed May 16, 2016, https://college.cengage.com/history/ayers_primary_sources/new_haven_women%20act_1861.htm.

72. William Tecumseh Sherman, "The March to the Sea," *Memoirs of General William T. Sherman*, vol. 2 (New York: D. Appleton and Co., 1875), 2.

73. "Frightful News! Lincoln Assassinated," (New Haven) *Daily Register*, April 15, 1865, 2nd ed., 1; "Assassination of Lincoln 67 Years Ago," *New Haven Register*, April 10, 1932, 3.

74. "Mr. Lincoln Called Them Wide-Awakes," *New York Times*, April 14, 1895, 28, quoted in Daniel D. Bidwell, "Lincoln in Hartford," in *Abraham Lincoln: Tributes from His Associates*, ed. William H. Ward (New York: Crowell, ca. 1895), 182–83.

75. "Mr. Lincoln Called Them Wide-Awakes," *New York Times*, April 14, 1895, 28.

76. Floyd M. Shumway and Richard Hegel, "Abraham Lincoln's Visit to New Haven," *Journal of the New Haven Historical Society* 39, no.1 (Fall 1992): 13–24.

77. Atwater, *History of the City of New Haven*, 163.

Part III: The 1872 Yale College Scientific Expedition

1. T. Mitchell Prudden, foreword by Lillian E. Prudden, *Biographical Sketches and Letters of T. Mitchell Prudden, M.D.* (New Haven, Conn.: Yale University Press, 1927), 15–16. The descriptions are Prudden's, taken from his "Autobiographical Notes." In a September 2, 2015, email Yale Peabody Museum archivist Barbara Narendra told the author that the autobiographical notes have disappeared.

2. "The Expedition to Martha's Vineyard," *Yale Literary Magazine: Conducted by the Students of Yale College* 37 (October 1872–July 1872).

3. "What to Do Next?," *College Courant: A Weekly Journal Devoted to the Interests of Colleges, Universities and the Higher Education,* June 15, 1872, 284.

4. Holt, *Garrulities,* 79.

5. Russell H. Chittenden, *History of the Sheffield Scientific School of Yale University, 1846–1922,* vol. 1 (New Haven, Conn.: Yale University Press, 1928), 165.

6. The offer Prudden received to teach freshman chemistry is mentioned in Prudden, *Biographical Sketches and Letters,* 17. The *Hartford Daily Courant* on October 11, 1872, reported that, according to the New Haven *Journal and Courier,* Marsh and two or three others were to meet up in St. Louis. These "others" were not identified, however, and the Yale expedition ultimately comprised Marsh, Russell, MacNaughton, Hoppin, and Hill.

7. Richard Conniff, *House of Lost Worlds: Dinosaurs, Dynasties, and the Story of Life on Earth* (New Haven, Conn.: Yale University Press, 2016), 54.

8. Holt, *Garrulities,* 84.

9. Ernest Howe notes, Marsh Papers, manuscript group 343, series 5, microfilm reel 26, frames 308–442, Yale University Library.

10. William Whitney Hawkes, MD, "Thomas H. Russell, M.D.," in *Proceedings of the Connecticut State Medical Society,* ed. Marvin McR. Scarbrough (New Haven: Connecticut State Medical Society, 1916): 237–40.

11. Letter from Rev. Charles A. Tibbals to Edwin R. Embree, Director of the Class Secretaries Bureau at Yale, February 7, 1916, Yale Alumni Records Office, Yale University, RU 830, 2000-A-007/2, series 2, box 637, folder 25.

12. Prudden, *Biographical Sketches and Letters,* 19. In their biography of Marsh, Schuchert and LeVene say, however, that Oscar Harger, the first permanent assistant in paleontology at the Peabody, served "as a sort of quartermaster" on the 1873 trip (*O. C. Marsh,* 298).

13. Schuchert and LeVene, *O. C. Marsh,* 126. The inflation calculator at https://www.in2013dollars.com, which draws on records published by the U.S. Department of Labor, was used to convert dollar amounts to 2021 values.

14. Henry W. Farnam, recollections of Professor Marsh sent to Ernest Howe, May 5, 1931, pp. 7, 8, Marsh Papers, manuscript group 343, series 5, microfilm reel 26, frame 462, Yale University Library.

15. Elsewhere, MacNaughton is spelled McNaughton.

16. Untitled article, *Hartford Daily Courant,* October 11, 1872, 2, column 6.

17. In an email to the author on June 9, 2016, Michael Lotstein, head of university archives in the Manuscripts and Archives Division at Yale University Library, said: "It does seem unusual for a student to start in December at any school at Yale at any time in its history. I cannot speak to how this might have happened other than his possible acceptance to start in the fall and then spending that semester with O. C. Marsh abroad? Unfortunately we do not have student records for Sheffield for this period so I cannot say for sure what transpired."

18. *Ninth Census—Volume I, The Statistics of the Population of the United States* (Washington, D.C., 1872), 16, cited in James P. Collins, "Native Americans in the Census, 1860–1890," *Prologue Magazine* 38, no. 2 (Summer 2006), https://www.archives.gov/publications/prologue/2006/summer/indian-census.html#nt16.

19. "A Leap to Death: Shocking Trapeze Accident," *Titusville* (Penn.) *Morning Herald*, August 16, 1872, http://www3.gendisasters.com/missouri/21400/st-louis -mo-circus-trapeze-accident-aug-1872; William Lawrence Slout, *Olympians of the Sawdust Circle: A Biographical Dictionary of the Nineteenth-Century American Circus* (San Bernardino, Calif.: Borgo Press, 1998).

20. Dr. John Arthur Horner, "Know Your KC History: Strange Goings on at Exposition Fair, 1872, part 1," October 26, 2011, Kansas City Public Library, http://www.kclibrary.org/blog/kc-unbound/know-your-kc-history-strange -goings-exposition-fair-1872-pt-1; Dr. Jason Roe, "A Myth Is Born," Kansas City Public Library, September 21, 2015, http://www.kclibrary.org/blog/week -kansas-city-history/myth-born.

21. Albany and New Haven population figures are from "Population of the 100 Largest Urban Places: 1870, table 10," U.S. Bureau of the Census, Inter- net Release date June 15, 1998, http://www.census.gov/population/www /documentation/twps0027/tab10.txt. Statistics on the largest U.S. cities are from City Mayors Statistics, "The Largest U.S. Cities, Cities Ranked 1 to 100," accessed April 22, 2021, http://www.citymayors.com/gratis/uscities_100.html.

22. "Our State Institutions: The Albany Iron Foundries," *New York Times*, January 2, 1872, 5.

23. Hamilton Child, compiler, *Gazetteer and Business Directory of Albany and Schenectady, N.Y., for 1870–71* (Syracuse: The Journal Office, 1870): 95, 100, 107, 110–11.

24. Sylvia McNamara, Julian Sagastume, and Ronald Taitz, "Energy: Elec- tricity," in "A People's Guide to Infrastructure in New Haven," Yale Univer- sity Campus Press, accessed January 26, 2017, https://campuspress.yale.edu /infrastructurenewhaven/energy/.

25. George A. Crofutt, *Crofutt's Trans-Continental Tourist's Guide*, vol. 4, 3rd rev. ed. (New York: George A. Crofutt, 1872).

26. Information about the 1872 expedition is compiled from the following sources: February 1877 Kansas Pacific Railway timetable, Kansas Memory, accessed January 26, 2017, http://img.kansasmemory.org/00213609.jpg; report of six days' travel for the 1871 Yale College Scientific Expedition, from "Geol- ogy on the Plains," dateline Fort Wallace, July 21, 1871, *Lawrence* (Kansas) *Daily Journal*, July 25, 1871, 2.

27. Special Orders No. 103, Headquarters Fort Wallace Kansas, U.S. Army Commands, Record Group 393, National Archives and Records Administra- tion, Washington, D.C.

28. "How We Spent Christmas," *Wallace News*, December 27, 1870, 3.

29. Description of the hotel from *Western Kansas World* (WaKeeney), Novem- ber 21, 1885, 4; May 29, 1873, letter to the *Topeka Daily Commonwealth* by an unidentified writer, published in *Atchison Daily Globe*, June 6, 1973, 8.

30. Jayne Humphrey Pearce, president, Fort Wallace Memorial Association, email to the author, February 20, 2017.

31. "Madigans Pioneers Wallace County," *Sherman County* (Kansas) *Herald*, June 27, 1957, based on an article written in 1923. Copy courtesy of the Fort Wal- lace Memorial Association.

32. "Geology on the Plains," *Lawrence Daily Journal*, July 25, 1871, 2.

33. "Kurt Cox, Uniform Specialist," Western Costume Company, accessed February 8, 2017, http://westerncostume.com/about-us/bios. Kurt Cox is still costuming movies but no longer works at Western Costume.

34. Quoted in Leo E. Oliva, *Fort Wallace: Sentinel on the Smoky Hill Trail* (Topeka: Kansas State Historical Society, 1998), 41.

35. Elizabeth Bacon Custer and Mary E. Burt, ed., *The Boy General: Story of the Life of Major-General George A. Custer, as Told by Elizabeth B. Custer* (New York: Charles Scribner's Sons, 1901), 28–29.

36. Oliva, *Fort Wallace*, xi.

37. Mrs. Frank C. Montgomery, "Fort Wallace and Its Relation to the Frontier," *Kansas Historical Collections* 17 (1926–28): 191.

38. "Time Line of the American Bison," U.S. Fish and Wildlife Service, accessed July 1, 2014, https://www.fws.gov/bisonrange/timeline.htm.

39. Reader "jussmartenuf, Dallas, Texas," comment on June 23, 2012, 3:43 P.M., to Tony Perrottet, "Chasing a Prairie Tale," *New York Times*, June 22, 2012, http://www.nytimes.com/2012/06/24/travel/buffalo-the-pawnee-and-an-old -story-on-a-trip-across-the-plains.html?_r=1&pagewanted=3&.

40. Tim Heffernan, "Where the Buffalo Roamed, A Strange and Morbid Economy," *Bloomberg*, August 31, 2012, https://www.bloomberg.com/view/articles /2012-08-30/where-the-buffalo-roamed-a-strange-and-morbid-economy.

41. Robert M. Utley, *Frontier Regulars: The United States Army and the Indian, 1866–1891* (New York: Macmillan, 1973), 213, 218n54, citing E. Douglas Branch, *The Hunting of the Buffalo* (New York: Appleton and Co., 1929), 169.

42. "The Bison: From 30 Million to 325 (1884) to 500,000 (Today)," Flat Creek Inn website, accessed May 27, 2021, https://www.flatcreekinn.com/bison -americas-mammal/.

43. Samuel A. Macdonald, *The Agony of an American Wilderness: Loggers, Environmentalists, and the Struggle for Control of a Forgotten Forest* (Lanham, Md.: Rowman & Littlefield, 2005), 13–14.

44. The description of buffalo grass is from the early Wallace, Kansas, merchant Peter Robidoux, quoted in W. F. Thompson, "Peter Robidoux: A Real Kansas Pioneer," *Kansas Historical Collections* 17 (1928): 289, https://www.kshs.org/p /kansas-historical-quarterly-first-newspapers-in-kansas-counties-4/12881.

45. Montgomery, "Fort Wallace and Its Relation to the Frontier," 198.

46. Montgomery, "Fort Wallace and Its Relation to the Frontier," quotes in full the telegram from "G. A. Custer, Bvt. Major Gen'l U.S.A.," from Hays City, Kansas, May 31, 1870, to Colonel Tilford (246–47). It was found, according to Montgomery, in "a mass of manuscripts in the adjutant general's correspondence and governor's correspondence, in the archives of the Kansas Historical Society, from General Pope and the military."

47. Betts, "Yale College Expedition of 1870," 663–71; Schuchert and LeVene, *O. C. Marsh*, 104–5.

48. Montgomery, "Fort Wallace and Its Relation to the Frontier," 247. Fort Wallace was not closed for eleven more years.

49. Quoted in Schuchert and LeVene, *O. C. Marsh*, 122.

50. David L. Browman and Stephen Williams, *Anthropology at Harvard: A Biographical History, 1790–1940* (Cambridge, Mass.: Harvard University Press, 2013), 162.

51. Montgomery, "Fort Wallace and Its Relation to the Frontier," 251; Lee A. Farrow, *Alexis in America: A Russian Grand Duke's Tour, 1871–1872* (Baton Rouge: Louisiana State University Press, 2014), 160.

52. The unidentified *New York Herald* correspondent is quoted in Farrow, *Alexis in America*, 160.

53. Montgomery, "Fort Wallace and Its Relation to the Frontier," 251; Louise Barnett, *Touched by Fire: The Life, Death, and Mythic Afterlife of George Armstrong Custer* (Lincoln: University of Nebraska Press, 2006), 180.

54. Interview with John Sipes Jr., Norman, Oklahoma, November 1996, posted by "Gary," American-Tribes.com, accessed March 3, 2017, https://amertribes.proboards.com/thread/21/stone-calf.

55. Peter Cozzens, introduction to Grace E. Meredith, *Girl Captives of the Cheyenne: A True Story of the Capture and Rescue of Four Pioneer Girls, 1874* (Mechanicsburg, Penn.: Stackpole Books, 2004), xiv. Unlike others who have written about the German girls' treatment at the hands of their captors, Cozzens gives a no-holds-barred account.

56. Linda Mowery-Denning, "Friendship Rises from Bitter Past," *Salina (Kansas) Journal*, September 10, 1990, 1.

57. Mowery-Denning, "Friendship Rises," *Salina Journal*, September 10, 1990, 1.

58. Linda Mowery-Denning, telephone conversation with the author, March 3, 2017.

59. Suzanne Walker, "Bob Hopper Gives Family Account Involving Cheyenne Indians," Chattanoogan.com, October 12, 2005, https://www.chattanoogan.com/2005/10/12/74056/Bob-Hopper-Gives-Family-Account.aspx.

60. Walker, "Bob Hopper Gives Family Account," Chattanoogan.com, October 12, 2005.

61. John Adler, "Background: Harper's Weekly," Harpweek.com, accessed March 28, 2017, http://www.harpweek.com/02About/about.asp.

62. Montgomery, "Fort Wallace and Its Relation to the Frontier," 245.

63. Leo E. Oliva email to the author, February 28, 2017.

64. John O'Donnell, introduction to *Prelude to Tragedy: Vietnam, 1960–1965*, eds. Harvey Neese and John O'Donnell (Annapolis, Md.: Naval Institute Press, 2001), viii.

65. United States Agency for International Development, "'Quiet War' Is Vital Part of Vietnam Struggle," *Front Lines* (October 1964): 7.

66. Maj. John M. Sullivan Jr., "Infantry on the Kansas Frontier, 1866–1880" (master's thesis, U.S. Army Command and General Staff College, Fort Leavenworth, Kans., 1997), 34–35, https://apps.dtic.mil/dtic/tr/fulltext/u2/a331801.pdf.

67. Oliva, *Fort Wallace*, 30.

68. Jeremy Agnew, *Life of a Soldier on the Western Frontier* (Missoula, Mont.: Mountain Press Publishing, 2008), 123.

69. Oliva, *Fort Wallace*, 113.

70. Agnew, *Life of a Soldier*, 124; E. A. Bode, *A Dose of Frontier Soldiering: The Memoirs of Corporal Emil A. Bode, Frontier Regular Infantry, 1877–1882*, ed. Thomas T. Smith (Lincoln: University of Nebraska Press, 1994), 50.

71. Oliva, *Fort Wallace*, 113.

72. Oliva, *Fort Wallace*, 105.

73. Montgomery, "Fort Wallace and Its Relation to the Frontier," 224.

74. Bvt. Maj.-Gen. George W. Cullum, "James W. Pope," *Biographical Register of the Officers and Graduates of the U.S. Military Academy at West Point, N.Y.*, 3rd ed., no. 2257 (Boston: Houghton, Mifflin, 1891), 122, https://babel.hathitrust .org/cgi/pt?id=uc1.b4233760&view=image&seq=132&q1=Pope.

75. Quotes from the James W. Pope journal, 1868–1869, mssHM 74606, the Huntington Library, San Marino, California. Online records indicate that the Huntington purchased the journal at auction in 2010 for $9,000. It was described at the time of sale as a rare record of conflict on the southern plains and "a tremendous piece of Americana." "440: Lt. James W. Pope Indian Wars Diary, 1868–1869," liveauctioneers, accessed October 14, 2016, https://new .liveauctioneers.com/item/7478378. Jenny Watts, the former and now retired curator of photography and visual culture at the Huntington Library, assisted the author in reading Pope's handwriting.

76. Marsh, "Ride for Life in a Herd of Buffalo," 2.

77. Schuchert and LeVene, *O. C. Marsh*, 129.

78. Marsh, "Ride for Life in a Herd of Buffalo," 2.

79. Marsh, "Ride for Life in a Herd of Buffalo," 2.

80. John D. Billings, *Hardtack and Coffee: Or, The Unwritten Story of Army Life* (Boston: George Smith and Co., 1888), 48. See also Joseph K. Barnes, Joseph Janvier Woodward, Charles Smart, George Alexander Otis, David Lowe Huntington, and United States Surgeon-General's Office, *The Medical and Surgical History of the War of the Rebellion (1861–65)* (Washington, D.C.: U.S. Government Printing Office, 1870) vol. 3, no. 2, 920.

81. Billings, *Hardtack and Coffee*, 47.

82. National Guard, New York, *History of Company "E," 107th Infantry 54th Brigade, 27th Division, U.S.A.* (New York: War Veterans' Association, 1920), 53.

83. Billings, *Hardtack and Coffee*, 47.

84. Henry W. Farnam, recollections of Professor Marsh sent to Ernest Howe, May 5, 1931, 6, Marsh Papers, manuscript group 343, series 5, microfilm reel 26, frame 462, Yale University Library.

85. "The Yale Exploring Expedition; Return of Professor Marsh's Party— Sketch of Their Trip to the Fossil Regions of the West," *Hartford Daily Courant*, December 12, 1872, 1. "The Yale Exploring Expedition," an article published December 14, 1872, in the *College Courant: A Weekly Journal*, 257–58, is nearly identical to the *Hartford Daily Courant* account. It corrects the Hartford newspaper's misspelling of Hill as Bill and adds a few words about the salted rubies that were "said to have been gathered on the fields" of the Green River area. It omits the concluding words stating that Marsh, Russell, and Hill arrived back in New Haven "on Saturday night." A few other discrepancies are inconsequential.

86. On "a good shot," see Mary Faith Pankin, "The Yale Scientific Expeditions in Kansas," *Heritage of the Great Plains* 35 (Fall–Winter 2002), 24. Pankin is the great-granddaughter of George G. Lobdell Jr., a Marsh assistant on the 1871 Yale expedition. George Bird Grinnell also remarked on Marsh's marksmanship in a letter to Ernest Howe on February 19, 1929, p. 3, Marsh Papers, manuscript group 343, series 5, box 49, folder 7, Yale University Library.

87. Sullivan, "Infantry on the Kansas Frontier, 1866–1880," 37.

88. Schuchert and LeVene, *O. C. Marsh*, 172–73. Marsh printed the directions in 1875.

89. Leo E. Oliva, an authority on Fort Wallace, kindly assisted with explanations of details related to the 1872 expedition's time in Kansas, based on Fort Wallace records on microfilm, a copy of which he purchased from the National Archives and Records Administration.

90. It is possible that additional specimens were found on any given date. Fossils and the dates they were found were not necessarily recorded in the field or entered definitively at the Yale Peabody Museum when the shipment of six boxes from Kansas reached New Haven. Of the 410 cataloged specimens from the 1872 Yale College Scientific Expedition, 266 were not attributed to any individual or team of collectors but to the expedition in general. Once the expedition moved on to Colorado, fewer collectors' names appear in the record. When the Colorado specimens reached New Haven, they were given the accession date of December 21, 1872. By that date the expedition had returned from the West. The Peabody's list of catalogued specimens also includes occasional errors, such as the collector of some specimens being identified as someone who was not a member of the 1872 expedition. Overall, however, record-keeping was good given the challenges, according to Daniel L. Brinkman in a communication to the author on October 16, 2020.

91. O. C. Marsh, "My First Pterodactyle," 4, Marsh Papers, manuscript group 343, series 5, box 49, folder 4, Yale University Library. Marsh described birds and what he called "dragons" as having "exchanged characters." In other words, birds once had teeth and reptiles once flew, but these characters are now reversed.

92. Schuchert and LeVene, *O. C. Marsh*, 126.

93. Schuchert and LeVene, *O. C. Marsh*, 132.

94. "Lost on the Plains" is listed as one of the Kansas stories in the Marsh Papers, no. 9, 1872, manuscript group 343, series 5, microfilm reel 26, frames 234–307, Yale University Library.

95. Schuchert and LeVene, *O. C. Marsh*, 126–27.

96. Schuchert and LeVene, *O. C. Marsh*, 127.

97. Henry W. Farnam, recollections of Professor Marsh sent to Ernest Howe, May 5, 1931, 1, Marsh Papers, manuscript group 343, series 5, microfilm reel 26, frame 462, Yale University Library.

98. Conniff, *House of Lost Worlds*, 55, 31.

99. Timothy Dwight, *Memories of Yale Life and Men*, quoted in Charles Schuchert, *Biographical Memoir of Othniel Charles Marsh, 1831–1899*, National Academy of Sciences of the United States of America, Biographical Memoirs,

vol. 20 (Washington, D.C.: National Academy of Sciences, 1939), 10, www
.nasonline.org/publications/biographical-memoirs/memoir-pdfs/marsh
_othniel.pdf.

100. George Bird Grinnell letter to Ernest Howe, February 19, 1929, p. 1, Marsh Papers, manuscript group 343, series 5, box 49, folder 7, Yale University Library.

101. William Clark's letter is quoted in Robert A. Saindon, ed., *Explorations into the World of Lewis and Clark*, vol. 3, *Essays from the Pages of* We Proceeded On, *the Quarterly Journal of the Lewis and Clark Trail Heritage Foundation* (Great Falls, Mont.: Lewis and Clark Trail Heritage Foundation, 2003) 194.

102. Clay Jenkinson, interviewed by Peter Coyote for "Meriwether Lewis: A Complex Captain," episode 101 of *Unfinished Journey: The Lewis and Clark Expedition*. Jenkinson said his thinking about Lewis was shaped by author Barry Lopez, to whom he attributes the question. Oregon Public Broadcasting, transcript p. 15, accessed April 8, 2017, https://www.yumpu.com/en/document /view/24678299/download-transcript-oregon-public-broadcasting.

103. Michael J. Everhart, "Rediscovery of the *Hesperornis regalis* Marsh 1871 Holotype Locality Indicates an Earlier Stratigraphic Occurrence," *Transactions of the Kansas Academy of Science* 114, no. 1–2 (2011): 61.

104. Schuchert and LeVene, *O. C. Marsh*, 361.

105. George Sternberg describes his discovery in July 1908 of a duck-billed dinosaur in Converse County, Wyoming, north of the town of Lusk, along the banks of the Cheyenne River. See "Thrills in Fossil Hunting," *Journal of Geoscience Education* 15, no. 2 (1967): 78–79.

106. Sternberg, "Thrills in Fossil Hunting," 79.

107. Sternberg, "Thrills in Fossil Hunting," 79.

108. Sternberg, "Thrills in Fossil Hunting," 79.

109. Charles Kingsley, *Glaucus: Or the Wonders of the Shore* (Cambridge: Macmillan and Co., 1855), cited in Conniff, *House of Lost Worlds*, 62. In an email to the author on May 26, 2016, Conniff described Kingsley as "a genius on the psychology of naturalists."

110. Everhart, *Oceans of Kansas*, 1st ed., 20.

111. Marsh, "Notice of a New and Remarkable Fossil Bird," *American Journal of Science*, ser. 3,4, no. 22 (1873): 344, cited in Everhart, *Oceans of Kansas*, 1st ed., 220.

112. Marsh, "On a New Sub-class of Fossil Birds (Odontornithes)," *American Journal of Science*, ser. 3,5, no. 25 (1874): 161–62, cited in Everhart, *Oceans of Kansas*, 1st ed., 221; also Marsh, "The Vertebrae of Recent Birds," *American Journal of Science*, ser. 3, no. 17 (1879): 266, http://marsh.dinodb.com/marsh/, Marsh 1879 - The vertebrae of recent birds.pdf.

113. Keith Thomson, *The Legacy of the Mastodon: The Golden Age of Fossils in America* (New Haven: Yale University Press, 2008), 213.

114. Meeting between Daniel L. Brinkman, vertebrate paleontologist at the Yale Peabody Museum, and the author, June 12, 2015.

115. Schuchert and LeVene, *O. C. Marsh*, 298.

116. Marsh, "Notice of a New and Remarkable Fossil Bird," cited in Everhart, *Oceans of Kansas*, 1st ed., 221.

117. Everhart, *Oceans of Kansas*, 1st ed., 216. This description of *Hesperornis regalis* comes primarily from Everhart.

118. Laura Geggel, "Ancient Water Bird Survived Attack by Short-Necked 'Sea Monster,'" *Live Science*, April 7, 2016, http://www.livescience.com/54335 -plesiosaur-attacked-ancient-water-bird.html; Larry D. Martin, Bruce M. Rothschild, David A. Burnham, "*Hesperornis* Escapes Plesiosaur Attack," *Cretaceous Research* 63 (August 2016): 178–80.

119. Bill Redekop, "New Species of Ancient Water Fowl Found in Morden," *Winnipeg Free Press*, March 15, 2016, https://www.winnipegfreepress.com/local /new-species-of-ancient-water-fowl-found-in-morden-372142941.html, citing Canadian Fossil Discovery Center's (Morden, Winnipeg, Canada) field and collection manager Victoria Markstrom after *Hesperornis* remains were found in the stomach contents of a mosasaur fossil at the South Dakota School of Mines and Technology. Email correspondence between Mike Everhart and the author, October 12, 2017.

120. The gender of the *Hesperornis regalis* individual found by Thomas H. Russell is not known, according to an email from Daniel L. Brinkman to the author, November 25, 2014.

121. Email from Mike Everhart to the author, April 14, 2017.

122. Schuchert, *Biographical Memoir of Othniel Charles Marsh*, 19; Marsh, "Introduction and Succession of Vertebrate Life in America" *American Journal of Science and Arts*, Ser. 3 (1877): 837–78, quoted in Conniff, *House of Lost Worlds*, 70.

123. Schuchert, *Biographical Memoir of Othniel Charles Marsh*, 19.

124. Everhart, "Rediscovery of the *Hesperornis regalis*," 62. According to Everhart, "Marsh initiated some confusion with the naming of his flying reptiles, first by calling them *Pterodactylus Oweni*, then renaming them, and then assigning several species names to what turned out to be one species, *Pteranodon longiceps*." Email from Michael J. Everhart to the author, October 11, 2017.

125. "Catalogued YPM Specimens from the 1872 Yale College Scientific Expedition," included in an email from Daniel L. Brinkman to the author, April 28, 2015. Pinpointing the localities of specimens collected by the 1872 expedition is problematic, due to a combination of past curating inaccuracies at the Peabody Museum, the names of counties in western Kansas changing over time, and sketchy or inaccurate field notes, as Michael J. Everhart explains in "Rediscovery of the *Hesperornis regalis*." After a discussion of all-but-impossible localities in the curation records, Everhart concludes that the county names Trego, Ellis, and Logan "were added to the records long after the specimens were deposited in the museum" (61).

126. *OutWest*, November 14, 1872, 8, https://www.coloradohistoricnewspapers .org/cgi-bin/colorado?a=d&d=OWT18721114.2.60#.

127. *Denver Daily Times*, November 13, 1872, 4, https://www.coloradohistoric newspapers.org/cgi-bin/colorado?a=d&d=DTM18721113.2.70.

128. "Christmas Dinner at the Tefft House," *Topeka* (Kansas) *Daily Blade*, December 27, 1873, 3, quoted in Paul Freedman, "American Restaurants and Cuisine in the Mid-Nineteenth Century," *New England Quarterly* 84 (March 2011): 26, http://www.mitpressjournals.org/doi/pdf/10.1162/TNEQ_a_00066.

129. *Denver Daily Times*, November 13, 1872, 4, https://www.coloradohistoric newspapers.org/cgi-bin/colorado?a=d&d=DTM18721113.

130. *Denver Daily Times*, November 13, 1872, 4.

131. On the population increase, see Mark A. Barnhouse, *Denver's Sixteenth Street* (Charlestown, S.C.: Arcadia Publishing, 2010), 9. According to Kansas historian and author Leo E. Oliva, the arrival of the Kansas Pacific Railway at Denver in 1870 created the first true transcontinental connection. The Union Pacific–Central Pacific connection in Utah, completed in 1869, was not truly transcontinental because no bridge crossed the Missouri River at Omaha, and passengers had to debark and cross the river by ferry. The Kansas Pacific–Denver Pacific connection thus provided true transcontinental railroad service, because passengers could now travel coast to coast by rail without disembarking to a ferry. Email from Leo E. Oliva to the author, June 11, 2017.

132. Denver Board of Trade, "Weather Record" and "Growth of the City," in *Denver Board of Trade for the Year Ending December 31, 1873* (Denver: Tribune Steam Book and Job Printing House, 1874).

133. Suzanne Thumhart (elsewhere Sue Thumbart), "Tourism," in *The Colorado Chronicles*, vol. 6, *Colorado Businesses* (Frederick, Colo.: Platte 'N Press, American Traveler Press, 1984), 27.

134. The photographers are listed by last name at "Langdon's List of 19th & early 20th Century Photographers," LangdonRoad.com, accessed April 26, 2009, https://www.langdonroad.com/colorado.

135. *Out West*, November 14, 1872, 8.

136. Cowan's Auctions website, accessed January 13, 2021, http://www .cowanauctions.com/lot/members-of-yale-paleontological-expedition-of-1872 -photograph-81435.

137. Description of "Lot 445, Members of Yale Paleontological Expedition of 1872 Photograph," Cowan's Auctions website, accessed January 13, 2021, https://www.cowanauctions.com/auction/2010-american-history-including -the-civil-war-june-11/lots.

138. In 2019 Cowan's was acquired by the Hindman family of auction houses.

139. Telephone call from Mark Greaves to the author and emails exchanged on April 26, 2019.

140. Peter E. Palmquist and Thomas R. Kailbourn, "William Gunnison Chamberlain," in *Pioneer Photographers of the Far West: A Biographical Dictionary, 1840–65* (Stanford, Calif.: Stanford University Press, 2000), 169.

141. Palmquist and Kailbourn, "William Gunnison Chamberlain," 170. The fire destroyed the work of two other photographers, along with Chamberlain's.

142. Christina Kotchemidova, "Why We Say 'Cheese': Producing the Smile in Snapshot Photography," *Critical Studies in Media Communication* 22, no.1 (March 2005): 2–25.

143. On changes in photography and for the quotation from the advertisement, see Terry Wm. Mangan, *Colorado on Glass: Colorado's First Half Century as Seen by the Camera. With a Directory of Early Colorado Photographers by Opal Murry Harber* (Denver: Sundance Limited, 1975), 64.

144. Hawkes, "Thomas H. Russell, M.D.," 237–40.

145. Lisa Robinson, "An Oral History of Laurel Canyon, the '60s and the '70s Music Mecca," *Vanity Fair*, February 8, 2015, https://www.vanityfair.com /culture/2015/02/laurel-canyon-music-scene.

146. Joni Mitchell, "Sweet Bird," *The Hissing of Summer Lawns* (Crazy Crow Music, November 1975), https://jonimitchell.com/music/song.cfm?id=29.

147. John Lukavic, emails with the author, May 31, 2019.

148. This is the pronunciation according to Mi'kmaq Spirit, a website accessed January 24, 2021, http://www.muiniskw.org/pgCulture0.htm. Additional information about the Mi'kmaq people and culture was provided in emails to the author from Diane Chisholm, director of the Mi'kmaq Resource Centre in Nova Scotia, June 26–27, 2019.

149. Vera Longtoe Sheehan, "The Double Curve Motif," Elnu Abenaki Tribe, accessed October 18, 2019, http://www.elnuabenakitribe.org/essays_and _articles/the_double_curve_motif.

150. "Yale Exploring Expedition," *Hartford Daily Courant*, December 12, 1872, 1.

151. "Yale Exploring Expedition," *Hartford Daily Courant*, December 12, 1872, 1.

152. Patricia Stallard, *Glittering Misery: Dependents of the Indian Fighting Army* (Norman: University of Oklahoma Press, 1992), 51.

153. 1st Lt. John Bradshaw, "Fort Russell, 1867–1900," in *A History of Francis E. Warren Air Force Base and Its Predecessors, Fort David A. Russell and Fort Francis E. Warren*, ed. Maj. Stephen L. Holland (Francis E. Warren Air Force Base, Wyo.: Warren ICBM and Heritage Museum, 1983), 13, http://www .warrenmuseum.com/mules-to-missiles/.

154. G. B. Dobson, "Fort D. A. Russell," Wyoming Tales and Trails website, accessed April 24, 2021, http://www.wyomingtalesandtrails.com/russell.html.

155. Marguerite Herman, "Laramie County, Wyoming," November 8, 2014, Wyoming State Historical Society, https://www.wyohistory.org/encyclopedia /laramie-county-wyoming.

156. Special Orders No. 190, November 14, 1872, Preliminary Inventory of the Records of United States Army Continental Commands, 1821–1920, Record Group 393, vol. 5, Military Installations, Fort D. A. Russell, Wyo., box 10, General Orders, Special Orders, and Orders, Quartermaster Depot, National Archives, Washington, D.C.

157. "Yale Exploring Expedition," *Hartford Daily Courant*, December 12, 1872, 1.

158. Conniff, *House of Lost Worlds*, 5.

159. Herman, "Laramie County, Wyoming," 3.

160. Celinda Reynolds Kaelin, "Tava: A Ute Cultural History," *A Sense of Place in the Pikes Peak Region*, Colorado College (Colorado Springs, 2002), accessed May 24, 2021. https://web.archive.org/web/20170924045624/https://www.coloradocollege .edu/other/senseofplace/cultural-history/ute-history-of-tava.html.

161. "Yale Exploring Expedition," *Hartford Daily Courant*, December 12, 1872, 1.

162. The same article was reprinted December 4, 1872, in the *Deseret News*. An email from Brittany Chapman Nash, Church History Library Reference Department, Church of Jesus Christ of Latter-Day Saints, Salt Lake City, to the author, April 5, 2016, confirms the identical newspaper accounts and the dates that the Yale party, minus Marsh, was in Salt Lake City.

163. "Yale Exploring Expedition," *Hartford Daily Courant*, December 12, 1872, 1.

164. Betts, "Yale College Expedition of 1870," quoted in Schuchert and LeVene, *O. C. Marsh*, 112.

165. "The Crisis in Utah: The Arrest of Brigham Young," *New York Herald*, October 4, 1872.

166. Benson John Lossing, Woodrow Wilson, eds., *Harper's Encyclopaedia of United States History from 458 A.D. to 1912*, vol. 9 (New York: Harper and Brothers, 1912), 2142; R. Guy McClellan, "Mormonism and the Mormons," in *The Golden State: A History of the Region West of the Rocky Mountains* (Philadelphia: W. Flint and Co., 1872), 588–89, https://archive.org/stream/goldenstatehistoomccl.

167. Ardis E. Parshall, "Philadelphia Matron Recalled Robust Mormon Thanksgiving," *Salt Lake Tribune*, November 22, 2008, http://www.sltrib.com.

168. The *San Francisco Chronicle* is quoted in Robert Wilson, "The Great Diamond Hoax of 1872," *Smithsonian* (June 2004): 1, https://www.smithsonianmag.com/history/the-great-diamond-hoax-of-1872-2630188/.

169. *Courier-Journal* article is quoted in Wilson, "Great Diamond Hoax," 2.

170. Frank N. Schubert, "The Great Surveys and the End of an Era," in *Vanguard of Expansion: Army Engineers in the Trans-Mississippi West, 1819–1879* (Washington, D.C.: USACE, Historical Division, 1980), n.p., https://www.nps.gov/parkhistory/online_books/shubert/chap8.htm.

171. Schubert, "Great Surveys."

172. "The Great Diamond Fraud," *Wilmington* (Ohio) *Journal*, December 19, 1872, 1, reprinted from the *New York Tribune*, December 19, 1872.

173. Wilson, "Great Diamond Hoax," 6.

174. Daniel Joseph Boorstin, *The Americans: The National Experience* (New York: Random House, 1965), 236.

175. *Olathe* (Kansas) *Mirror*, December 19, 1872, 1.

176. "The Land Leaguers," The *Wyandott Herald* (Kansas City, Kansas), November 28, 1872, 2.

177. *Colorado Mining Review*, December 1872, quoted in Richard A. Bartlett, *Great Surveys of the American West* (Norman: University of Oklahoma Press, 1962), 203–4.

178. "Science and Literature in a Daily Paper," *New York Tribune*, August 2, 1873, 6.

179. Martha A. Sandweiss, *Passing Strange: A Gilded Age Tale of Love and Deception across the Color Line* (New York: Penguin Press, 2009), 50.

180. *Chicago Tribune*, Personal column, December 6, 1872, 4.

181. "Return of the Yale College Expedition," *American Naturalist* 7, no. 1 (January 1873): 49, https://www.jstor.org/stable/2448128?refreqid=excelsior%3Aecc8cbb8d32c594dfb2364678130cc48&seq=1#metadata_info_tab_contents.

182. General news, *Reading* (Penn.) *Times*, April 1, 1873, 4.

183. "The Old New World," (Washington, D.C.) *Evening Star*, June 16, 1873, 2.

184. "Scientific Notes—Home and Foreign Notes," *Appletons' Journal of Literature, Science, and Art* 9 (February 8, 1873): 222.

Part IV: I Go to Kansas

1. "Youth in Action: May Boeve, Climate Change Activist," *The Nation*, April 20, 2009, http://www.thenation.com/article/youth-action-may-boeve-climate-change-activist.

2. "Kit Carson Park in New Mexico Renamed over American Indian Concerns," June 13, 2014, Associated Press, Fox News, http://www.foxnews.com/us/2014/06/13/kit-carson-park-in-new-mexico-renamed-over-american-indian-concerns/.

3. "Economic Impact of the Kansas Livestock Industry," Kansas Livestock Association, accessed June 24, 2014, http://www.kla.org/industryeconomics.aspx.

4. William Pentland, "Kansas Makes Renewable Energy Standard Voluntary," *Forbes*, May 29, 2015, https://www.forbes.com/sites/williampentland/2015/05/29/kansas-makes-renewable-energy-standard-voluntary/#20e03a07ce00.

5. Alan Claus Anderson, Scott W. White, Britton Gibson, and Luke Hagedorn in partnership with Polsinelli Shughart and Kansas Energy Information Network, "The Economic Benefits of Kansas Wind Energy," November 19, 2012, 27, https://www.renewableenergylawinsider.com/wp-content/uploads/sites/165/2012/11/Kansas-Wind-Report.pdf.

6. Steven Mufson and Tom Hamburger, "A Battle Is Looming over Renewable Energy, and Fossil Fuel Interests Are Losing," *Washington Post*, April 25, 2014, 6, http://www.washingtonpost.com/business/economy/a-battle-is-looming-over-renewable-energy-and-fossil-fuel-interests-are-losing/2014/04/25/24ed78e2-cb23-11e3-a75e-463587891b57_story.html.

7. Anderson, White, Gibson, and Hagedorn, "Economic Benefits of Kansas Wind Energy," 17.

8. "The Ten Best College Presidents," *Time*, November 11, 2009, http://content.time.com/time/specials/packages/printout/0,29239,1937938_1937933_1937919,00.html#.

9. Dave Barker, "Madd about Midd Warming up to the Issues," *Middlebury Campus*, November 17, 2005, http://middleburycampus.com/article/madd-about-midd-warming-up-to-the-issues/.

10. Libuse Binder, *Ten Ways to Change the World in Your Twenties* (Naperville, Ill.: Sourcebooks, Inc., 2009), 108.

11. "1872 U.S. Flag," North American Vexillological Association, accessed June 24, 2014, http://www.nava.org/flag-information/qa/1872-us-flag.

12. Cutter et al., "General William Huntington Russell," 426–31.

13. "Evolution of the Company Symbol, Identification with Dinosaurs" and "Dino Becomes Big Star," Sinclair Oil, accessed August 20, 2014, https://www.sinclairoil.com/history/symbol_01.html.

14. "Evolution of the Company Symbol."

15. Bill McKibben, Will Bates, May Boeve, Jamie Henn, Jeremy Osborn, and Jon Warnow, *Fight Global Warming Now: The Handbook for Taking Action in Your Community* (New York: Holt, 2007), 50, 52.

16. Everhart, "Rediscovery of the *Hesperornis regalis*," 64.

17. Everhart, "Rediscovery of the *Hesperornis regalis*," 64.

18. Travis Taggart, email correspondence with the author, October 12, 2010.

19. Forrest L. Mitchell and James L. Lasswell, *A Dazzle of Dragonflies* (College Station: Texas A&M University Press, 2005), 46–47, 20.

20. Gary Buffalo Horn Man and Sherry Firedancer, "Dragonfly," in *Animal Energies* (Rainelle, Wyo.: Dancing Otter Publishing), 1992.

Part V: Diaspora

1. "Yale Exploring Expedition," *Hartford Daily Courant*, December 12, 1872, 1.

2. Col. Norris Galpin Osborn, ed., "Thomas Hubbard Russell," in *Men of Mark in Connecticut: Ideals of American Life Told in Biographies and Autobiographies of Eminent Living Americans*, vol. 2 (Hartford: William R. Goodspeed, 1906), 427.

3. Thomas Hubbard Russell, "Talipes Equines" (thesis, Yale School of Medicine, 1875), photocopy provided to the author by Florence Gillich, Historical Library Assistant, Cushing/Whitney Medical Historical Library Yale University, June 3, 2016.

4. Yale University, Sheffield Scientific School, *Biographical Record, Classes from Eighteen Hundred and Sixty-eight to Eighteen Hundred and Seventy-two of the Sheffield Scientific School* (New Haven, Conn.: Class Secretaries Bureau, Yale University, 1910), 216–23, https://catalog.hathitrust.org/Record/006504005.

5. Kevin Falvey, "The New Haven Dispensary," *Yale Medicine* (Autumn 2010), https://medicine.yale.edu/news/yale-medicine-magazine/the-new-haven-dispensary/.

6. "Made a Professor," *New Haven Evening Register*, June 27, 1883, 1.

7. Hawkes, "Thomas Hubbard Russell," 237.

8. Osborne, "Thomas Hubbard Russell," 427–28.

9. Hawkes, "Thomas Hubbard Russell," 239.

10. Hawkes, "Thomas Hubbard Russell," 239.

11. "It Was Not Asiatic Cholera," *New York Times*, July 28, 1894, 1.

12. "Saved by X Ray," *Boston Post*, April 4, 1896, 13.

13. "Girl's Death Charged to Dr. Elijah Bond: Grace Dearborn Comes to an Awful End," *New Haven Register*, December 18, 1897, 1.

14. "Miss Conlon's Death," *Naugatuck* (Conn.) *Daily News*, October 9, 1899, 2.

15. "May Save His Life: Surgical Operation on a Young Athlete," (Rochester, N.Y.) *Democrat and Chronicle*, August 2, 1902, 1.

16. "Saves Athlete with Broken Neck: John Nichols, Jr., About to Die, Is Restored to Consciousness by Operation," *Scranton* (Penn.) *Republican*, August 1, 1902, 1.

17. "Saves Athlete with Broken Neck," *Scranton Republican*, August 1, 1902, 1.

18. "May Save His Life," *Democrat and Chronicle*, August 2, 1902, 1.

19. "May Save His Life," *Democrat and Chronicle*, August 2, 1902, 1.

20. "General [news]," *Baltimore Sun*, August 1, 1902, 6.

21. "Broken Neck Was Fatal," *Hartford Daily Courant*, August 4, 1902, 9.

22. "Rock Climbing at West Rock," West Rock Ridge State Park, accessed July 10, 2020, https://westrocktrails.blogspot.com/p/rock-climbing.html. During the time of the COVID-19 outbreak in 2020, climbers were advised not to attempt West Rock because of the risk of spreading infection and straining the capacity of hospitals in the event of a fall.

23. "Pneumonia Fatal to Local Doctor," *Boston Morning Herald*, February 3, 1916.

24. "Funeral of Dr. Russell: Services for Distinguished Local Physician to Be Held Saturday; His Active Career," *New Haven Register*, February 3, 1916; "Dr. Thomas H. Russell, Famous Surgeon, Dies," *New York Evening Journal*, February 4, 1916.

25. Akiko Busch, *How to Disappear: Notes on Invisibility in a Time of Transparency* (New York: Penguin Press, 2019), 9.

26. "Othniel Charles Marsh," U.C. Museum of Paleontology, Berkeley, accessed July 12, 2020, https://ucmp.berkeley.edu/history/marsh.html.

27. Edward Drinker Cope letter to Henry Fairfield Osborn, quoted in Conniff, *House of Lost Worlds*, 136, 306n1 (to chapter 14).

28. Mark J. McCarren, *The Scientific Contributions of Othniel Charles Marsh: Birds, Bones, and Brontotheres* (New Haven, Conn.: Peabody Museum of Natural History, Yale University, 1993), 1.

29. Schuchert and LeVene, *O. C. Marsh*, 495.

30. Schuchert and LeVene, *O. C. Marsh*, 503–26.

31. Conniff, *House of Lost Worlds*, 79.

32. Schuchert and LeVene, *O. C. Marsh*, 166, citing "The Red-Cloud Report," *The Nation*, October 28, 1875.

33. Schuchert and LeVene, *O. C. Marsh*, 167.

34. William Wyckoff, "Red Cloud Visits a Friend: The Great Indian Chief the Guest of Prof Marsh in New Haven," *New York Times*, January 21, 1883, 1. To learn English would have caused Red Cloud to "lose caste," according to Wyckoff.

35. "MacNaughton Mountain," Lake Placid website, accessed July 15, 2020, https://www.lakeplacid.com/do/hiking/macnaughton-mountain.

36. "Was Handling a Revolver," *Boston Globe*, May 1, 1898, 16; "Handling a Revolver, Charles D. Hill, a Prominent Calais Merchant, Accidentally Killed," *Portland* (Maine) *Transcript*, May 4, 1898, http://mainelygenealogy.blogspot.com/2015/11/the-portland-transcript-may-4-1898_27.html, accessed Sept. 1, 2016.

37. Marsh, "Ride for Life in a Herd of Buffalo," 1.

38. Daniela Breitman, Deborah Byrd, and Paul Scott Anderson, "Sally Ride: 1st American Woman in Space," Human World/Space, *Earth Sky News* (June 18, 2020), https://earthsky.org/space/sally-ride-1st-american-woman-in-space-june-18-1983.

39. William C. Wyckoff, "A Perilous Fossil Hunt: Professor Marsh's Last Trip to the Bad Lands," *New York Tribune*, December 22, 1874, 2.

40. Wyckoff, "Perilous Fossil Hunt," *New York Tribune*, December 22, 1874, 2.

41. Schuchert, *Biographical Memoir of Othniel Charles Marsh*, 17.

42. Everhart, "Rediscovery of the *Hesperornis regalis*," 66.

43. P. D. Gingerich, "Evolutionary Significance of the Mesozoic Toothed Birds," *Smithsonian Contributions to Paleobiology* 27 (1976): 23–34.

44. Michael J. Everhart, personal communication with Daniel L. Brinkman in 2011, cited in Everhart, "Rediscovery of the *Hesperornis regalis*," 66.

45. Schuchert and LeVene, *O. C. Marsh*, 308.

46. Arthur Lakes, "A Walk through the Misty Museum and Other Departments: Yale College: Curiosities from the Rocky Mountains," *Denver Tribune*, February 12, 1879.

47. "Scientists Wage Bitter Warfare," *New York Herald*, January 12, 1890, quoted in Conniff, *House of Lost Worlds*, 140, 306n8.

48. Wyckoff, "Perilous Fossil Hunt," *New York Tribune*, December 22, 1874, 2.

49. Lukas Rieppel, "Plaster Cast Publishing in Nineteenth-Century Paleontology," *History of Science* 53, no. 4 (2015): 456–91 (478, fig. 8).

50. Annual fund appeal letter from David Skelly, director of the Yale Peabody Museum of Natural History, December 1, 2019.

51. Matt Dwyer, "Peabody Museum's Great Hall Closing for Major Renovation," WNPR.org, December 31, 2019, https://www.wnpr.org/post/peabody-museums-great-hall-closing-major-renovation.

52. Email from Daniel L. Brinkman to the author, June 18, 2020.

53. Rieppel, "Plaster Cast Publishing," 457.

54. O. C. Marsh, *Birds with Teeth*, extract from the *Third Annual Report of the Director, Department of the Interior, U.S. Geological Survey, J. W. Powell, Director* (Washington, D.C.: Government Printing Office, 1883), 65–68. Unless otherwise noted, the descriptions of *Hesperornis* are from Marsh.

55. Marsh, *Birds with Teeth*, 67.

56. Marsh, *Birds with Teeth*, 65.

57. Conniff, *House of Lost Worlds*, 59.

58. Rieppel, "Plaster Cast Publishing," 456.

59. Rieppel, "Plaster Cast Publishing," 475–76.

60. Executive Committee of the Society of the Alumni, *Yale College in 1881. Some Statements Respecting the Late Progress and Present Condition of the Various Departments of the University for the Information of Its Graduates, Friends, and Benefactors* (New Haven, Conn.: Tuttle, Morehouse, and Taylor, 1868–86), 29, https://babel.hathitrust.org/cgi/pt?id=mdp.39015075991854&view=image&seq=29.

61. Rieppel, "Plaster Cast Publishing," 460.

62. Receipt sent by Tobias Kappeler to O. C. Marsh April 5, 1881, O. C. Marsh Correspondence, box 18, folder 748, Peabody Museum of Natural History, https://peabody.yale.edu/collections/vertebrate-paleontology/correspondence-o-c-marsh.

63. Telephone call and email to the author from William L. Lassetter, Economic Geology Projects Manager, Virginia Department of Mines, Minerals and Energy, Charlottesville, Virginia, June 18, 2020.

64. O. C. Marsh letter to Joseph Leidy, April 27, 1881, Coll. 567: ANSP, Correspondence, Archives Collection, Academy of Natural Sciences of Drexel University.

65. "3-D Printed Dinosaurs: 8 Best Curated Models," All3DP.com, accessed June 23, 2020, https://all3dp.com/2/3d-printed-dinosaur-best-curated-models/.

66. "Best STL [stereolithography] Files of Dinosaurs to Make with a 3D Printer," cults3d.com, accessed June 23, 2020, https://cults3d.com/en/collections /best-stl-files-dinosaur-3d-printing.

67. R. W. Schufeldt, MD, "The Fossil Remains of a Species of Hesperornis Found in Montana," *The Auk* 32, no. 3 (July 1915): 290–94, http://www.jstor.com /stable/4072679.

68. The exact numbers are a matter of debate, according to Alyssa Bell and Louis M. Chiappe; see "A Species-Level Phylogeny of the Cretaceous Hesperornithiformes (Aves: Ornithuromorpha): Implications for Body Size Evolution amongst the Earliest Diving Birds," *Journal of Systematic Paleontology* 14, no. 3 (May 2015): 5, 2, https://www.researchgate.net/publication/277974710 _A_species-level_phylogeny_of_the_Cretaceous_Hesperornithiformes_Aves _Ornithuromorpha_Implications_for_body_size_evolution_amongst_the _earliest_diving_birds/link/564dfod908aefe619b0efda4/download.

69. The name Schreckengost is variously translated from German as "frightening guest," "startled guest," "frightening innkeeper," and "afraid of a ghost."

70. Marianne Rohrlich, "Belatedly, Stardom Finds a 20th-Century Master," *New York Times*, May 11, 2006, https://www.nytimes.com/2006/05/11/garden /belatedly-stardom-finds-a-20thcentury-master.html.

71. Mark Gottlieb, "Viktor Schreckengost, Industrial Designer and Painter, 1906–2008," Clevelandartsprize.org, accessed July 18, 2020, http://clevelandartsprize .org/awardees/viktor_schreckengost.html.

72. Rohrlich, "Belatedly," *New York Times*, May 11, 2006.

73. Rohrlich, "Belatedly," *New York Times*, May 11, 2006.

74. Clevelanders' longstanding interest in bird life is commented on in "The Bird Building at the Cleveland Zoological Park," a four-page brochure sent with an email to the author on January 18, 2019, by Wendy Wasman, librarian and archivist at the Cleveland Museum of Natural History. On the Cleveland Academy of Natural Sciences's ornithology collection, see "Proceedings of the Cleveland Academy of Natural Science, 1845–1859," published by a Gentleman of Cleveland (Cleveland: Academy of Natural Sciences, 1874): 13, https:// archive.org/details/proceedingsclevoosciegoog.

75. Henry Adams and Sunny Morton, ed., *Viktor Schreckengost and 20th-Century Design* (Cleveland: Cleveland Museum of Art, 2001), 74.

76. Adams and Morton, *Viktor Schreckengost*, 76.

77. Gottlieb, "Viktor Schreckengost," 1.

Part VI: I Return to Kansas

1. Clara Holzmark Wolf, "Bibles and Rifles," *Overland Monthly* 55, 2nd ser. (January–June 1910): 362, https://archive.org/details/overlandmonthly551910sanf

/page/362/mode/2up. Wolf quotes Beecher's letter written from Brooklyn on Friday, March 28, 1856, to C. B. Lines, Esq., New Haven, Conn., which was published in *New York Daily Tribune*, Friday, April 4, 1856, 5.

2. Frank Decker, *Brooklyn's Plymouth Church in the Civil War Era: A Ministry of Freedom* (Charleston, S.C.: History Press and Arcadia Publishing, 2013), chapter 5, "The Church of the Holy Rifles," photo caption for Sharps rifle, n.p.

3. "Sharps Model 1853 Single Shot Breechloading Percussion Carbine," NRA National Firearms Museum, accessed July 14, 2017, http://www.nramuseum .org/guns/the-galleries/a-nation-asunder-1861-to-1865/case-15-union-muskets -and-rifles/sharps-model-1853-single-shot-breechloading-percussion-carbine .aspx.

Adams, Henry. *Viktor Schreckengost and Twentieth-Century Design*. Edited by Sunny Morton. Cleveland, Ohio: Cleveland Museum of Art, 2001.

Ambrose, Stephen. *Duty, Honor, Country: A History of West Point*. Baltimore: Johns Hopkins University Press, 1999.

Atwater, Edward Elias. *History of the City of New Haven to the Present Time*. New York: W. W. Munsell, 1887.

Bartlett, Richard A. *Great Surveys of the American West*. Norman: University of Oklahoma Press, 1962.

Betts, Charles Wyllys. "The Yale College Expedition of 1870." *Harper's New Monthly Magazine* 257 (October 1871): 663–71.

Billings, John D. *Hardtack and Coffee: Or, The Unwritten Story of Army Life*. Boston: George Smith and Co., 1888.

Binder, Libuse. *Ten Ways to Change the World in Your Twenties*. Naperville, Ill.: Sourcebooks, 2009.

Black, Riley. "The Many Ways Women Get Left Out of Paleontology." *Smithsonian Magazine*, June 7, 2018. https://www.smithsonianmag.com/science-nature/many-ways-women-get-left-out-paleontology-180969239/.

Busch, Akiko. *How to Disappear: Notes on Invisibility in a Time of Transparency*. New York: Penguin Press, 2019.

Conniff, Richard. *House of Lost Worlds: Dinosaurs, Dynasties, and the Story of Life on Earth*. New Haven, Conn.: Yale University Press, 2016.

Cutter, William Richard, Edward Henry Clement, Samuel Hart, Mary Kingsbury Talcott, Frederick Bostwick, Ezra Scollay Stearns, eds. "General William Huntington Russell." *Genealogical and Family History of the State of Connecticut: A Record of the Achievements of Her People in the Making of a Commonwealth and the Founding of a Nation*. Vol. 1. New York: Lewis Historical Publishing, 1911.

Davidson, Jane P., and Michael J. Everhart. "Scattered and Shattered: A Brief History of the Early Methods of Digging, Preserving and Transporting Kansas Fossils." *Transactions of the Kansas Academy of Science* 120, nos. 3–4 (October 1, 2017): 247–58. https.//doi.org/10.1660/062.120.0416

Erlich, Gretel. *The Solace of Open Spaces*. New York: Penguin Books, 1986.

Everhart, Michael J. *Oceans of Kansas: A Natural History of the Western Interior Sea*. 2nd ed. Bloomington: Indiana University Press, 2017.

———. *Oceans of Kansas: A Natural History of the Western Interior Sea*. 1st ed. Bloomington: Indiana University Press, 2005.

———. "Rediscovery of the *Hesperornis regalis* Marsh 1871 Holotype Locality Indicates an Earlier Stratigraphic Occurrence." *Transactions of the Kansas Academy of Science* 114, no. 1–2 (2011): 59–68.

Fowler, William Chauncey. *The Historical Status of the Negro in Connecticut: A Paper Read before the New Haven Colony Historical Society (in 1873), Copied from*

Henry B. Dawson, ed., *the Historical Magazine, and Notes and Queries concerning the Antiquities, History and Biography of America, 1874–75*. Charleston, S.C.: Walker, Evans & Cogswell, 1901.

Frazier, Ian. *Great Plains*. New York: Farrar, Strauss and Giroux, 1989.

Grinnell, George Bird. "The Blackfeet." In *Pawnee, Blackfoot, and Cheyenne: History and Folklore of the Plains from the Writings of George Bird Grinnell*, 81–156. New York: Charles Scribner's Sons, 1961.

——. "From Yale to the Wild West: An Old-Time Bone Hunt: An Account of the Expedition Undertaken by Prof. O. C. Marsh in 1870 to the Then Wild West." In *Pawnee, Blackfoot, and Cheyenne: History and Folklore of the Plains from the Writings of George Bird Grinnell*, 3–12. New York: Charles Scribner's Sons, 1961.

Hall, Peter. "Middletown: Streets, Commerce, and People, 1650–1981." *Sesquicentennial Papers Number 8: A Pamphlet Written for the 150th Anniversary of Wesleyan University*. Middletown, Conn.: Wesleyan University, 1981.

Hanrahan, Brendan. *Great Day Trips in the Connecticut Valley of the Dinosaurs*. Wilton, Conn.: Perry Heights Press, 2004.

Hawkes, William Whitney, MD. "Thomas H. Russell, M.D." In *Proceedings of the Connecticut State Medical Society*, edited by Marvin McR. Scarbrough, 237–40. New Haven: Connecticut State Medical Society, 1916.

Hill, Everett Gleason. *A Modern History of New Haven and Eastern New Haven County*. Vol. 1. New Haven, Conn.: S. J. Clarke, 1918.

Holt, Henry. *Garrulities of an Octogenarian Editor: With Other Essays Somewhat Biographical and Autobiographical*. New York: Houghton Mifflin, 1923.

Hunting, Jill. *Finding Pete: Rediscovering the Brother I Lost in Vietnam*. Middletown, Conn.: Wesleyan University Press, 2009.

Ise, John. *Sod and Stubble: The Story of a Kansas Homestead*. New York: Wilson-Erickson, 1936.

Jones, Carol. *Balancing Three*. N.p.: Acme Publishing, 2017.

Marcy, Randolph B. *The Prairie Traveler: The 1859 Handbook for Westbound Pioneers*. Reprint, Mineola, N.Y.: Dover Publications, 2006.

Marsh, Othniel Charles. "A Ride for Life in a Herd of Buffalo." Othniel Charles Marsh Papers, manuscript group 343, series 5, box 49, folder 4. Manuscripts and Archives, Yale University Library.

McKibben, Bill, Phil Aroneanu, Will Bates, May Boeve, Jamie Henn, Jeremy Osborn, and Jon Warnow. *Fight Global Warming Now: The Handbook for Taking Action in Your Community*. New York: Holt Paperbacks, 2007.

Meredith, Grace E. *Girl Captives of the Cheyennes: A True Story of the Capture and Rescue of Four Pioneer Girls, 1874*. 1923. Reprint, with a new introduction by Peter Cozzens, Mechanicsburg, Penn.: Stackpole Books, 2004.

Mitchell, Mary H. "Slavery in Connecticut and Especially in New Haven." *Papers of the New Haven Colony Historical Society* 10 (1951): 286–312.

Montgomery, Mrs. Frank C. "Fort Wallace and Its Relation to the Frontier." *Kansas Historical Collections* 17 (1926–28): 189–283.

Munkittrick, Alain, and Deborah Shapiro. *Middletown's High Street and Wesleyan University*. Charleston, S.C.: Arcadia Publishing, 2020.